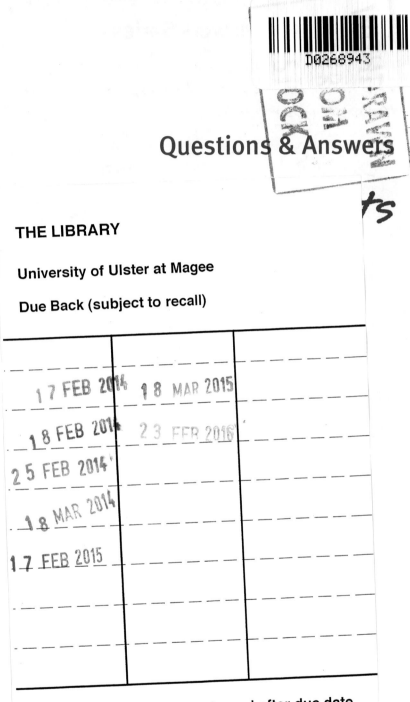

Questions & Answers Series

Series Editors: Rosalind Malcolm and Margaret Wilkie

The ideal revision aid to keep you afloat through your exams

Q&A Company Law
Stephen Judge

Q&A Criminal Law
Mike Molan

Q&A Employment Law
Richard Benny, Michael Jefferson,
and Malcolm Sargeant

Q&A Equity and Trusts
Margaret Wilkie, Rosalind Malcolm,
and Peter Luxton

Q&A EU Law
Nigel Foster

Q&A Evidence
Maureen Spencer and John Spencer

Q&A Family Law
Ruth Gaffney-Rhys, with Chris Barton,
Mary Hibbs, and Penny Booth

Q&A Human Rights and Civil Liberties
Steve Foster

Q&A International Law
Susan Breau

Q&A Land Law
Margaret Wilkie, Peter Luxton,
and Rosalind Malcolm

Q&A Law of Contract
Adrian Chandler with Ian Brown

Q&A Law of Torts
David Oughton and Barbara Harvey

Q&A Public Law
Richard Clements and Philip Jones

- **advice on exam technique**
- **summary of each topic**
- **bullet-pointed answer plans**
- **model answers**
- **diagrams and flowcharts**
- **further reading**

Titles in the series cover all compulsory law subjects and major options.

Buy yours from your
campus bookshop,
online, or direct
from OUP

www.oxfordtextbooks.co.uk/law/revision

Questions & Answers

Equity and Trusts

EIGHTH EDITION

Margaret Wilkie
Formerly Visiting Lecturer in Law,
University of Sheffield

Rosalind Malcolm
Barrister, Professor of Law,
University of Surrey

Peter Luxton
Professor of Law,
Cardiff University

2012 and 2013

OXFORD
UNIVERSITY PRESS

OXFORD
UNIVERSITY PRESS

Great Clarendon Street, Oxford ox2 6DP

Oxford University Press is a department of the University of Oxford.
It furthers the University's objective of excellence in research, scholarship,
and education by publishing worldwide in

Oxford New York

Auckland Cape Town Dar es Salaam Hong Kong Karachi
Kuala Lumpur Madrid Melbourne Mexico City Nairobi
New Delhi Shanghai Taipei Toronto

With offices in

Argentina Austria Brazil Chile Czech Republic France Greece
Guatemala Hungary Italy Japan Poland Portugal Singapore
South Korea Switzerland Thailand Turkey Ukraine Vietnam

Oxford is a registered trade mark of Oxford University Press
in the UK and in certain other countries

Published in the United States
by Oxford University Press Inc., New York

© Margaret Wilkie, Rosalind Malcolm, Peter Luxton 2012

The moral rights of the authors have been asserted
Database right Oxford University Press (maker)

Contains public sector information licensed under the Open Government Licence v1.0
(http://www.nationalarchives.gov.uk/doc/open-government-licence/open-government-licence.htm)

Crown Copyright material reproduced with the permission of the Controller, HMSO
(under the terms of the Click Use licence)

Fifth edition 2006
Sixth edition 2008
Seventh edition 2010

British Library Cataloguing in Publication Data
Data available

Library of Congress Cataloging in Publication Data
Library of Congress Control Number: 2011943539

Typeset by Laserwords Private Ltd, Chennai, India
Printed in Great Britain
on acid-free paper by
Ashford Colour Press Ltd, Gosport, Hampshire

ISBN 978–0–19–969763–2

10 9 8 7 6 5 4 3 2 1

Contents

The Q&A series

Key features

The Q&A series provides full coverage of key subjects in a clear and logical way.

This book contains the following features:

- Questions
- Commentaries
- Bullet-pointed answer plans
- Full model answers
- Further reading suggestions

 online resource centre
www.oxfordtextbooks.co.uk/orc/qanda/

Every book in the Q&A series is accompanied by an Online Resource Centre, hosted at the URL above, which is open access and free to use.

The Online Resource Centre for this book contains revision and exam advice, a glossary of equity & trusts terms, and links to websites useful for the study of Equity & Trusts.

Preface

This is the eighth edition of the first book in the series. We are delighted that the book has sold so well, and assume that this is a testimony to its usefulness to students of this difficult, and often academic, subject. The feedback from lecturers has indicated that the book is generally considered to be a good revision aid and a support to tutorial work—no doubt particularly so where tutorials involve large numbers of students or are infrequent (as on distance learning courses).

The law of equity and trusts continues to develop and we have updated the book to take account of recent developments, substituting and re-writing where appropriate.

On the statutory side, the Perpetuities and Accumulations Act 2009 came into force on 6 April 2010. Section 18 expressly excludes from its effect the rule of law that limits the duration of non-charitable purpose trusts. The Act does not therefore change the previous law on this area: purported non-charitable purpose trusts that might tie up land or capital beyond a permitted period of perpetuity are, and will remain, void for perpetual trust. Otherwise, it is prospective only and applies to instruments taking effect from 6 April 2010 (except for wills which are only affected by the Act when executed from that date). The Equality Act 2010 will abolish the presumption of advancement but, at the time of writing, is still awaiting implementation. At the time of writing, the Charities Bill 2011 was progressing through Parliament. We have made the bold assumption that this consolidating Bill was eventually enacted during the course of 2011, and we have, therefore, made references throughout to the Charities Act 2011.

Developments in case law include the Court of Appeal decision on constructive trusts in *Jones v Kernott* [2010]—the appeal decision of the Supreme Court is awaited. More unusually, a decision on mutual wills has emerged from the Court of Appeal in *Olins v Walters* [2009].

The purpose of the book remains unchanged—it is intended as a student aid in structuring answers to examination-type problems, and in elucidating some of the subject's more difficult areas. Further reading is included at the end of chapters to assist with the study of the subject, particularly with the preparation of coursework.

Margaret Wilkie
Rosalind Malcolm
Peter Luxton
1 August 2011

Table of cases

Table of legislation

Introduction

This book has been written by three lecturers with many years' experience of researching and teaching equity and trusts on different law degree courses at various universities. It is an attempt to give guidance to students on what is expected in the answer to typical questions on the topic (and also, in some instances, on what is superfluous and irrelevant!). We have, in places, pointed out what might distinguish a good answer (class 2(i) or better) from one of a lower quality.

We are acutely aware that many institutions are now adopting assessed coursework as part of their total mark for a subject at the end of the year. Where we feel that the topic is one which might lend itself to this type of coursework, we have included, in the introduction to the question, references to academic articles and further cases which would assist in a deeper study of the area. Very often, assessed coursework will stipulate a maximum limit on the number of words you should write. If this is the case, then you should keep within such limits. This may well require careful planning and balancing of the material in your answer, part of the exercise being to test your ability to write clearly and concisely.

Although the material in all equity and trusts courses will have a large part in common, individual lecturers may accord parts of the subject more extensive treatment. It would be a foolish student indeed who did not heed the emphasis given by his or her lecturer to any particular parts of the course. If your lecturer has, for instance, written a book on charities, it is likely to be a subject dear to the heart and one which will be taught and examined.

Many of the questions on equity and trusts are likely to be problem questions. In dealing with a problem-type examination paper in particular, it is wise to spend a good few minutes at the beginning carefully reading the questions. Ignore the student next to you with a scratchy pen who turns over the first page of the answer book while you are still thinking. There is nothing more deflating than realising, on an examination post mortem, that there was a question on the paper in which you could have done well ... much better than one you did attempt!

Equally important for essay and problem questions is to spend a few minutes, before you actually embark on writing your answer, in jotting down a rough plan of what should be included. This should be brief—perhaps just a few key words or case names, which you can then expand to a paragraph in your answer. You will have been intelligent enough to calculate the time available for each question (after allowing time for reading the paper thoroughly at the beginning) and you should then keep to your plan: avoid writing excessively on a point which interests you to the detriment of other parts of the question. It is a common experience for examiners to find that the first two or three pages of some examination scripts contain nothing of relevance at all. We suspect those are the scripts of candidates who start writing from the first moment, without allowing prior pause for thought.

There are a few other obvious techniques which will endear you to your examiner. Leave the margins on your answer book clear—they are for your examiner's use and not yours. Start each question on a new page and number not only the question clearly, but also the different parts of it. Leave a line between each part. Illegible writing is a handicap in life, but especially so in the examination room. It may not in itself lose you marks, but it will irritate your examiner. Also, an examiner whose attention is directed to deciphering a barely legible script is less likely to be able to follow the argument you are putting forward, which could result in lost marks. Spelling has been called a low form of cunning, but it is important and if it is not your forte, it is worth working on it. This is especially so with legal terms and judges' names. If you do not wish to give the impression you have never opened a law book in your life, you should try to avoid crass errors. (Candidates attempting charity answers, please note: the judge who laid down the four heads of charity was Lord Macnaghten—there is no 'u' in the name and the 'n' is not capital.)

If you suffer from dyslexia, or have an impairment which might affect your ability to write, you might consider it a good idea to mention it to your tutor in advance of your examination. Most institutions are willing to make allowances for this. Some, for example, are prepared to give extra time at the examination, or extra facilities such as the provision of an amanuensis.

The most important point of all is to be sure to ANSWER THE QUESTION YOU ARE ASKED rather than the question you would like to have been asked (perhaps because you revised it in detail the night before). You are unlikely to get marks for irrelevant material and you risk trying the patience of your examiner, which may be wearing thin by the hundred and first script—which just happens to be yours. Avoid writing a treatise on the law on the subject raised by the question—seldom do questions say, 'Write all you know about …'. Above all, assume that all legalities relating to the problem are in order, unless the question specifically suggests otherwise: do not look a gift horse in the mouth. For example, it is not necessary to set out the requirements for a valid will or a valid trust if the question simply states that a will or a trust was made with no indication of any flaws.

Good reading, and good luck!

The nature of equity and the law of trusts

Introduction

The topics covered by this chapter are, by their very nature, bound to be broad and discursive. If you took the opportunity at the beginning of your course (or even during the preceding summer vacation) to undertake some of the general reading recommended by your lecturer, you will reap your reward here. Success in answering these questions depends on a broad reading of the available literature and an historical, even philosophical, approach. You may largely ignore the minutiae of the law reports in favour of a jurisprudential understanding of the development of equity and its doctrinal bases.

For relevant literature, see the Further reading section at the end of this chapter, and check your own reading list for additional material recommended by your lecturer.

The chapter contains four essay questions. The usual principles apply in tackling such questions in exam conditions: draw up a plan in rough and stick to it; do not ramble; make a series of points; write a conclusion.

However, there is a difference in answering essay questions of this type and some of the essay questions covered in the rest of the book. Essays that require discussion of substantive law do, at least, start with something on which to hang your hat. An essay, for example, on the development of the search order, or on the constructive trust, requires an analysis of a sequence of case law. If you know half a dozen cases on the point, then the art is to angle them at the question. Different essay titles on the same area of substantive law usually require the same case law but with a different nose! Essay questions on highly theoretical subjects do require a different style. They require a factual base and plenty of examples of the points you are making, but for high marks they need a touch of original thinking. Even if your thinking is not original, they require a thoughtful intellectual analysis of other people's thinking. If you have not thought about the issues raised by these questions before you enter the examination room, then you are not going to achieve high marks on these questions. If you have the makings of a highly practical lawyer, then select a problem question!

It is quite likely that these topics could crop up as assessed essay questions. If so, then a long session in the library is the starting point. Conduct your preparation for the essay as if you were undertaking a piece of research. Survey the literature noting carefully your sources. Then think over your arguments. Do you agree with X that there has been a fusion of law and equity or do you agree with Y that there has not? Why do you agree or disagree? Do you see both sides of the argument? Argue the case with your friends then write it up while the adrenaline is flowing.

Question 1

The innate conservatism of English lawyers may have made them slow to recognise that by the Judicature Act 1873 the two systems of substantive and adjectival law formerly administered by courts of law and courts of equity ... were fused. As at the confluence of the Rhone and the Saone, it may be possible for a short distance to discern the source from which each part of the combined stream came, but there comes a point at which this ceases to be possible. If Professor Ashburner's fluvial metaphor is to be retained at all, the confluent streams of law and equity have surely mingled now. (Lord Diplock in *United Scientific Holdings Ltd v Burnley Borough Council* [1978] AC 904.)

Discuss.

Commentary

The reference is to Ashburner, *Principles of Equity*, 2nd edn, Butterworths, 1933, at p. 18. Further useful references are Lord Evershed MR (1954) 70 LQR 326; V. Delaney (1961) 24 MLR 116; and J. E. Martin, 'Fusion, fallacy and confusion' [1994] Conv 13. It is interesting to note that there are several statements from judges of the highest seniority which concur with the statement of Lord Diplock quoted above, at least to the extent that they consider that this issue is redundant and the combined effect of the systems should be considered. See, for example, Lord Evershed (1948) JSPTL 180, Lord Denning (1952) CLP 1, and in *Landmarks in the Law* (Butterworths, 1984). Academic writers seem, in general, to take a different view. So, the question is provocative, even controversial. A good modern example of the conflict is provided by the House of Lords' decision in *Tinsley v Milligan* [1994] 1 AC 340 and the ensuing case law. For a criticism of this decision, see R. Buckley (1994) 110 LQR 3.

Answer plan

Establishing the case, *United Scientific Holdings Ltd v Burnley Borough Council*, in context

- Discussion of view that law and equity have mingled with supporting commentary from judges

- Identification of the problem in the separate development of common law and equity with historical survey

- Discussion of effect of **Judicature Acts 1873–1875**

- Critique of Lord Diplock's view with examples

- Discussion of situations and examples of statutes where the difference between legal and equitable interests has been eroded

- Distinction between legal rights and remedies and equitable ones

- Case examples, e.g., *Tinsley* v *Milligan*; *Tribe* v *Tribe*

Suggested answer

The statement by Lord Diplock was accepted unanimously by the judges in the House of Lords. The case concerned the timing of the service of notices triggering rent-review clauses. The notice to trigger a rent review had been served late by the landlord and the question arose as to whether time was of the essence. The **Law of Property Act 1925, s. 41** provides that 'stipulations in a contract, as to time or otherwise, which according to rules of equity are not deemed to be or to have become of the essence of the contract, are also construed and have effect at law in accordance with the same rules'. The section clearly states that a rule of equity is to be adopted within the body of legal rules. Lord Diplock proclaimed that the systems had, quite simply, become fused and that no distinction was to be drawn between law and equity.

This view is at the most extreme, yet it is one apparently shared by other eminent judges. Lord Denning, in *Landmarks in the Law*, states that 'the fusion is complete'. Sir George Jessel MR in *Walsh* v *Lonsdale* (1882) 21 ChD 9, one of the first cases on this issue to be heard subsequent to the **Judicature Acts 1873–1875**, said 'there are not two estates as there were formerly, one estate at common law by reason of the payment of rent from year to year, and an estate in equity under the agreement. There is only one court, and the equity rules prevail in it.' In *Tinsley* v *Milligan* [1994] 1 AC 340, Lord Browne-Wilkinson said that English law was now a single law which was made up of legal and equitable interests, and a person owning either type of estate had a right of property amounting to a right *in rem* not merely a right *in personam*. The approach of Lord Goff in *Napier and Ettrick (Lord)* v *Hunter* [1993] AC 713 is in accord with this: 'No doubt our task nowadays is to see the two strands of authority, at law and in equity, moulded into a coherent whole.'

The difficulty originates from the early development of equity as a separate system from the common law. The common law courts emerged in the centuries following the Norman Conquest. Intervention by the Lord Chancellor gradually developed into a separate body of law, known as equity, which had, by the fifteenth century, become well established. The Chancellor's jurisdiction was exercised through what became the

Court of Chancery. The two systems were sometimes in conflict. Parties seeking common law relief would need to seek the jurisdiction of the common law courts. If they wanted equitable relief they would go to the Court of Chancery. This might occur during the course of the same litigation. The common law courts only had limited jurisdiction to grant equitable relief. The Common Law Procedure Act 1854, s. 79, gave the common law courts a limited power of granting injunctions; the Chancery Amendment Act 1858 gave power to the Court of Chancery to award damages instead of (or in addition to) injunctions or specific performance.

The problem became acute in the nineteenth century, and a series of Parliamentary reports led eventually to the Judicature Acts 1873 and 1875. These Acts amalgamated the superior courts into one Supreme Court of Judicature. The Courts of Queen's Bench, Exchequer and Common Pleas and the Court of Chancery, the Court of Exchequer Chamber and the Court of Appeal in Chancery, were all replaced by the Supreme Court. The Supreme Court consisted of the Court of Appeal and the High Court, which originally had five divisions (subsequently reduced to three). The Supreme Court could administer both rules of common law and equity. Thus, there is no question as to the fusion of the courts. The two distinct sets of courts fused on 1 November 1875. Sir George Jessel MR, who, as Solicitor-General, was the government officer largely responsible for the Judicature Acts, said in *Salt v Cooper* (1880) 16 ChD 544, that the main object of the Acts was not the fusion of law and equity, but the vesting in one tribunal of the administration of law and equity in all actions coming before that tribunal.

Yet it is difficult to pursue Lord Diplock's dictum further to the point of saying that the substantive rules of law and equity are themselves indistinguishable. In trusts there is a distinction between legal and equitable interests and the right to trace property in equity depends on the existence of a fiduciary relationship. In property law the equitable doctrine of part performance was only enforceable by an equitable remedy. Except where statute has intervened, legal and equitable interests are distinguishable in that legal interests are rights *in rem* that bind the whole world whereas equitable rights are lost against equity's darling (the bona fide purchaser of a legal estate for value without notice). In land with unregistered title, the Land Charges Act 1972 made a number of equitable interests registrable (and one legal interest—the puisne mortgage) and indeed had the effect of determining that such interests which are not registered are void against certain types of purchasers. Nevertheless, a group of equitable interests still fall outside the ambit of this statute and are subject to the equitable doctrine of notice. Equitable interests behind a trust, pre-1926 equitable easements and restrictive covenants fall into this category.

It is possible to cite examples, however, where the distinction has become irrelevant. In registered land, the categories of registered, minor and overriding interests imposed by the Land Registration Act 1925 cut across the distinction between legal and equitable interests. In turn, the importance of the Land Registration Act 2002 which repealed the Land Registration Act 1925, does not rest on distinctions between these interests. Statute has rendered the distinction redundant.

Remedies present some interesting examples of the distinction which has grown up between law and equity; a distinction which arose as 'an accident of history' according to Lord Nicholls in *A-G v Blake* [2000] 3 WLR 625, p. 634. In general, legal rights and remedies remain distinct from equitable ones. Some overlap does, however, occur; for example, an injunction, an equitable remedy, can be sought for an anticipatory breach of contract, or to stop a nuisance, both common law claims. In *A-G v Blake* [2000] 3 WLR 625, the House of Lords allowed the equitable remedy of account of profits for a claim for breach of contract where the common law remedy of damages would have been inadequate. The equitable remedy of account of profits is normally available where there is a fiduciary relationship but the House of Lords permitted its application otherwise in exceptional cases where it was the effective way to remedy a wrong. By contrast, in *Seager v Copydex Ltd* [1967] 1 WLR 923, CA, an action was brought for breach of confidence in respect of confidential information revealed by the defendants about a carpet grip. Such a claim is equitable and normally the equitable remedies of injunction and account are available. However, an injunction would have been ineffective and the judge awarded damages. It would seem, therefore, that a common law remedy is available for an equitable claim for breach of confidence. See, for example, the *Spycatcher* case, *A-G v Guardian Newspapers Ltd (No. 2)* [1990] 1 AC 109 (p. 286 per Lord Goff).

In *Tinsley v Milligan* [1994] 1 AC 340, it was held that the equitable principle governing when title to property was affected by illegality had now merged into the rule of common law. A claimant can therefore enforce a property right acquired pursuant to an illegal contract, provided that he does not need to bring evidence of the illegality to establish his title.

In *Tinsley v Milligan*, the conflict between law and equity became apparent in a modern setting. Two women agreed that a house they shared should be held in the name of one so that the other could fraudulently claim housing benefit. When they later disagreed, the legal owner sought to evict her partner. The defendant claimed that she had an equitable interest. The House of Lords held that the defendant had a right to assert her equitable ownership. The principle that a litigant cannot rely on an illegal purpose to rebut the presumption of advancement was confirmed, but, in this case, the equitable presumption of the resulting trust was held to apply. Thus, the defendant did not need to rely on her own illegal conduct and the equitable maxim that 'he who comes to equity should come with clean hands' did not have to be invoked. This case, seeking to balance illegality and unjust enrichment, has created difficulties in application. In *Tribe v Tribe* [1996] Ch 107, a case concerning a transfer of shares from father to son, the matter was complicated by the effect of the presumption of advancement. (Note that, when s. 199 of the Equality Act 2010 comes into effect, it will abolish the presumption of advancement.) *Tinsley v Milligan* had confirmed the principle that a litigant cannot rely on his or her own fraud or illegality to rebut this presumption except where there is some act of repentance. But in *Tribe v Tribe*, the Court of Appeal held that, in the circumstances of this particular case, the father would be able to rely on an illegal purpose to rebut the presumption of advancement because the illegality (the avoidance of the cost by the tenant of a schedule of dilapidations) had not proved necessary and had not been carried out. This result meant that the two cases were consistent: the defendant (Miss Milligan) had recovered her interest in the house even though she had acted fraudulently; the father (David Tribe) had also recovered his shares although he had planned a fraudulent act. To have come to a different result simply because the relationship between the parties in *Tribe* v *Tribe* gave rise to the presumption of advancement, was not considered appropriate by the Court of Appeal. This area of illegal transactions has also been the subject of a Law Commission consultation: (see Law Com Consultation Paper No. 154 (1999) *Illegal Transactions: The Effect of Illegality on Contracts and Trusts*).

Thus, the systems are administered in the same courts, but in general the distinction remains relevant and continues to produce conflicts.

Question 2

Equity is not past the age of child bearing (per Lord Denning MR, *Eves* v *Eves* [1975] 1 WLR 1338, CA).

Discuss.

 Commentary

This question may sometimes appear as an assessed essay. Confronted in the examination room, it may seem daunting. What should be included? Clearly the source of the quotation should be considered. In context, it is being used to justify a new development in equity; in the particular case cited, the new model constructive trust. It would be justifiable to limit the answer to this particular topic, but, on the other hand, it could be broadened to include all the new developments over recent years in the field of equity. To select one or the other approach cannot be wrong. However, as in many situations, in attempting to produce the answer the examiner wants, you should consider the approach in lectures. Did the lecturer use this as a general theme throughout the course? This might indicate the wide-ranging approach. Or was particular attention paid to the novelty of the new model constructive trust?

If the question is set as coursework there is a greater argument for adopting the broad approach. There is scope for a powerful dissertation. In the examination room it may be safer to adopt the narrow approach rather than attempt to be too ambitious. It could, of course, be a gift of a question if you know a little about everything, rather than a lot about a limited subject.

The answer suggested here takes the broad approach.

Answer plan

- Discussion of equity and its flexible nature
- List of equitable innovations
- Judicial justifications of equitable innovations
- Equitable remedies: search orders; freezing injunctions
- Constructive trusts: the new model
- Proprietary estoppel
- Undue influence in mortgage cases

Suggested answer

When equity originally developed as a gloss on the common law it was innovative; it developed new remedies and recognised new rights where the common law failed to act. The efficacy of equity was largely due to its ability to adapt and innovate, yet inevitably, this development itself became regulated in a similar way to the development of the common law. There are maxims of equity which may determine the outcome of disputes. Although the judge has a discretion in the granting of an equitable remedy, that discretion is exercised according to settled principles. Thus, it might be said that equity can develop no further; the rules of precedent predetermine the outcome.

Yet, this is belied by a number of new developments in equity, for example, the recognition of restrictive covenants, the expansion of remedies, the development of doctrines such as proprietary estoppel, the enhanced status of contractual licences and, as referred to in the quotation from the judgment of Lord Denning MR, the new model constructive trust, are all illustrations of developments in equity.

There is an attempt, however, to justify these new developments, which are all examples of judicial creativity, by precedent. As Bagnall J said in *Cowcher* v *Cowcher* [1972] **1 WLR 425** at p. 430: 'This does not mean that equity is past childbearing; simply that its progeny must be legitimate—by precedent out of principle. It is well that this should be so; otherwise no lawyer could safely advise on his client's title and every quarrel would lead to a law-suit'.

Equity developed the remedies of the injunction, specific performance, account, rectification and rescission. The injunction has been a growth area. The search order (developed in the case *Anton Piller KG* v *Manufacturing Processes Ltd* [1976] Ch 55), reflects the growth of new technology and the need to protect ownership rights in that property. Intellectual property such as video and audio tapes and computer programs can easily be destroyed before an action for breach of copyright can be brought. Confidential information relating to industrial processes can disappear leaving a claimant with no means of proof. The search order developed to allow a claimant to enter a defendant's premises to search for and seize such property where there was a clear risk that such property would be destroyed before trial. As an area of equitable creativity, it is still being refined by the judges, with cases such as *Columbia Picture Industries Inc.* v *Robinson* [1986] 3 All ER 338 and *Universal Thermosensors Ltd* v *Hibben* [1992] 1 WLR 840 laying down guidelines for the exercise of such a Draconian order.

The freezing injunction is another example of a refined application of an established remedy developed in the case of *Mareva Compañía Naviera SA* v *International Bulk Carriers SA* [1975] 2 Lloyd's Rep 509 following *Nippon Yusen Kaisha* v *Karageorgis* [1975] 1 WLR 1093. While a claim may succeed, if it is impossible to enforce a judgment because there are no assets, then the judgment is worthless. In international disputes, assets may be transferred abroad to make the judgment debt impossible, or at least, very difficult, to follow. Recognising this dilemma, the judges in the *Mareva* case were prepared to grant an order freezing the defendant's assets. Further cases have now demonstrated that the courts are prepared to make this order available worldwide in certain circumstances (see, for example, *Derby & Co. Ltd* v *Weldon (No. 3 and No. 4)* (1989) 139 NLJ 11 and *Republic of Haiti* v *Duvalier* [1990] 1 QB 202).

Equity initially recognised the trust. This was one of the original developments of equity. However, the protection granted to equitable owners behind a trust has developed significantly over the last 30 years with the new model constructive trust, the contractual licence and the doctrine of proprietary estoppel.

The constructive trust of a new model developed largely because of the creative activity of Lord Denning MR. In *Hussey* v *Palmer* [1972] 1 WLR 1286, CA, Lord Denning described the constructive trust as one 'imposed by law wherever justice and good conscience require it'. Cases such as *Eves* v *Eves* [1975] 1 WLR 1338, CA, where the woman was given an equitable interest in the property representing her contribution in terms of heavy work, and *Cooke* v *Head* [1972] 1 WLR 518, CA, a similar case, took this development further. Several cases, including *Lloyds Bank* v *Rosset* [1991] 1 AC 107, have re-established earlier principles in this field relating to the existence of a common intention that an equitable interest should arise, and the existence of a direct financial contribution. These principles are more akin to those relating to the establishment of a resulting trust. Nevertheless, the House of Lords in *Stack* v *Dowden* [2007] UKHL 17 re-introduced some of the earlier flexibility into the constructive trust showing that equity is alive and well.

The new model constructive trust has been most alive in the field of licences. At common law, a contractual licence was controlled by the doctrine of privity of contract, and failed to provide protection against a third party. Equitable remedies have been made available to prevent a licensor breaking a contractual licence and to enable a licence to bind third parties. It has been accepted that certain licences may create an equitable proprietary interest by way of a constructive trust or proprietary estoppel. In *Binions* v *Evans* [1972] Ch 359, CA, it was held by Lord Denning MR that purchasers were bound by a contractual licence between the former owners and Mrs Evans, an occupant. A constructive trust was imposed in her favour as the purchasers had bought expressly subject to Mrs Evans' interest and had, for that reason, paid a reduced price. Also in *Re Sharpe* [1980] 1 WLR 219, a constructive trust was imposed on a trustee in bankruptcy in respect of an interest acquired by an aunt who lent money to her nephew for a house purchase on the understanding that she could live there for the rest of her life.

The fluidity of these developing areas is shown in case law which appears to hold back from a development which may have pushed the frontiers too far. Obiter dicta by the Court of Appeal in *Ashburn Anstalt v W. J. Arnold & Co.* [1989] Ch 1, approved in *Habermann v Koehler* (1996) 73 P & CR 515, suggest that a licence will only give rise to a constructive trust where the conscience of a third party is affected. It will be imposed where their conduct so warrants. Judicial creativity in equitable fields is thus made subject to refinements by judges in later cases.

Proprietary estoppel is another example of an equitable doctrine which has seen significant developments in the interests of justice since its establishment in the leading case of *Dillwyn v Llewelyn* (1862) 4 De GF & J 517. The doctrine is based on encouragement and acquiescence whereby equity was prepared to intervene and adjust the rights of the parties. Its application has been further enhanced by the Court of Appeal in *Gillett v Holt* [2001] Ch 210, where a broader approach to the doctrine was taken that depended, ultimately, on the unconscionability of the action. Two House of Lords' decisions in *Yeoman's Row Management v Cobbe* [2008] UKHL 55 and *Thorner v Major* [2009] UKHL 18 have also injected new approaches into the doctrine and have both generated a lively discussion. Again, it is a development which stands outside the system of property rights and their registration established by Parliament.

Cases such as *Jennings v Rice* [2002] EWCA Civ 159, [2003] 1 P & CR 8, *Matharu v Matharu* (1994) 68 P & CR 93, *Costello v Costello* (1995) 70 P & CR 297 and *Durant v Heritage* [1994] EGCS 134 show that the doctrine of proprietary estoppel and the protection of licences by estoppel remain an effective method used by the judges for the protection of licences and equitable rights. The degree to which the right receives protection is variable depending on the circumstances of the particular case. For instance, in *Matharu v Matharu*, the licence did not confer a beneficial interest but gave the respondent a right to live in the house for the rest of her life. In *Durant v Heritage* the court ordered the house to be transferred to the applicant under the doctrine of proprietary estoppel. In *Jennings v Rice* [2002] EWCA Civ 159, [2003] 1 P & CR 8, by contrast, the equity was satisfied by monetary compensation.

Another development in equity resulted from the decisions of the House of Lords in *Barclays Bank plc v O'Brien* [1994] 1 AC 180 and *CIBC Mortgages plc v Pitt* [1994] 1 AC 200. These two cases heralded the re-emergence in a broad sense of the equitable doctrine of notice. They provide that, where there is undue influence over a co-mortgagor or surety, this may give rise to a right to avoid the transaction. This right to avoid the transaction amounts to an equity of which the mortgagee may be deemed to have constructive notice. This resurrection of the equitable doctrine of notice in a very modern context demonstrates clearly the flexibility of equity. A number of cases followed these two decisions. In *Royal Bank of Scotland* v *Etridge (No. 2)* [2001] **4 All ER 449** (a case in which eight conjoined appeals were heard), the House of Lords laid down general guidelines for the application of the doctrine of notice in this context.

So, although there may be setbacks and refinements in the development of new doctrines when later judges seek to rationalise and consolidate new principles, nevertheless it is clear that equity maintains its traditions.

Question 3

Explain and discuss the maxim, 'equity looks upon that as done which ought to be done'. To what extent (if any) does this maxim operate to impose a trust on any person?

 Commentary

This discussion question requires an examination of the various applications of the maxim. It touches upon a number of different fields. In relation to trusts of land, its operation was affected by the **Trusts of Land and Appointment of Trustees Act 1996**. On the application of the doctrine in the context of *Williams & Glyn's Bank Ltd* v *Boland* [1981] AC 487, HL, see Stuart Anderson (1984) 100 LQR 86.

Some aspects of this are esoteric, for example, the rule in *Lawes* v *Bennett* (1785) 1 Cox 167. Many lecturers do not cover this rule in their courses. If that is the case then you may not be expected to deal with it in a question of this sort. The guidance on the suggested content of this answer offered here must be tempered by what you have been expected to cover in your syllabus.

Answer plan

- Explanation of maxims of equity as body of principles
- Explanation of maxim 'equity looks upon that as done which ought to be done'
- Examples of contract of sale for land; specifically enforceable agreements; contracts for leases and rule in *Walsh* v *Lonsdale*; doctrine of conversion; rule in *Lawes* v *Bennett*; conditional contracts; rule in *Howe* v *Earl of Dartmouth*

Suggested answer

The maxims of equity operate as guidelines for the exercise of judicial discretion. Although equity did not acquire the rigidity of the common law, it did develop a body of principles. An equitable remedy is available at the discretion of the judge. The judge is assisted in the exercise of this discretion by these principles. They provide, for example, that for claimants to be granted equitable remedies, they must come to court with clean hands; they must have behaved equitably and must not have delayed in seeking the intervention of equity. These principles, known as maxims, do not operate as binding precedent but provide a basis for the development of equity. Some of them have, however, formed the basis for certain rules which are binding. There are 12 maxims in addition to some general principles.

The maxim 'equity looks upon that as done which ought to be done' demonstrates the principle that, where there is a specifically enforceable obligation, equity will enforce it as though the obligation had been carried out. The common law is rigid in that, if the proper formality has not been carried out (for example, the execution of a deed for the transfer of an interest in land) then it will not recognise the interest. Equity is prepared, nonetheless, to enforce the obligation as though all due formalities are present.

For example, a contract for the sale of land is specifically enforceable if it has been effected in accordance with the rules laid down in the **Law of Property (Miscellaneous Provisions) Act 1989, s. 2**. It is an estate contract which creates an equitable interest in favour of the purchaser, and is binding on third parties if protected by registration. Until completion, the vendor holds the legal estate upon constructive trust for the purchaser.

It is arguable, on the authority of *Oughtred* v *IRC* [1960] AC 206, HL, and *Re Holt's Settlement* [1969] 1 Ch 100, that, once an agreement has been entered into which is specifically enforceable, then the equitable interest passes without the need for formalities, as provided by the **Law of Property Act 1925, s. 53(2)**. This view was held to be sound in *Neville* v *Wilson* [1997] Ch 144, CA.

A contract for a lease, provided it complies with the contractual requirements, is enforceable in equity under the rule in *Walsh* v *Lonsdale* (1882) 21 ChD 9. Although the due formality of a deed required at law has not been complied with, equity sees as done that which ought to be done, and enforces the contract for the lease.

The maxim underlies the doctrine of conversion. Before the implementation of the **Trusts of Land and Appointment of Trustees Act 1996**, this doctrine stated that where there was a trust for the sale of land, equity assumed that the sale had already taken place. This meant, therefore, that the beneficiaries' interests were deemed to have been converted into personalty already, even if the land had not been sold. Since many trusts for sale arose where couples purchased a home for their joint occupation, their interests were frequently held in this manner long before the property was sold. The problem was considered in *Williams & Glyn's Bank Ltd* v *Boland*

[1981] AC 487, HL. Mrs Boland was deemed to have an interest behind a trust for sale. The contest arose between her equitable interest and the interest of the bank, as mortgagee of the legal estate. If Mrs Boland had an interest in land then she would have an overriding interest under the **Land Registration Act 1925, s. 70(1)(g)** (now repealed and replaced by the **Land Registration Act 2002**). However, if her interest had already been converted into personalty, she would not have an overriding interest since the sub-section only protects rights in land. It was held that the purpose of the doctrine was to simplify conveyancing in cases where the intention was to sell the land immediately. The doctrine should not be extended beyond that to a case where it was clearly a fiction.

The **Trusts of Land and Appointment of Trustees Act (TLATA) 1996** provides that trusts for the sale of land are replaced by trusts of land with the power of sale. This means that the interest behind the trust is an interest in land until the power is exercised (s. 3(1)). This applies to trusts for sale arising before or after the commencement of the TLATA 1996, except in relation to trusts created by will where the testator died before commencement (s. 3(2), (3)).

A more obscure application of the doctrine is the rule in *Lawes* v *Bennett* (1785) 1 Cox 167, which applies to the exercise of an option. If a leaseholder is granted an option to purchase the freehold and the freeholder dies before the option is exercised, then the disposition of the rents pending the exercise of the option, and the eventual purchase price, must be determined. The rents will go to the person entitled to the freehold. This would be either a residuary or a specific devisee. The proceeds of sale, however, which are payable when (and if) the option is exercised, pass to the residuary legatee as conversion into personalty is deemed to have taken place.

The maxim was applied to conditional contracts in *Re Sweeting (deceased)* [1988] 1 All ER 1016. A contract for the sale of land, subject to conditions, was not completed until after the vendor's death. It was held that the proceeds of sale went to the residuary legatee as the interest had already been converted into personalty.

The maxim also underlies the rule in *Howe* v *Earl of Dartmouth* (1802) 7 Ves 137, which relates to the duty to convert (*inter alia*) wasting assets. The rule is limited in that it only applies to residuary personalty settled by will in favour of persons with successive interests. The duty is that, where there are hazardous, wasting or reversionary assets they must be converted into authorised investments. Where there is a duty to convert, there is also a duty to apportion between the life tenant and remainderman until sale. The scope of the rule in *Howe* v *Earl of Dartmouth* is now of more limited significance, however, as the **Trustee Act 2000** has greatly widened the range of investments that are available to trustees.

So, the maxim applies to a variety of cases where equity is prepared to act as though the common law requirements had been fully complied with, or to convert property where it is equitable to do so.

Question 4

What is equity?

Commentary

This question requires an historical and jurisprudential analysis of the meaning and position of equity in the legal system.

It is important to use examples to avoid an undirected discussion. The approach suggested here is to deal with the historical side first, using this as a vehicle for a discussion of the contribution which equity has made to the legal system.

Answer plan

- Explanation of the term 'equity'
- Equitable maxims
- Contrast between the development of equity and the common law
- Principle in cases of conflict established in **Senior Courts Act 1981, s. 49**
- Equitable remedies
- The development of common law courts and courts of equity

Suggested answer

Equity to the layman means fairness and justice, but in the legal context its meaning is much more strictly defined. There are rules of equity: it must obey the rules of precedent as does the common law, and its development may appear equally inflexible and rigid.

Yet, because of its historical development and the reasons underlying this, there does remain an element of discretion and the potential for judges to retain some flexibility in the determination of disputes.

There are well-established principles which govern the exercise of the discretion but these, like all equitable principles, are flexible and adaptable to achieve the ends of equity, which is, as Lord Selborne LC once remarked, to 'do more perfect and complete justice' than would be the result of leaving the parties to their remedies at common law: *Wilson v Northampton and Banbury Junction Railway* Co. (1874) LR 9 Ch App 279, 284 (and see Lord Hoffmann, *Co-operative Insurance Society Ltd v Argyll Stores (Holdings) Ltd* [1998] AC 1).

Equity developed as a result of the inflexibility of the common law; it 'wiped away the tears of the common law' in the words of one American jurist. When the common law developed the strictures of the writ system through the twelfth and the thirteenth centuries and failed to develop further remedies, individuals aggrieved by the failure of the common law to remedy their apparent injustice petitioned the King and Council. The King was the fountain of justice and if his judges failed to provide a remedy then the solution was to petition the King directly. The King, preoccupied with affairs of state, handed these petitions to his chief minister, the Chancellor. The Chancellor was head of the Chancery, amongst other state departments. The Chancery was the office which issued writs and, therefore, when the courts failed to provide a remedy, it was appropriate to seek the assistance of the head of the court system. Originally the Chancellor was usually an ecclesiastic. The last non-lawyer was Lord Shaftesbury who retired in 1672. Receiving citizens' petitions, the Chancellor adjudicated them, not according to the common law, but according to principles of fairness and justice; thus developed equity.

Early on, each individual Chancellor developed personal systems of justice giving rise to the criticism that equity had been as long as the Chancellor's foot. The Lord Chancellor did indeed sit alone in his court of equity, or Chancery, as it became known. It was not until 1813 that a Vice-Chancellor was appointed to deal with the volume of work. Equity began to emerge as a clear set of principles, rather than a personal jurisdiction of the Chancellor, during the Chancellorship of Lord Nottingham in 1673. By the end of Lord Eldon's Chancellorship in 1827 equity was established as a precise jurisdiction.

But the development of a parallel yet separate system of dispute resolution was inevitably bound to create a conflict. An individual aggrieved by a failure of the common law to remedy a gross injustice would apply to the court of equity. The Chancellor, if the case warranted it, would grant a remedy preventing the common law court from enforcing its order.

The catharsis occurred in the *Earl of Oxford's Case* (1615) 1 Rep Ch 1, where the court of common law ordered the payment of a debt. The debt had already been paid, but the deed giving rise to the obligation had not been cancelled. The court of equity was prepared to grant an order preventing this and rectifying the deed.

The clash was eventually resolved in favour of equity; where there is a conflict, equity prevails. This rule is now enshrined in the **Senior Courts Act 1981, s. 49.**

A series of maxims underlies the operation of equity, establishing a series of principles. For example: 'equity looks upon that as done which ought to be done'; 'he who comes to equity must come with clean hands'; 'equity will not allow a statute to be used as a cloak for fraud', are all examples of the maxims.

The remedies developed by equity, such as injunctions and specific performance, are, unlike the common law remedy of damages, subject to the discretion of the judge. Thus a judge may decide that, although a breach of contract has been established, the conduct of the claimant is such that an equitable remedy should not be granted. In addition, if damages are an adequate remedy, then there is no need to substitute an equitable remedy.

In substantive law, equity has frequently reflected the reality of transactions between private citizens. It recognised the trust when the common law had refused to acknowledge the existence of a beneficiary and provide remedies for breach of trust against a defaulting trustee. The concept of the trust has been the vehicle for much creative activity on the part of the courts of equity. The trust has developed from an express agreement between parties to situations where the conduct of parties has led the courts to infer or to impose a trust.

So, equity remains a separate system of rules operating independently of the common law. Until the late nineteenth century it operated in a separate set of courts. So, a plaintiff seeking both legal and equitable remedies would be obliged to pursue an action in separate courts. Much delay and expense ensued. The position was eventually resolved in the **Judicature Acts 1873** and **1875** which established a system of courts in which both the rules of equity and common law could be administered. The position had already been ameliorated to some degree by the **Common Law Procedure Act 1854**, which gave the common law courts power to grant equitable remedies, and the **Chancery Amendment Act 1858 (Lord Cairns' Act)**, which gave the Court of Chancery power to award damages in addition to, or in substitution for, an injunction or a decree of specific performance. A claimant can, therefore seek both damages and an injunction in the same court.

The equitable jurisdiction is, in fact, a personal jurisdiction operating against the conscience of the individual, whereas the common law jurisdiction operates against real property. Thus, an order from a court based on equitable principles preventing a legal order being enforced operates against the conscience of the defendant. In theory, therefore, there is no clash between the jurisdictions. In practice, there is a significant constraint on the common law jurisdiction.

The historical distinction does remain, however, in the existence of separate divisions of the High Court, viz., the Chancery Division (which deals primarily with matters which involve equitable rights and remedies) and the Queen's Bench Division (which deals primarily with matters involving rights and remedies at common law).

So, equity represents a later development of law, laying an additional body of rules over the existing common law which, in the majority of cases, provides an adequate remedy: 'Equity, therefore, does not destroy the law, nor create it, but assists it' (per Sir Nathan Wright LJ in *Lord Dudley and Ward* v *Lady Dudley* (1705) Pr Ch 241 at p. 244).

Further reading

Anderson, S. (1984) 100 LQR 86.

Ashburner, *Principles of Equity*, 2nd edn, Butterworths, 1933.

Buckley, R. (1994) 110 LQR 3.

Delaney, V. (1961) 24 MLR 116.

Gardner, S., 'Two maxims of equity' [1995] CLJ 60.

Holdsworth, W., *History of English Law*, 7th edn, Sweet & Maxwell, 1966.

Lord Denning (1952) CLP 1.

Lord Denning, *Landmarks in the Law*, Butterworths, 1984.

Lord Evershed (1948) JSPTL 180.

Lord Evershed MR (1954) 70 LQR 326.

Maitland, F. W., *Equity*, 2nd edn, Cambridge University Press, 1936.

Pettit, P. H., 'He who comes to equity must come with clean hands' [1990] Conv 416.

Pollock, F., *Jurisprudence and Legal Essays*, Macmillan, 1961.

Snell, E., *Principles of Equity*, 30th edn, Sweet & Maxwell, 2000.

Watkin, T. (1977) 6 AALR 119.

3

The three certainties and formalities

Introduction

Questions on certainties are usually problem-type questions. Frequently all three of the certainties—intention, subject-matter and objects—will be included in one question. The classic form of a question in this area involves a will with a series of gifts, each of which raises a separate issue on certainty; the testator will have just died and you will be asked to advise the executors.

The question may be confined to certainty within trusts. However, you may be expected to make a comparison with the rules for certainty for powers, particularly if the question also concerns certainty of objects (see question 3(c)). If you intend to answer a question on certainty therefore, you should also know the distinction between trusts and powers.

Some of the cases highlight the distinction between a trust and other transactions such as a gift, and illustrate the application of the rule of equity that 'equity will not construe an invalid gift as a trust'. You should therefore be aware of the requirements for a valid gift.

A wide knowledge of case law is essential for answering these problems. Frequently, parts of the question may appear to be based directly on one case. Avoid the temptation to start your answer with a reference to the case. Establish the general principle, apply it to the particular problem, and then support it with a reference to the particular case.

Sometimes there is a trap in these apparently straightforward questions. If the question seems to fit very obviously into a particular precedent, look out for a later precedent which may distinguish it. See question 1(a) for an example of this. Apart from this possibility, these problem questions are usually plain sailing if you know the basic principles and some of the cases. It is more important to remember the wording used in a case than the name. If you find names difficult to memorise, you can always write: 'In a decided case …'. You will lose some marks but not as many as you would if you were to omit the case altogether.

When dealing with different parts of the question avoid repeating yourself. If you have dealt with certainty of intention in part (a), for example, then do not run through the points again for part (b). The examiner would not want more than a brief reference to the point if it occurred in a different form in part (b) and would not give you marks for regurgitating the same law again. Part (b) will invariably involve a different issue, perhaps another certainty, and you should deal with this at more length. If you think both parts are on certainty of intention and nothing else, then you are probably in trouble and should choose another question.

Problem questions are relatively easy to devise and discussion questions are quite rare in this field—unless your examiners happen to be gifted creative writers. We have therefore included three problem-type questions in this chapter. Any essay question which your examiner devised is likely to be straightforward and you could use the material in these problem questions for it.

Generally, these problem questions are gifts to the reasonably well-prepared examinee. No such person should get less than a 2(ii) on such a question. Conversely, it is quite difficult to get a first. You would really need to impress the examiner with a detailed knowledge of the cases, perhaps even referring to distinguishing judgments (as in question 1(a) with the reference to *Comiskey v Bowring-Hanbury* [1905] AC 84).

Not infrequently, examiners have been known to include certainty in 'pick 'n' mix'-type questions. Tread warily! Certainty could be mixed in with questions on topics such as constructive trusts, charities or trusts of imperfect obligation. For an example, see question 4 in Chapter 9.

The formality requirements for trusts are contained in **LPA 1925, s. 53.** You should be aware of the basic requirements of this section. A more in-depth consideration of the section's application to various transactions is required by question 4, and the cases on this are complex and difficult for the reasons explained in the Commentary. For further reading on s. 53 and the cases on it discussed in question 4, see the Further reading section at the end of this chapter.

Question 1

Lucien, who died recently, left a will appointing Bill and Ben his executors and trustees. The will contained the following dispositions:

(a) 'My freehold house to my wife Harriet absolutely in full confidence that she will hold it for either my daughter Tessa or my son James as she sees fit.'

(b) 'The income from my blue-chip shares to my trustees Bill and Ben from which they must ensure that my old Uncle Tom has a reasonable standard of living.'

(c) 'Three of my five Van Gogh paintings to my trustees to hold one of them in trust for my sister Pearl, whichever she may choose, and the other two in trust for my sister Jewel.' Pearl died before the testator.

Advise Bill and Ben as to the validity of these dispositions.
    Would your answer in (c) differ if Pearl had survived the testator but died before choosing?

Commentary

This question is an example of how two parts of a question, **(a)** and **(b)**, may both include different examples of uncertainty as to words or intention. You should therefore state the general law on this subject fairly fully in your answer to **(a)**, but merely refer to it briefly and apply it in your answer to **(b)**.

Both parts **(b)** and **(c)** include uncertainty as to subject-matter, and again any general statement of law on this should be made under **(b)** and avoid repetition of this under **(c)**.

It may be appropriate to mention some cases briefly in **(a)** and discuss them further in **(b)** and **(c)**, but make sure that they are relevant ones, e.g., *Mussoorie Bank* v *Raynor* **(1882) 7 App Cas 321**, where the words 'feeling confident that she will act justly to our children in distributing the same' were held not to create a trust. However, as well as looking for an understanding of the requirement of certainty of intention, the examiner will be looking for a proper application of the law to the problem set and not a general discussion of cases which are dissimilar. Remember that there are three parts to the question and you should not spend an undue amount of time on one part at the expense of the other parts.

Answer plan

(a)
- Do the words 'in full confidence' impose a trust or are they merely precatory?
- Cases on certainty of words
- If a trust, then a discretionary trust
- If no trust, then operates as an absolute gift to Harriet

(b)
- Possible uncertainty of subject-matter both as to the trust itself and as to the amount to be used for Uncle Tom
- Possible that uncertainty as to Tom's share may be resolved by *Re Golay*, where the court said that 'reasonable income' was capable of objective determination

(c)
- Possible uncertainty as to subject-matter again as to which three of the five Van Gogh paintings
- Also uncertainty of subject-matter as to which two paintings Jewel is to have as Pearl, with the power to choose, has died before choosing (*Boyce* v *Boyce*)
- If Pearl survives the testator but dies without choosing, there is still uncertainty of subject-matter. There are possible, but untried, arguments which might persuade the court to decide differently

Suggested answer

(a) In *Knight* v *Knight* (1840) 3 Beav 148, Lord Langdale MR said that three certainties were required to establish a valid trust, namely, certainty of words (or intention), subject-matter and objects. The essence of a trust is that it imposes a binding obligation on the trustees, and the question to consider here is whether the words used are sufficiently obligatory to impose a trust. Until the Executors Act 1830, courts were very ready to find a trust, as property to which a trust was not attached would remain in the hands of the executors. The Executors Act 1830 changed this, however, and from then on the courts were less willing to find a trust where the words used could be construed as merely precatory. *Lambe* v *Eames* (1871) 6 Ch App 597 is generally regarded as the turning-point, where the court refused to construe merely precatory words as creating a trust. In *Re Steele's Will Trusts* [1948] Ch 603 it was said that the exception to this would be where a testator had used identical wording to that previously held to create a trust. This case has been criticised, however, for replacing a search for the testator's intention with a mechanical application of legal rules; furthermore it ignores the fact that the meaning of words can change over time.

There are two conflicting cases where words used were similar to those found here. In *Re Adams & Kensington Vestry* (1884) 27 ChD 394 a gift 'to the absolute use of my wife ... in full confidence that she will do what is right as to the disposal thereof between my children' was held not to impose any trust upon the wife but was construed by the court to be an absolute gift to her. In *Comiskey* v *Bowring-Hanbury* [1905] AC 84, however, the House of Lords (Lord Lindley dissenting) considered a bequest to the testator's wife of 'the whole of my real and personal estate absolutely in full confidence that she will make use of it as I should have made myself and that at her death she will devise it to such one or more of my nieces as she may think fit and in default to my nieces equally'. This was held to create a trust for the widow for life, remainder to the nieces as she might by will appoint, but otherwise equally between them, as the testator had shown a clear intention to benefit his nieces in any event.

In *Re Hamilton* [1895] 2 Ch 370 it was said by Lindley LJ that each disposition must be construed on its own merits. The disposition in this problem appears to be nearer to *Re Adams & Kensington Vestry* than to *Comiskey* v *Bowring-Hanbury* on the ground that there is no gift over in default. Nevertheless it may be possible to distinguish the disposition in (a) from *Re Adams & Kensington Vestry* on the specificity of the ultimate beneficiaries—in which case it could be construed as imposing a trust.

If there is a trust, it is a discretionary trust for either Tessa or James, and there is therefore no uncertainty of objects. If the words are held not to impose a trust, then the disposition operates as an absolute gift to Harriet.

(b) For a trust to be valid, the subject-matter must also be certain. This includes both the property and the beneficial interests which the beneficiaries are to take. If either of these is uncertain, the trust will fail. In this case, it is possible that both are uncertain.

In *Re Kolb's Will Trusts* [1962] Ch 531 it was said that a reference to stocks and shares 'in the blue-chip category' was insufficiently certain because the term 'blue chip', whilst used to indicate a very good share, has no precise meaning. If so, the trust will fail for uncertainty of subject-matter, which means that all Lucien's shares (and the income therefrom) not otherwise validly and specifically bequeathed, will form part of Lucien's residuary estate. If, however, the reference to blue-chip shares is held sufficiently certain it becomes necessary to consider other parts of this disposition.

The wording 'they must ensure' might well be sufficiently obligatory to impose a trust on the income in the hands of the trustees, as it indicates that the trustees were not intended to enjoy the whole of the income beneficially. It would appear, however, that they are not to use the whole of the income for Uncle Tom. Sufficient income for a reasonable standard of living might appear to be uncertain, but in *Re Golay's Will Trusts* [1965] 1 WLR 969 it was held that 'a reasonable income' was capable of being quantified objectively in relation to a person's lifestyle. Presumably, therefore, a sufficient income relating to Uncle Tom's lifestyle could be ascertained.

(c) The problem in this part of the question is again to determine the subject-matter of the trust. There is an initial uncertainty as to the subject-matter of the trust as a whole, that is, as to which three of the five Van Gogh paintings are to be held on trust for Pearl to choose from. This is similar to *Palmer* v *Simmonds* (1854) 2 Drew 221, where a gift of 'the bulk of my estate' failed for uncertainty. Additionally, the interests of Pearl and Jewel are uncertain until Pearl has made her choice; death means that no choice can now be made. In *Boyce* v *Boyce* (1849) 16 Sim 476, a testator left three houses in his will, 'one to Maria, which she may choose; the others to Charlotte'. Maria pre-deceased the testator, and the trust for Charlotte, which was dependent upon Maria's choice, was held to fail for certainty of subject-matter. Pearl having predeceased the testator, it is impossible to determine which paintings should be held in trust for Jewel. All three paintings will therefore fall into residue. In the absence of a residuary gift, they will pass, as on intestacy, to Lucien's next-of-kin.

If Pearl had survived the testator but died before making a choice, although prima facie there is still an uncertainty of subject-matter, it is possible that this would enable the circumstances to be distinguished from *Boyce* v *Boyce*. The *Boyce* v *Boyce* situation has an element of ademption about it as the testator is presumed to know that Pearl has predeceased him and is therefore unable to make a choice. However, if the testator has no reason to suppose that Pearl will not choose, and dies in the belief that he has set up a valid trust, it might be possible for equity to intervene, although it is not clear how. The maxim 'Equity is equality' would not reflect the testator's intentions.

One tenuous argument might be that Lucien intended to make Pearl a trustee of the power of selection, i.e., that it is a trust power to select. This would mean that the maxim 'Equity will not allow a trust to fail for want of a trustee' could be applied, and someone else (or even the court) could make the choice. On the wording of the disposition, however, there seems little to favour such a construction.

Question 2

Clockwise Ltd is a mail order company selling a particularly popular line of talking alarm clocks. It received numerous orders with accompanying cheques but, because of difficulties with the suppliers of certain components, was unable to dispatch the orders. On the advice of the company's accountants, the cheques were paid into a separate bank account which the bank was instructed to call the 'Customers' Trust Deposit Account'. Owing to an error by the bank clerk, the account was called instead 'Clockwise No. 2 Account'.

Clockwise Ltd also wished to purchase some new machinery, and one of its business associates, Ticktock plc, agreed to lend the company the sum of £10,000 solely for this purpose. This money was paid into another separate account called 'Clockwise No. 3 Account'. Clockwise Ltd signed an agreement for the purchase of the machine and paid a deposit of £3,000 from this account, leaving in it £7,000.

Unfortunately, the problems with Clockwise's suppliers became more acute and Clockwise Ltd has now gone into liquidation. The bank (which is owed money by the company) and the liquidator are claiming the monies in the No. 2 and No. 3 accounts.

(a) Advise the bank and the liquidator.

(b) Would your answer differ if the monies paid by the customers, and lent by Ticktock plc had, by an error of Clockwise Ltd, been paid instead into Clockwise Ltd's general trading account?

Commentary

This question on certainties is based on a number of commercial cases where the existence of a trust has been pleaded successfully to prevent money paid to a company for a particular purpose being available for distribution generally to its creditors. The cases have been criticised in academic articles (see, for example, Goodhart and Jones, 'The Infiltration of Equitable Doctrine into English Commercial Law' (1980) 43 MLR 489 and P. J. Millett, 'The Quistclose Trust: Who Can Enforce It? (1985) 101 LQR 266). They are, however, defensible on the practical grounds that if potential customers or lenders who are helping a company to survive are not allowed to protect their property, they will not be prepared to deal with the company at all. In *Re Kayford Ltd* **[1975] 1 WLR 279**, where Megarry J found that a trust had been created, he made the point in his judgment that, although it was quite proper for the mail order company to have done what it did with money received from members of the public, he was not so sure that the same considerations should apply to commercial creditors. The distinction has not been drawn in subsequent cases, however, where the courts have found trusts in favour of commercial creditors also (see *Carreras Rothmans Ltd* v *Freeman Matthews Treasure Ltd* **[1985] Ch 207** and *Re Lewis's of Leicester* **[1995] 1 BCLC 428**).

Answer plan

(a) • Are the monies in the Clockwise No. 2 account held on trust for the customers of the company?

　　• In *Re Kayford*, Megarry J said that a 'manifestation of an intention' to establish a trust is sufficient, and held on similar circumstances to this that money received by a mail order company was held on trust for the customers

- If there is a trust, then the money at no time belongs to Clockwise Ltd and cannot be claimed by the liquidator

- The fact that the account was not called 'trust account' is probably not fatal to establishing a trust

- Was the money lent by Ticktock plc solely to purchase the new machinery? If so, then it is stamped with a trust for this purpose, and on failure of the trust will go on a resulting trust back to Ticktock plc

- It does not matter whether the purpose fails initially or subsequently. The £7,000 held by Clockwise Ltd and any of the £3,000 deposit retained will go on a resulting trust back to Ticktock plc

(b) • Although the necessary intention to create a trust is still present, there is no certainty of subject-matter and the trust has not been fully constituted

- It would therefore be much more difficult for the customers and Ticktock plc to claim for the return of their money, which would be available with the general assets of the company to the liquidator

Suggested answer

(a) One of the three certainties essential to establish a valid trust is the certainty of words or intention. Words are not themselves necessary: the person in whom the property is vested may manifest a clear intention to create a trust by actions.

In *Paul v Constance* [1977] 1 WLR 527 a man said on several occasions that funds in a deposit account in his name belonged both to himself and his mistress. **Section 53** of the **Law of Property Act 1925** does not require any formality for the creation of a trust of personalty, and these oral statements were held to be sufficient to create a trust for his mistress of half of the money in the account.

In *Re Kayford Ltd* [1975] 1 WLR 279, a mail order company, which was experiencing financial difficulties, paid cheques received from customers into a separate dormant account which only at a later date was called 'Customers' Trust Deposit Account'. Megarry J held that this appellation was a sufficient manifestation of intention to create a trust of the monies therein for the customers. Being a trust of personalty, no written formalities were required by the **Law of Property Act 1925, s. 53**, for its creation. The monies having been kept separately meant that there was certainty of subject-matter; the objects of the trust (the customers) were also certain.

Although in the question the account into which the monies have been paid does not bear the name 'Trust Account', the fact of segregation of the money received from the customers may be sufficient evidence of certainty of intention to create a trust. As the money has been kept separately there is also certainty of subject-matter; the beneficiaries are the customers. The money would not therefore be available to the bank or the liquidator.

Similarly, where property is handed over for a particular purpose only, this may be sufficient to impress it with a trust for that purpose. In *Barclays Bank Ltd* v *Quistclose Investments Ltd* [1970] AC 567, Quistclose lent some £200,000 to Rolls Razor Ltd (which was in financial difficulties) for the sole purpose of paying a dividend on its ordinary shares. The money was paid into a separate bank account. Rolls Razor went into liquidation before the dividend was paid. It was held that the money was not available to the bank with whom the account was opened, nor for distribution by the liquidator to the general creditors of the company. It had from the start been impressed with a trust for a particular purpose (the payment of a dividend) and had therefore never belonged to Rolls Razor beneficially. When the trust failed because the liquidation prevented the payment of the dividend, the money was held on a resulting trust for Quistclose.

Applying these principles to the question, it would seem that the money paid by Clockwise Ltd into a separate account for the purpose of purchasing machinery would similarly be impressed with a trust for that purpose, and again would not be available to the bank or the liquidator. As mentioned in the Commentary on this question, Megarry J's distinction between the money of members of the public and trade creditors has not been observed in subsequent cases.

Does the fact that part of this money has already been appropriated for the purpose affect the trust as to the remainder? In *Re EVTR Ltd* [1987] BCLC 646, money lent for the purchase of a machine was paid to the borrower company's solicitors. When the borrower company went into liquidation, it had already paid part of the money to the suppliers under a contract of purchase. The Court of Appeal found no reason to distinguish between the resulting trust, which would have arisen if the purpose for which the money was paid had failed initially, and the failure of the purpose only subsequently. Money returned by the suppliers was held to go on a resulting trust for the lender. In the question it is likely that the £7,000 still held by Clockwise Ltd, and any money repayable to them from the £3,000 deposit paid, will go on a resulting trust for Ticktock plc.

(b) What if the monies in either case are paid into Clockwise Ltd's general trading account by error? In such circumstances, although the necessary intention to create a trust might be there, there would be no certainty or segregation of the subject-matter and it would almost certainly be impossible to find a trust. In the case of the customers' cheques, presumably if a trust were intended, it would affect only funds paid into the designated account. Payment into a different account would therefore prevent the trust being constituted. In the case of Ticktock's money, although the money would be impressed with a trust from the start, there would be the practical problem that money paid into the general trading account might not be traceable. The case of *Hunter* v *Moss* [1994] 1 WLR 452 (referred to in the answer to question 3(d)) suggests that segregation of the subject-matter of a trust is not essential if the subject-matter is all identical. It might be argued on behalf of the customers of Clockwise Ltd that Clockwise Ltd has done everything in its power to constitute a trust so that the principle in *Re Rose* [1952] Ch 499 should apply. If it is possible to establish a trust in favour of the customers and Ticktock plc then they may be able to trace the trust monies into Clockwise

Ltd's general trading account. They will only have a claim however to the extent that their monies are still in the account and not deemed to have been paid out under the rule in *Clayton's Case* (*Devaynes* v *Noble* (1816) 1 Mer 572). If the account has been overdrawn at any time since the monies were paid in, then their claim will be defeated. (For a more detailed explanation of the rules relating to tracing see Chapter 13.)

Question 3

Consider whether a trust has been created in the following circumstances:

(a) Eliza orally declared herself a trustee of her house, Dunroamin, for her son Percy. She subsequently wrote a letter to Percy informing him that she had done so.

(b) Oliver, on visiting his only niece, Alison, aged 10, handed her an emerald ring which had belonged to her grandmother. As he handed it over, Oliver told Alison that she was to have the ring. When Oliver left, he took the ring with him, and when he died shortly afterwards, it was found among his effects.

(c) Simon, who died recently, made a will leaving, *inter alia*, 'the residue of my estate to my dear wife Sarah trusting that she will dispose of whatever she does not want between such of my relatives and friends as she shall select'.

(d) One Friday, Paul bought ten tickets in the National Lottery. He immediately declared himself a trustee of nine of them for his son Steve, and of the remaining one for his girlfriend Gladys, but without indicating which of the ten was to be held for Gladys. The following day, when the draw was made, one of Paul's tickets won the top prize of £40 million.

Advise Gladys.

Commentary

This is a certainty question mixed with other areas of trust law. In **(a)** all three certainties are satisfied, but you are required to consider whether the necessary formalities for the creation of a trust of land have been complied with. Part **(b)** raises the question of the constitution of a trust and the difference between a trust and a gift. Part **(c)** raises doubts about all three certainties, but also requires a knowledge of the test for certainty of objects for discretionary trusts and powers, and some of the cases on this. In part **(c)** you will probably consider certainty of words and subject-matter first. If you come to the conclusion that the trust would fail on either or both of these, do not of course be deterred from discussing certainty of objects also. The examiner will undoubtedly be looking for a discussion of all three certainties. Part **(d)** deals with certainty of subject-matter in the light of *Hunter* v *Moss* [1994] 1 WLR 452.

Answer plan

(a) • A trust of land must be *evidenced* in writing (but not necessarily made in writing) and signed by the person creating it (**LPA 1925, s. 53(1)(b)**)

  • The declaration evidenced by the subsequent letter will be sufficient

  • As the legal title to the house is already vested in Eliza, the trust is fully constituted

(b) • A gift of a chattel is incomplete unless it is handed over or there is a deed of gift. As Oliver takes the ring back, the gift is not complete

  • The wording does not indicate a trust

(c) • 'Trusting' may be a precatory word and not sufficiently obligatory to impose a trust on Sarah

  • Although 'residue' is certain as the subject-matter of the trust, 'whatever she does not want' is uncertain, and any trust would therefore fail for uncertainty of subject-matter

  • If it had been a valid trust, it would have been a discretionary one. The test for certainty of objects of a discretionary trust is individual ascertainability. 'Relatives' satisfies this test but 'friends' would fail it

(d) • Although *Hunter v Moss* is authority that there is certainty where the subject-matter is identical, this cannot apply to lottery tickets which all bear a different identifying number

  • The trust will therefore fail for uncertainty of subject-matter

Suggested answer

(a) The three certainties for a trust are satisfied, but the **Law of Property Act 1925, s. 53(1)(b)**, requires that 'a declaration of trust respecting any land or any interest therein must be manifested and proved by some writing signed by some person who is able to declare such trust or by his will'. Although the oral declaration of trust by Eliza is therefore ineffective, the subsequent letter testifying to the oral declaration signed by Eliza would be sufficient for the purpose of **s. 53**. The section does not require that the trust should be created in writing, but merely that its creation should be evidenced in writing.

(b) If Oliver had declared himself to be a trustee of Alison's ring, this would have been effective as it is possible to create a trust of personalty by words alone. As the ring is still in his possession, he would have held it as trustee and the trust would have been fully constituted. His words would have had the effect of severing the beneficial ownership in the ring, thereby creating the duality of ownership essential to a trust.

However, Turner LJ stated in *Milroy v Lord* (1862) 4 De GF & J 264 at p. 274 that the court will not allow a purported gift which is ineffective because there is no delivery of the subject-matter to take effect as a trust. In *Jones v Lock* (1865) LR 1 Ch App 25, a father put a cheque into the hand of his nine-month-old son saying, 'I give this to baby for himself'. When he later died and the cheque was found among his effects, it was held that there had been no effective gift; nor had any effective trust of the cheque been created. Similarly, in *Richards* v *Delbridge* (1874) LR 18 Eq 11 where a grandfather endorsed a lease of property he had with the words 'This deed and all thereto belonging I give to [his grandson] from this time forth' it was ineffective to transfer the lease by way of gift as a deed was required to transfer a legal estate in land, but the words of gift could not be construed either as an intention to create a trust.

If Oliver's words on handing over the ring to Alison indicate an intention to make a present gift, the gift is thereby perfected and his taking back the ring cannot recall such gift. In such circumstances, he would, at most, be a bailee of the ring for Alison.

On the other hand, Oliver's words on handing over the ring might indicate merely an intention to make a gift of it in the future. In these circumstances, Alison has merely custody or bailment of the ring, and Oliver is free to take it back (which he does).

If Oliver had made it clear when he left that he was taking the ring with him for safe-keeping but he regarded it as belonging to Alison, this might have been sufficient intent to create a trust of it for Alison with himself as trustee, or else merely a bailment with himself as bailee. However, there is no evidence to support such interpretation, and it is therefore probable that there will be an ineffective gift and an ineffective trust.

(c) First, it might be argued that the word 'trusting' in this context is a more colloquial expression than the legal words 'on trust for', implying merely reliance upon Sarah's integrity rather than imposing an obligation on her. If this is argued successfully, then the words are precatory in nature and fail to satisfy the certainty of words necessary to create a trust.

Secondly, 'the residue of my estate' is sufficiently capable of ascertainment to form the subject-matter of a trust (the residue being the remainder of a person's estate not specifically disposed of). Nevertheless there is uncertainty of subject-matter here because the share which the friends and relatives are to receive ('whatever she does not want') is necessarily uncertain. In *Sprange* v *Barnard* (1789) 2 Bro CC 585, a gift to the testatrix's husband with a provision that 'at his death, the remaining part of what is left, that he does not want for his own wants and use' was to be divided between the testatrix's brother and sisters, failed as a trust for uncertainty of subject-matter.

The third certainty, that of objects, also has to be considered here. If the requirements of certainty of words and subject-matter were satisfied, there might still be a problem with regard to certainty of objects. This would be a discretionary trust and the test for certainty of objects is that laid down by the House of Lords in *McPhail* v *Doulton* [1971] AC 424, namely, can it be said of any given postulant that they are, or are not, within the scope of the discretion? When the Court of Appeal considered the application of this test to the word 'relatives' in *Re Baden's Deed Trusts (No. 2)* [1973] Ch 9, the Court of Appeal decided that the expression 'relatives' was conceptually certain enough to satisfy the test, although the judges had differing reasons for deciding this. We therefore have high judicial authority that the word 'relatives' is conceptually certain.

In *Re Barlow's Will Trusts* [1979] 1 WLR 278, the testatrix directed that 'any friends of mine' might buy a painting from her collection at a reduced price. This was held valid, but only because the court interpreted this as a series of individual gifts to apply conditionally to anyone who was able to satisfy the trustees that he or she was a friend. The test for certainty of objects of conditional gifts is, however, more relaxed than that applicable to certainty of objects of discretionary trusts. Had the provision been construed as a discretionary trust (or fiduciary power) to select amongst the testator's friends, it would not have satisfied the test in *McPhail* v *Doulton*. As part (c) involves a discretionary trust, the disposition might well fail the *McPhail* v *Doulton* test for conceptual certainty.

(d) A declaration of trust relating to property other than land may be made orally, so that the declaration of trust made by Paul does not offend the **Law of Property Act 1925, s. 53**. It would seem however that the purported declaration of trust is void for uncertainty of subject-matter, in that the interests of the intended beneficiaries, Steve and Gladys, have not been specified. In other words, Paul has not indicated which tickets he is holding for which beneficiary.

In *Hunter* v *Moss* [1994] 1 WLR 452, the Court of Appeal held that a declaration of trust of 50 shares from a holding of 950 did not fail for uncertainty of subject-matter, even though the settlor had not specified which particular shares out of his holding were to be subject to the trust. A different result had been reached in the earlier decision of *Re London Wine Co. (Shippers) Ltd* (1975) 126 NLJ 977, where a purported allocation of some bottles of wine in a wine cellar was held insufficient to confer a property interest, since no bottles had actually been segregated and set aside for a particular customer. *Re London Wine Co.* was applied by the Privy Council in *Re Goldcorp Exchange Ltd* [1995] 1 AC 74, where it was affirmed that on the purchase of unascertained goods, there was no fixed and identifiable bulk created by a deemed appropriation, and therefore no property to which any tracing claim could apply. The purchasers of unascertained goods (as in *Goldcorp*) may now have a better claim as against creditors in a liquidation under the **Sale of Goods (Amendment) Act 1995**, which provides that purchasers who have paid for such goods acquire property rights as tenants in common in them. This would not of course affect a declaration of trust of identifiable and ascertained goods.

The *London Wine Co.* case was distinguished in *Hunter* v *Moss* on the ground that the bottles of wine might not be of equal quality, whereas the shares were all of the same class and carried the same rights. This is not true of tickets in the National Lottery, since the particular number selected for each ticket is an intrinsic part of its potential value. *Hunter* v *Moss* is therefore distinguishable. The suggestion in *Hunter* v *Moss* that the tracing remedy could be used to cure uncertainty of subject-matter has been criticised: Luxton, 'Certainty of subject-matter: a problem shared?' (1994) 28 Law Teacher 312. In any event, it is difficult to see how the tracing rules could be used to identify which beneficiary is entitled to the winnings.

Therefore, the only way in which certainty of subject-matter could be satisfied would be if the declaration could be construed as creating not one trust for Steve of nine tickets and another for Gladys of one ticket, but rather a single trust of all ten tickets under which Steve and Gladys share the beneficial interest in the ratio of 9:1 in Steve's favour. The winnings would then be held in trust for them both in the same ratio. This does not seem, however, to be what Paul intended. The trust is therefore probably void for uncertainty of subject-matter, and Paul is entitled to keep the winnings for himself.

Question 4

Last year, as part of his estate planning, Wurzel, a wealthy farmer, wished to dispose of some of his property for the benefit of his family. His first step was to set up a family trust, of which his friends, Oats and Rye, agreed to be the trustees and to hold any property which Wurzel might transfer to them upon any trusts that Wurzel might declare.

Wurzel transferred the freehold title to six holiday cottages in Wales into the names of Oats and Rye, and sent them the deeds. Upon Wurzel's recent oral instructions, his solicitor wrote to Oats and Rye directing them to hold the cottages and the shares in trust for Wurzel's two grandchildren, Turnip and Carrot, in equal shares.

Two years ago, Wurzel transferred his holding of 5,000 shares in Racine Ltd into the name of the Cube Bank plc as security for a loan which the bank made to him. Six months ago, Wurzel repaid all sums due under the loan, and at the same time wrote to the bank instructing it to transfer the shares into the names of Oats and Rye.

Last month Wurzel orally declared himself a trustee for his son, Spinach, of his (Wurzel's) beneficial interest under the Root Trust.

Consider the validity and consequences of Wurzel's actions.

Commentary

The **Law of Property Act 1925, s. 53**, specifies certain formalities relating to the declaration of trusts and the disposition of beneficial interests. The section has been interpreted on a number of occasions in the House of Lords, namely in *Grey* v *IRC* **[1960] AC 1**, *Vandervell* v *IRC* **[1967] 2 AC 291** and *Oughtred* v *IRC* **[1960] AC 206**, and, in the Court of Appeal, in *Re Vandervell's Trusts (No. 2)* **[1974] Ch 269**. In each of these cases it fell to be determined whether a particular transaction attracted *ad valorem* stamp duty or income tax.

Stamp duty is a tax on documents only; it has in recent years been restricted in scope, but it still applies to transfers of land and to sales of shares. The consequence of failure to have a document stamped is that it cannot be produced as evidence in court.

Ad valorem duty varies according to the value of the property transferred. Such duty is payable on a conveyance or transfer on sale. Until 1985, *ad valorem* duty was payable on a voluntary disposition as if it were a transfer on sale, which meant that stamp duty was frequently payable on the creation of a trust. Prima facie, *ad valorem* duty (as opposed to a fixed duty of 50p) was payable only if the document was effective to dispose of the beneficial interest. No *ad valorem* duty was payable, therefore, if only the legal interest passed on a transfer, e.g., on a change of trustees. On the other hand, *ad valorem* duty was payable on a transfer of shares to a donee by a full (i.e., legal and beneficial) owner, because the transfer passed the beneficial interest as well as the legal title.

A donor or settlor might therefore have attempted to avoid stamp duty by effecting a transfer of the beneficial interest without having to use a document. Unfortunately for the taxpayer, many of those schemes which involved a disposition of a subsisting equitable interest were held to be ineffective to avoid *ad valorem* duty because of the **Law of Property Act 1925, s. 53(1)(c)**. The effect of that sub-section requiring a disposition of an equitable interest to be effected in writing was that there was a document on which *ad valorem* duty was payable. Taxpayers sometimes argued that **s. 53(2)** dispensed with the need for writing; but this did not assist the taxpayers in either *Grey* **v** *IRC* (discussed in the answer) or *Oughtred* **v** *IRC*.

In *Oughtred* **v** *IRC*, it was argued that no *ad valorem* stamp duty was payable on a transfer of shares (in that case an exchange) on the ground that the equitable interest had already passed under the prior contract for sale by virtue of a constructive trust, for which no writing was required because of **s. 53(2)**. The majority of the House of Lords held that, in any event, *ad valorem* duty was payable on the share transfer because it ranked as a transfer on sale. This was sufficient to dispose of the case, so that the views expressed on **s. 53** were obiter. Lord Radcliffe accepted the taxpayer's argument on **s. 53(2)**; and his opinion was adopted by Megarry J in *Re Holt's Settlement* **[1969] 1 Ch 100**. In *Neville* **v** *Wilson* **[1997] Ch 144**, the Court of Appeal applied Lord Radcliffe's dissenting judgment and held that an oral agreement between the shareholders of a company to divide between themselves the shares of another company, which were held beneficially for them, created constructive trusts between them. The agreements were therefore valid under **s. 53(2)** of the **Law of Property Act 1925** and did not need to be in writing to comply with **s. 53(1)(c)**. (The shareholders also agreed to strike the company off the register, so that had the agreement been void, the shares would have gone to the Crown as *bona vacantia*.)

If a settlor retains any beneficial interest under a trust, or any possibility of benefiting under a trust, the income arising under it is treated as the settlor's for income tax purposes. In some cases the Revenue have argued that the settlor retains a beneficial interest through having failed to dispose of it in writing as required by **s. 53(1)(c)**. This was the point at issue in both *Vandervell* **v** *IRC* (which was a victory for the Revenue) and *Re Vandervell's Trusts (No. 2)* (which was a victory for the taxpayer).

The scope of **s. 53(1)(c)** as explained by these decisions seems, therefore, to reflect the courts' need to interpret the section so as not to allow too broad a circumvention of the taxing statutes.

For a further consideration of these difficult cases, see the articles and case note referred to in the Further reading section at the end of this chapter.

Answer plan

- The cottages are held on a resulting trust for Wurzel
- Wurzel's solicitor's letter would probably satisfy **LPA 1925, s. 53(1)(b)** for the creation of a trust in land

- But the instructions may be a transfer of Wurzel's interest, in which case the formality requirement is **s. 53(1)(c)**, which may or may not be satisfied

- **Section 53(2)** will not operate to exempt the transfer from writing (**Grey v IRC**)

- The Cube Bank hold the shares for Wurzel on a bare trust

- The transfer of the legal title by the bank on the instructions of the owner of the equitable interest (Wurzel) will operate to transfer the equitable interest without any separate disposition in writing

- If Wurzel's oral declaration of trust creates a sub-trust, it is valid; if it is a transfer of Wurzel's interest, it is void as it falls within **s. 53(1)(c)**

Suggested answer

When Wurzel transferred the legal title to the six cottages to his trustees without informing them of the names of the beneficiaries, the trustees would have held the legal title to the cottages on a resulting trust for Wurzel: **Grey v IRC** [1960] AC 1. A resulting trust arises whenever there is a gap in the beneficial ownership: as there was with the option to purchase back the shares given to the Vandervell Trustee Co. in **Vandervell v IRC** [1967] 2 AC 291.

Wurzel's declaration of the trusts of the cottages is subject to the **Law of Property Act 1925, s. 53**.

Section 53(1)(b) applies if Wurzel's equitable interest under the resulting trust ranks as an interest in land. It requires a declaration of a trust of land or any interest in land to be manifested and proved by some writing signed by some person who is able to declare such trust or by his will. The expression 'some person who is able to declare such trust' must be intended to include some person other than the settlor.

The question is whether the letter that Wurzel's solicitor sent to Oats and Rye could satisfy para. (b). There is no authority on this point; but the express inclusion of signature by an agent in paras (a) and (c) of **s. 53(1)** might suggest that signature by agent does not satisfy para. (b): *expressio unius exclusio alterius*. It would appear, however, that the transferee can sign: **Gardner v Rowe** (1828) 5 Russ 258. It would also appear that, unlike paras (a) and (c), para. (b) is merely an evidential requirement, i.e., non-compliance does not invalidate the declaration but merely means that, without signed writing, it cannot be proved: **Gardner v Rowe**. On this basis, Oats and Rye hold the cottages on a valid trust for the grandchildren, and are therefore, as trustees, obliged to provide the signed writing of the trusts in accordance with para. (b).

It is more likely, however, that the interest of which Wurzel is disposing is not an interest in land but a beneficial interest under a resulting trust. It was held by the House of Lords in **Grey v IRC**, that an instruction by a beneficiary to the trustee to hold his interest in trust for a third party is in substance a disposition, and must therefore comply with **s. 53(1)(c)**. Paragraph (c) states that a disposition of an equitable interest or trust subsisting at the time of the disposition must be in writing and signed by the disponor or by his agent thereunto lawfully authorised in writing. As the solicitor is Wurzel's agent, provided his letter to Oats and Rye complies with para. (c), there is a valid disposition of the beneficial interest.

If the solicitor's letter does not comply with para. (c) (if, for example, it is not signed), there is probably no valid disposition. It is not exempted from para. (c) by s. 53(2), i.e., it does not involve the 'operation of a resulting ... trust': see *Grey v IRC*, which itself concerned a direction to trustees to hold for a third party an interest under a resulting trust. Lord Denning MR's statement in *Re Vandervell's Trusts (No. 2)* [1974] Ch 269 that a resulting trust dies without the need for any writing at all is difficult to reconcile with *Grey v IRC*, but is perhaps distinguishable on the special facts: the option to purchase (which was the subject-matter of the resulting trust) ceased to exist when exercised, and a new beneficial interest arose in respect of the shares which were thereby purchased.

Wurzel's repayment of sums due under the loan from the Cube Bank plc means that the bank's legal mortgage of the shares comes to an end, and the bank holds the legal title to the shares on a bare trust for Wurzel. In *Vandervell v IRC*, Vandervell's bank held the legal title to shares on a resulting trust for him and, upon his instructions, transferred them to the Royal College of Surgeons. The House of Lords held that Vandervell's beneficial interest passed to the College contemporaneously with the legal title without the need for compliance with para. (c).

The decision in that case means that a direction by a beneficiary under a bare trust to the trustee to transfer the trust property beneficially to a third party is not a disposition within para. (c) because the direction does not itself dispose of the beneficiary's interest. Furthermore, the trustees' transfer pursuant to such direction, although effective to vest a full title (both legal and equitable) in the third party, is not a disposition for the purposes of para. (c) either. The explanation seems to be that, when the legal and equitable titles pass together, the equitable interest is not separately disposed of, but is subsumed in the passing of the legal title. There is, therefore, no disposition of a 'subsisting equitable interest'.

For these reasons, if the Cube Bank plc has transferred the shares in Racine Ltd to Oats and Rye, the gift is perfect both at law and in equity, and Wurzel cannot recall it. If, however, the bank has not yet effected the transfer, Wurzel can revoke his instructions to the bank and prevent the gift from being completed.

If the effect of Wurzel's declaration of trust in favour of Spinach would be that Wurzel would drop out of the picture (*Grey v IRC*) and the trustees of the Root Trust would hold the trust property in trust for Spinach instead (*Grainge v Wilberforce* (1889) 5 TLR 436), the declaration would rank as a purported disposition of a subsisting equitable interest. As such, because it is made only orally, it would be void for non-compliance with para. (c).

If, however, the declaration gives rise to a sub-trust, there is no disposition for the purposes of para. (c) because Wurzel retains his equitable interest under the Root Trust and a new beneficial interest is created in favour of Spinach.

It appears that the declaration will be treated as a purported disposition if no additional duties are imposed on the trustees; but otherwise, it will give rise to a sub-trust. Wurzel's declaration does not impose any express duties. If, however, Spinach is a minor, a sub-trust will be created because otherwise the trustees would be subject to additional duties, e.g., those imposed by the **Trustee Act 1925, s. 31**. If construed as a sub-trust, therefore, the declaration will be valid.

Further reading

Battersby, G., 'Formalities for the disposition of equitable interests under a trust' (1979) 43 Conv 17.

Clarke, P. J., 'Mr Vandervell again' (1974) 38 Conv 405.

Green, B., '*Grey, Oughtred* and *Vandervell*: a contextual reappraisal' (1984) 47 MLR 385.

Harris, J. W., 'The case of the slippery equity' (1975) 38 MLR 577.

Martin, J., 'Certainty of subject matter: a defence of *Hunter v Moss*' [1996] Conv 223.

Watkin, T. G., 'Doubts and certainties' (1979) 8 AALR 123.

4

Constitution of trusts

Introduction

Constitution of trusts is a fascinating area of equity which has produced a welter of academic discussion in articles and elsewhere: it is therefore a popular topic with examiners. Since, moreover, it naturally falls within the earlier part of a course on trusts, it is one which the student should have plenty of time to absorb. This is generally a good area in which hard-working students can gain high marks. Since constitution of trusts is an aspect of the creation of trusts, this topic may well be combined in an examination question with one or more of the three certainties and with formalities. But watch out for other combinations!

It used to be common for questions in this area to involve unfulfilled covenants to transfer property to be held for the benefit of third parties. Although this is a particularly interesting aspect of the topic, the issues tended to arise in relation to marriage settlements, which are far less common nowadays. The importance of establishing a trust of the benefit of a covenant has also been reduced by the **Contracts (Rights of Third Parties) Act 1999**. The modern tendency is therefore to concentrate on other aspects of the topic, notably on whether a settlor has done everything necessary to be done by him to vest the property in the intended trustee.

Some of the well-established principles in this area have been thrown into some confusion as a result of the decision of the Court of Appeal in *Pennington* v *Waine* [2002] 1 WLR 2075. The main reasoning of the Court of Appeal in that case is difficult to follow, out of line with all previous case law, and (with respect) wrong. A candidate should not be afraid to criticise a decision adversely, but it is important to state the precise criticisms clearly and cogently. Students would therefore be well advised to ensure that they have read *Pennington* v *Waine*, and also the slightly earlier decision of the Privy Council in *T. Choithram International SA* v *Pagarani* [2001] 1 WLR 1, upon which the Court of Appeal in *Pennington* v *Waine* purported to derive some support.

Superficially, *Pagarani* appeared to involve an imperfect transfer to trustees of a charitable trust. The difference from *Pennington* v *Waine*, however, was that the settlor was himself to be one of a number of trustees; and where there are several trustees of a trust, the trust can be completely constituted merely by vesting the property in the name of one of them. The effect of this principle in *Pagarani* was that, although the declaration contemplated a transfer to trustees, it took effect as a declaration by the settlor of himself as trustee without any need for the property to be transferred. It was in this context that Lord Browne-Wilkinson, giving the advice of the Privy Council, said: 'Although equity will not aid a volunteer, it will not strive officiously to defeat a gift': [2001] 1 WLR 1 at p. 12. The Court of Appeal in *Pennington* v *Waine* took this statement entirely out of context, and reached a decision that will no doubt provide a fruitful quarry for examination questions until it is either narrowed in scope in later cases or simply overruled by the Supreme Court. Reference to academic commentary on this development would be a sound addition to an examination question on this topic and would be essential in assessed coursework. For examples of such commentary, see the Further reading section at the end of this chapter.

Question 1

Equity will not assist a volunteer.

Explain and discuss.

Commentary

Superficially this may appear a simple question, but there is considerable opportunity for a student prepared to draw on their knowledge and understanding of different parts of the subject. The area is vast, but the secret is in selecting the material which most directly addresses the question. Note carefully that you are required not merely to explain the maxim, but to discuss it.

Answer plan

- Scope of maxim
  - meaning of 'volunteer' and 'consideration'
  - relevance to imperfect gifts/incompletely constituted trusts
  - relationship to actions at common law
- Exceptions to the maxim
  - rule in *Strong* v *Bird*
  - *donationes mortis causa*
  - proprietary estoppel
  - unconscionability?

Suggested answer

The quotation is one of the maxims of equity. It is a pithy way of stating that, where a trust is incompletely constituted or a gift is imperfectly made, equity will not give its remedy of specific performance to an intended beneficiary who is a volunteer, or to the intended donee. In the context of gifts, the maxim is often expressed in the form 'equity will not perfect an imperfect gift': see *Milroy v Lord* (1862) 4 De GF & J 264. A volunteer is a person who has not furnished consideration for the creation of the trust. Consideration in equity consists of both common law consideration (money or money's worth) and (in certain instances) marriage. It is clear that a covenant (although it may be enforceable at common law) does not comprise consideration in equity.

If marriage is to constitute consideration, the trust must be made either before and in consideration of a particular marriage, or (if made after the marriage) in pursuance of an ante-nuptial agreement to make such a trust. Furthermore, only certain persons within a marriage settlement are treated by equity as providing consideration: these are the spouses to the marriage and their issue. Issue of a former marriage and illegitimate children will prima facie fall outside the marriage consideration: *Re Cook's Settlement Trusts* [1965] Ch 902. But they may come within it if their interests are so closely inter-twined with those of the issue of the marriage in question that they cannot be separated: *A-G v Jacobs-Smith* [1895] 2 QB 341, CA. Next-of-kin are outside the marriage consideration: *Re Plumptre* [1910] 1 Ch 609.

The quotation needs to be treated with care, as equity will protect a beneficiary's interest under a completely constituted trust even if that beneficiary is a volunteer (as in *Paul v Paul* (1882) 20 ChD 742, where the settlor, having completely constituted the trust, was not permitted to reclaim the property on the ground that the beneficiaries were volunteers). The maxim also means that where a trust is completely constituted in regard to certain items of property, but incompletely constituted in regard to other items, volunteer beneficiaries cannot compel the settlor to transfer the latter into the trust: *Jefferys v Jefferys* (1841) Cr & Ph 138. However, if some of the would-be beneficiaries under an incompletely constituted trust have provided consideration for its creation, they may obtain specific performance. The consequence will be that the trust becomes completely constituted, thus also benefiting the volunteers, who could not have sued personally: *Davenport v Bishopp* (1843) 2 Y & C Ch Cas 451.

The modern approach has been expressed as being that 'Although equity will not aid a volunteer, it will not strive officiously to defeat a gift': *T. Choithram International SA v Pagarani* [2001] 1 WLR 1, PC at p. 12, per Lord Browne-Wilkinson. However, in some older cases it appears that equity went further than merely not assisting a volunteer, and would frustrate an action brought at common law to aid a volunteer. Thus, the court has directed covenantees of a voluntary covenant not to sue the covenantor for damages at common law since this would give the volunteers indirectly what they were not entitled to obtain directly: *Re Kay's Settlement* [1939] Ch 329. In principle, however, such a claim should be denied the covenantees only when they hold the benefit of the covenant on a resulting trust for the covenantor. A claim by them ought to be available if the covenant is itself the subject-matter of the express trust, as it was in *Fletcher* v *Fletcher* (1844) 4 Hare 67. In such a case the trust is completely constituted vis-à-vis the covenant, even though it is incompletely constituted as regards the property to which such covenant relates. Thus, although equity will not give specific performance vis-à-vis such property, it will not frustrate a claim brought by the trustee-covenantees for damages for breach of covenant at common law. Indeed, in such circumstances, equity will (if necessary) at the behest of the beneficiaries compel the covenantee to lend his name to a claim at common law against the covenantor. This problem does not arise in relation to covenants entered into at least six months after the passing of the Contracts (Rights of Third Parties) Act 1999, which enables a third party to enforce a contract in his or her own right, thus enabling the volunteer to sue for damages.

Equity has for many years recognised three so-called exceptions to the maxim that it will not assist a volunteer. The first is the rule in *Strong* v *Bird* (1874) LR 18 Eq 315 whereby, if the intended donee of an *inter vivos* gift becomes the executor, or even the administrator, of the intending donor upon the latter's death, the legal title passes to him. This, together with a continuing intention to make a gift on the deceased's part, perfects the gift. Arguably, however, this is not so much an exception to the maxim as an illustration of the means by which a gift can be perfected. This principle has been extended to trusts: *Re Ralli's Will Trusts* [1964] Ch 288.

The second exception is *donationes mortis causa*. Equity's assistance is not needed (and therefore the maxim is inapplicable) if the subject-matter of the gift is transferred to the intended donee during the donor's lifetime, albeit subject to the usual conditions to which such gifts are subject. If, however, the intended donee's title remains imperfect at the donor's death, equity's assistance will be required, and this constitutes a genuine exception to the maxim. This will be the case, for instance, if the subject-matter of the *donatio mortis causa* is a chose in action, and the donor hands over merely the indicia of title: *Birch* v *Treasury Solicitor* [1951] Ch 298.

A third exception is proprietary estoppel. If A encourages, or even acquiesces in B's acting to his detriment in the belief that he has rights in the property of A, equity may protect B should A act inconsistently with such rights. This is the principle which can be traced back to *Dillwyn* v *Llewelyn* (1862) 4 De GF & J 517. A modern (and perhaps startling) instance is *Pascoe* v *Turner* [1979] 1 WLR 431, where the Court of Appeal held that the equity raised by the estoppel could be satisfied only by a conveyance of the fee simple. Equity was there assisting a volunteer by perfecting an imperfect gift. In other cases, however, the equity has been satisfied by a lesser remedy, as by the award of a licence (*Inwards* v *Baker* [1965] 2 QB 29) or merely monetary compensation: *Dodsworth* v *Dodsworth* (1973) 228 EG 1115 and *Jennings* v *Rice* [2003] 1 P & CR 8, CA.

A fourth exception was recognised by the Court of Appeal in the rather unsatisfactory decision in *Pennington* v *Waine* [2002] 1 WLR 2075. In that case a purported gift of shares appeared to be imperfect because the intending donor, Ada, had not done everything necessary to be done by her in accordance with the rule in *Re Rose* [1952] Ch 499,

CA. She had merely put the completed share transfer form into the hands of her agent, Mr Pennington (who merely retained it): she had not thereby put her nephew, Harold (the intended donee), into the position of being able to take steps to obtain registration. The court nevertheless held that, in the circumstances, it would be unconscionable for Ada to go back on her gift.

This decision seems to cast into doubt principles that have been settled since *Milroy* v *Lord* (1862) 4 De GF & J 264. Furthermore, the notion of unconscionability is vague, and, with respect, smacks of palm-tree justice. This is why, whilst unconscionability no doubt underlies much equitable intervention, it finds expression only through settled principles. The result in *Pennington* v *Waine* might possibly have been explicable on the basis of proprietary estoppel, if it had been established that, by signing a consent form to act as a director, Harold had acted to his detriment in reliance upon a representation that the necessary qualification share was being transferred to him. The Court of Appeal, however, made no reference to estoppel. The result might also have been better (if rather shakily) founded on Arden LJ's alternative explanation: namely, that, when Mr Pennington wrote to inform Harold of the gift, Mr Pennington became Harold's agent for the purpose of submitting the transfer to the company. In any event, whilst *Pennington* v *Waine* treats unconscionability as a separate exception to the maxim 'Equity will not assist a volunteer', later cases may nevertheless prefer to follow more established principles. Indeed, in *Curtis* v *Pulbrook* [2011] EWHC 167 (Ch), Briggs J treated *Pennington* v *Waine* as a case of detrimental reliance.

Question 2

In 1998, A secured B's undertaking to hold any property which A might thereafter transfer to B in trust for A's niece, N. In 1999, A showed B a painting which was hanging on the wall in A's home, and told B that this was to be held on the trusts which he (A) had declared. A was owed the sum of £20,000 by C, and in 2000, A wrote to B saying: 'I hereby assign to you the debt owed to me by C.' A was himself a beneficiary under the FGH Trust, and in 2000, A orally directed the trustees of that trust to hold his interest thereunder in trust for B. In September 2004, A covenanted with B to transfer to B in trust for N any property which A might receive under the will of D, who was then still alive. D died early in 2006, bequeathing to A shares in XYZ Ltd.

A died last month, leaving all his property to E. At the date of his death, he had not transferred either the painting or the shares to B, and he had not notified C of the intended assignment of the debt.

Advise N which of the foregoing items (if any) are held in trust for her, and what steps (if any) she might take to enforce the covenant.

Commentary

This is a typical examination question on volunteers and incompletely constituted trusts. The student needs to identify the requirements for transferring different sorts of property into a trust. The area of the law relating to trusts of covenants is complex and involves apparently conflicting decisions upon which a variety of academic views has been expressed. It seems likely that much of the fire has gone out of this debate, however, with the enactment of the **Contracts (Rights of Third Parties) Act 1999**, which enables a third party to sue on a contract.

Answer plan

Valid declaration of trust, but transfer to trustee?

- Painting: deed or delivery
  - merely showing insufficient
- Debt: statutory assignment under **LPA 1925, s. 136**
  - absence of notice to debtor not necessary for assignment in equity
- Assignment of interest under the trust: **LPA 1925, s. 53(1)(c)**
  - oral, so ineffective
- Shares: transfer in books of company
  - no transfer or effort to transfer
  - but *covenant* to transfer?

  trust of benefit of covenant?

  impact of **Contracts (Rights of Third Parties) Act 1999**

Suggested answer

Since A intended to create a trust by transferring property to another person, B, as trustee, a trust will arise in favour of the intended beneficiary, N, only if there is a valid declaration of trust and an effective transfer of the property to the trustee: *Milroy v Lord* (1862) **4 De GF & J 264**, per Turner LJ. The terms of the undertaking which A secured from B are a clear declaration of trust. As regards transfer, however, it is necessary to take each item of property in turn.

The painting is a chattel, which is transferred either by delivery or deed. There is no evidence of a deed here. Delivery requires a physical handing over; merely showing the painting to B does not comprise a delivery: *Re Cole* [1964] Ch 175. The painting has therefore not been transferred into the trust, and will pass under A's will to E.

The benefit of the debt could not be assigned at common law, but under **s. 136** of the **Law of Property Act 1925**, the benefit of a debt can be assigned so as to enable the assignee to sue the debtor in his own name. For such a legal assignment to occur, the assignment must be in writing under the hand of the assignor, it must be absolute, and written notice must be given to the debtor. In the problem, it appears that the assignment was absolute, in that it was intended to be an unconditional assignment of the entire debt. Furthermore, it appears to have been in writing under the hand of the assignor, since A instructed B in a letter. There can be no statutory assignment, however, unless written notice (whether by A or somebody else) has been given to C. As A gave no such notice, it may be that no such notice has been received by C.

Even if C has not been notified, there will have been an assignment in equity. By executing an absolute assignment in writing, A has done all he needs to do; s. 136 does not require that notice to the debtor be given by the assignor. The assignment is therefore perfect in equity as soon as A executes the assignment: *Holt* v *Heatherfield Trust Ltd* [1942] 2 KB 1. The benefit of the debt in equity is therefore held by B in trust for N. In these circumstances, even after A's death, the assignment can become a statutory assignment if a third party (e.g., B) gives notice to C: *Walker* v *Bradford Old Bank Ltd* (1884) 12 QBD 511.

An instruction by a beneficiary to trustees to hold his interest in trust for a third party comprises a disposition of a subsisting equitable interest for the purposes of s. 53(1)(c) of the Law of Property Act 1925: *Grey* v *IRC* [1960] AC 1. It must therefore be in writing signed by the disponor or his agent. Since A's direction to the trustees of the FGH Trust was merely oral, the purported assignment is void. A's beneficial interest under that trust will therefore pass to E under A's will.

Lastly, as A did not transfer the shares in XYZ Ltd to B, the shares are not subject to the trust in favour of N. Equity does not regard a voluntary covenant as consideration, so B cannot compel A's estate to transfer the shares to him. It might, however, be argued that, by covenanting with B to transfer any property he might acquire under D's will, A has vested the benefit of the covenant in B. If this is so, it would seem to follow that N would be the beneficiary of a fully constituted trust of the benefit of the covenant, so that B would have to sue to enforce the covenant by suing for damages for breach of covenant, or else be liable to compensate N for breach of trust.

Whether the benefit of a covenant can comprise the subject-matter of a trust has been the subject of some judicial and much academic debate. The courts have shown their unwillingness to permit covenantees to sue on a covenant for the benefit of volunteers: *Re Kay's Settlement* [1939] Ch 329, *Re Cook's Settlement Trusts* [1965] Ch 902. In the latter case, Buckley J suggested that there can be no trust of the benefit of a covenant concerning future property. If this is correct, B cannot be holding the benefit of the covenant on trust for N, and the only possibility would be that B holds the benefit of the covenant on trust for A's estate. On the other hand, it has been argued that the benefit of a covenant will be held on trust for the intended beneficiaries where the covenantor makes it clear that this is his intention: see Hayton and Marshall, *Commentary and Cases on The Law of Trusts and Equitable Remedies*, 12th edn, Sweet & Maxwell,

2005, at p. 244. Such an intention might also be inferred, as where all the intended beneficiaries are volunteers, as in *Fletcher* v *Fletcher* (1844) 4 Hare 67, since otherwise there would be no point in entering into the covenant in the first place: Hornby (1962) 78 LQR 228.

Much of the significance of this argument would now appear to have been rendered obsolete by the Contracts (Rights of Third Parties) Act 1999, which applies to contracts entered into (like the covenant in the problem) at least six months after its enactment. Even a purely voluntary covenant (such as that in the problem) is a contract, and, under s. 1, a person who is not a party to a contract (N) may enforce a term of the contract in her own right if the contract expressly provides that she may, or if the term purports to confer a benefit on her (unless it appears that the parties did not intend the term to be enforceable by the third party). For the purpose of enforcing a term of the contract, the third party has the same remedies as would have been available to her in an action for breach of contract had she been a party to the contract: s. 1(5). Since the covenant was purely voluntary, N could not obtain specific performance to compel A's estate to transfer the shares to B, so that the shares would pass to E under A's will. However, N could sue A's estate for damages, the measure of the damages being the value of the shares that A failed to transfer.

Against this it might be argued that, even if N had been a party to the covenant, if the court were to follow the approach of Eve J in *Re Kay's Settlement*, she would not be entitled to damages. In that case, it appears that the court held that the benefit of a voluntary covenant was held on a resulting trust for the covenantor's estate. If the court took the same view in the question, so that the benefit of the covenant was held in trust for A's estate, this circumstance might indicate that the parties to the covenant did not intend it to be enforceable by the third party. This would effectively remove purely voluntary covenants for the benefit of third parties from the scope of the Contracts (Rights of Third Parties) Act 1999, since the Act would be available only in the very circumstance in which it is not needed, i.e., when equity treats the third party as a beneficiary under a trust of the covenant.

While this is a tenable argument, it is more likely that the courts will reject it and will use the opportunity afforded by the 1999 Act to abandon these refinements of equity, which were essentially designed for the now outmoded era of marriage settlements. The modern approach was expressed by Lord Browne-Wilkinson (albeit in a different context), when he said 'Although equity will not aid a volunteer, it will not strive officiously to defeat a gift': *T. Choithram International SA* v *Pagarani* [2001] 1 WLR 1, PC at p. 12. Long before the 1999 Act was passed, it was held that where the third party volunteer was herself a party to the covenant, she could recover substantial damages for breach of covenant in respect of her own loss: *Cannon* v *Hartley* [1949] Ch 213. It would therefore appear that, unless the covenantor indicates otherwise, the effect of the 1999 Act is to put every intended beneficiary under a voluntary covenant into the position of the covenantee in that case. On this footing, N could sue A's estate for damages to the value of the shares.

Question 3

In 2002, Acute handed his share certificate in respect of his shareholding in Diacritical Ltd to Cedilla, together with a share transfer form which Acute had completed in favour of Cedilla. As he handed these documents over, Acute instructed Cedilla to hold the shares in trust for Acute's nephew, Grave. Cedilla agreed. Shortly after, Cedilla attempted to obtain registration of the shares in her own name, but was defeated by the exercise by the directors of Diacritical Ltd of a power contained in the company's articles to refuse registration.

In 2003, Acute received back the share certificate from Cedilla. He handed it to his cousin, Umlaut, informing him that the shares were a gift to him.

Last month, Acute died with the shares still standing in his name. In his will he appointed Umlaut his executor and gave all his property to Cedilla.

Discuss who is entitled to the shares.

Commentary

This is a complex question, both because the relevant law itself is difficult, and also because you need to sort out in your mind the priorities of several claimants—never the easiest thing in the examination room. There is a lot to write so you will need to be economical with the facts of the cases. Cases should be cited to support legal principle; facts can be given sparingly in order to distinguish one case from another. See, for instance, the treatment in the suggested answer of the authorities which support, or which appear to conflict with, the principle of *Re Rose* **[1952] Ch 499, CA**. If you have a good understanding and keep a clear head, this is the sort of question where you could score very heavily.

Answer plan

- Grave's trust completely constituted *inter vivos*?
  - *Re Rose*
  - effect of refusal of registration?
  - Grave's priority over purported gift to Umlaut
  - if not perfect, equity will not assist Grave (a volunteer)
- Grave's trust completely constituted on Acute's death?
  - by bequest of shares to Cedilla (intended trustee)?
  - *Re Ralli*
- Umlaut's purported gift perfected on Acute's death?
  - Umlaut's appointment as executor
  - *Strong* v *Bird*

Suggested answer

Grave is beneficially entitled to the shares if he can establish that he is a beneficiary under a fully constituted trust of them. A trust is completely constituted only if there is compliance with the requirements laid down in *Milroy v Lord* (1862) 4 De GF & J 264. Where, as here, the settlor seeks to confer the benefit of property on a person by vesting it in a trustee, two things must be done. First, there must be a clear declaration by the settlor of the terms of the trust. Here, the instructions to Cedilla suffice. Secondly, the settlor must do all he can to vest the property in the intended trustee. The legal title to the shares will not pass to Cedilla unless and until the company registers Cedilla's name in its register of members. Since this has not been done, the legal title to the shares has not passed. The share transfer may nevertheless be perfect in equity if, in accordance with *Milroy v Lord*, the settlor has done everything necessary to be done by him to transfer the shares. In *Re Rose* [1952] Ch 499, the Court of Appeal held that a gift of shares was perfect in equity as soon as the donor had put the donee into the position of being able to take steps to complete the transfer: i.e., when the donor had handed to the donee the share certificate and executed share transfer form.

On this basis, the trust in favour of Grave would have been completely constituted from the date in 2002 when these documents were delivered to Cedilla. If so, from that date, Acute would have held the legal title to the shares in trust for Cedilla, who would herself have held the equitable interest thereunder on a sub-trust for Grave. This makes Cedilla a trustee of a completely constituted trust for Grave. She is therefore under a duty to ensure that the trust property is safeguarded—by taking steps to bring in the legal title to the shares (as she did attempt to do), and (if necessary) by compelling Acute to transfer to her any dividends he receives in respect of that holding.

The transfers in *Re Rose* were registered, but there is nothing in the case to suggest a different result where registration is refused. The principle in *Re Rose* has been attacked for thus saddling an intended donor with an unintended and potentially permanent trusteeship: see McKay (1976) 40 Conv (NS) 139. This objection carries some force; moreover a permanent trusteeship in this context contrasts sharply with a contract for the sale of shares where (if the company refuses to register the purchaser) the vendor cannot be fixed with a permanent trusteeship: see *Stevenson v Wilson* 1907 SC 445, considered (without criticism) by the House of Lords in *Scott Ltd v Scott's Trustees* [1959] AC 763.

A case difficult to reconcile with *Re Rose* is *Re Fry* [1946] Ch 312; but that case may be considered, perhaps, to turn on the effect of relevant Defence Regulations. Apart from that decision, the principle of *Re Rose* is consistent with a range of authorities: see, particularly, *Mallott v Wilson* [1903] 2 Ch 494 and *Mascall v Mascall* (1985) 49 P & CR 119. The principle was assumed correct by the House of Lords in *Vandervell v IRC* [1967] 2 AC 291, HL and it also operates in the case of equitable assignments of legal choses in action: *Holt v Heatherfield Trust Ltd* [1942] 2 KB 1.

If *Re Rose* applies, Grave is a beneficiary under a trust of the shares, and is entitled to the dividends which Diacritical Ltd will continue to pay to Acute (and, after

Acute's death, to Acute's personal representative). On this basis, the purported gift of the shares to Umlaut, even if ultimately perfected (as discussed below) is later in time, and is therefore subject to the rights of Grave. Similarly, Acute cannot by his will give to Cedilla property which he does not own beneficially. Thus the gift of all his property to Cedilla does not include the shares.

If, however, a court were to distinguish or overrule *Re Rose* and hold that the trust was incompletely constituted, then, unless Grave had provided consideration for the creation of the trust, he could not (as a volunteer) gain the assistance of equity: *Re Plumptre* [1910] 1 Ch 609. Since, however, Acute gave all his property in his will to Cedilla, the intended trustee of the shares, it is arguable that the trust in favour of Grave is completely constituted on Acute's death, since Cedilla then has a right as beneficiary under the will to see that the property is properly distributed: *Re Diplock* [1948] Ch 465, CA. She will ultimately obtain the legal title to the shares when the executor, Umlaut, transfers the shares into her name. It makes no difference that the legal title comes to Cedilla, the intended trustee, in a different capacity: *Re Ralli's Will Trusts* [1964] Ch 288.

There is, however, one further twist: Umlaut's appointment as executor. If it can be shown that Acute had a continuing intention to give the shares to Umlaut from 2003 until his death, the imperfect gift to Umlaut might be perfected under what is known as the rule in *Strong v Bird* (1874) LR 18 Eq 315 (i.e., by the acquisition by Umlaut of the legal title to the shares as executor). In principle, this would seem to postpone the equity of the beneficiaries under the will to that of the executor. It was upon this basis that Walton J in *Re Gonin* [1979] Ch 16 objected to the decision in *Re James* [1935] Ch 449, which had extended the rule to administrators. This objection may carry less weight where the intended donee becomes executor, since such appointment results from the testator's own voluntary act. The objection may not be entirely overcome, however, since an executor does stand in a fiduciary relationship to the beneficiaries under the will, and to permit him to have a prior claim seems to fly in the face of normal equitable principles designed to prevent a conflict of interest: cf *Holder v Holder* [1968] Ch 353, CA. Nevertheless, the application of the rule to executors is well established: *Re Stewart* [1908] 2 Ch 251. Umlaut will therefore be permitted to bring evidence outside the will that Acute intended to give him the shares. Since such evidence derives from the intended donee, however, it will need to be treated with caution: cf cases involving secret trusts: *Re Rees* [1950] Ch 204, CA, and *Re Tyler* [1967] 1 WLR 1269.

If, therefore, the intended trust in favour of Grave was not perfected in 2002, Umlaut may be able to satisfy the court that he is entitled to the shares under the rule in *Strong v Bird* in priority to both Cedilla and Grave.

Question 4

Three months ago, Lear, a keen rambler, caught a chill after spending a stormy winter's night wandering lost on the moors. He was taken to hospital suffering from pneumonia. When his eldest daughter, Goneril, visited him, he handed her the key to a deed box which was in his study at home. Lear told Goneril that he did not expect to live much longer and that, if anything were to happen to him, Goneril was to have the contents of the box.

Shortly after, when Lear's middle daughter, Regan, was by his bedside, Lear handed to her the Land Certificate relating to his country cottage in Gloucestershire, which he owned in fee simple. He advised Regan that, if he did not pull through, Regan was to have the cottage.

Last month, during a visit by his youngest daughter, Cordelia, Lear wrote a cheque for £10,000 in her favour. He informed her that this was to be her share of his property on his death.

Last week Lear, who remained seriously ill in hospital, deliberately took an overdose of sleeping pills, from which he died.

Goneril has now opened the deed box, and finds that it contains the keys and vehicle registration document to Lear's car, and a bank pass book relating to Lear's deposit account with the Serpent's Tooth Bank plc. It is discovered that, a couple of weeks before his death, Lear had leased the country cottage to Edmund for a term of 21 years. In his will, Lear gave all his property to charity.

Advise Lear's daughters.

Commentary

Those with little or no Latin should note that *donatio* is a noun meaning gift, so one can refer either to a '*donatio mortis causa*', or to a gift '*mortis causa*'. The plural is *donationes mortis causa*. Succour may be sought from remarks of Lord Simon of Glaisdale in **Brumby v Milner [1976] 1 WLR 1096**, a tax case, where his Lordship deprecated the unnecessary use by lawyers of Latin terms. In the present case, however, the English equivalent is slightly more of a mouthful, and the Latin reminds us of the Roman Law origins of this principle, which finds its modern counterpart in the Civil Law.

Answer plan

- Gifts *mortis causa*?
  - (1) Conditional on death
  - (2) In contemplation of death
    - *quere* if suicide
  - (3) Part with dominion
    - contents of deed box (handing key to deed box—the only key?)
- Car: delivery of evidence of ownership with physical possession
- Deposit account: pass book as indicia of title
- Cottage
  - **Sen v Headley**
  - granting of lease shows no parting with dominion?
  - lease subject to interest of donee?

- Cheque
- Unpresented cheque cannot be a gift *mortis causa*
  (merely revocable order to banker)

Suggested answer

Lear evidently intended the gifts to the daughters to take effect only in the event of his death. Such gifts would normally be testamentary in nature and valid only if made in accordance with the **Wills Act 1837** (as amended). Such formalities are absent here. Nevertheless, Lear's daughters will be able to take the property concerned if they can establish a valid *donatio mortis causa* in respect of each item.

To constitute a gift *mortis causa*, three elements must be satisfied. These have been affirmed by the courts many times (e.g., in *Cain v Moon* [1896] 2 QB 283, and, most recently, in *Sen v Headley* [1991] Ch 425).

First, the gift must be intended to be conditional upon death, so that it is not perfect until death, before which time it can be revoked by the donor. The gift must also be intended to be automatically revoked in the event of the donor's survival. Such conditions will be readily inferred where the gift is made in contemplation of death, which appears to be the case here.

Secondly, the gift must be made in contemplation of death, which must be more than a contemplation that the donor, like all living things, must some day die. This requirement is met where the donor is suffering from a life-threatening illness (*Saulnier v Anderson* (1987) 43 DLR (4th) 19) and seems therefore to be met in the instant case. However, in *Re Dudman* [1925] 1 Ch 553, it was held that a *donatio mortis causa* made in contemplation of suicide (at that time a crime) was not valid. Suicide is no longer a crime (**Suicide Act 1961**) and the present position is unclear. Such a purported *donatio* might still be invalid today on the ground that the requisite contemplation of death imports an element of uncertainty as to whether and when death will ensue. Such uncertainty is absent if the donor has the intention of taking his own life. In the problem, however, at the time he made the *donationes mortis causa*, Lear may have contemplated death by pneumonia, not by suicide. In *Wilkes v Allington* [1931] 2 Ch 104, it was held that it does not matter if death occurs from a disease other than that contemplated. A *donatio* might therefore not be invalidated if death occurs by suicide not contemplated at the time the *donatio* was made: see *Mills v Shields* [1948] IR 367.

Thirdly, the donor must part with dominion over the subject-matter of the *donatio*. Delivery to the intended donee of the only key to a locked receptacle which contains the subject-matter suffices, even if the subject-matter could have been handed over: *Re Mustapha* (1891) 8 TLR 160. It has, however, been stated obiter that there is no sufficient parting with dominion if the donor retains a duplicate key: *Re Craven's Estate* [1937] Ch 423. The statement in the question that 'the key' was handed over to Goneril implies that it was the only key, in which case this requirement is satisfied. Moreover, it does not matter if the box itself contains another key which opens a further box: *Re Lillingston* [1952] 2 All ER 184.

On this principle, since the deed box contains the key to Lear's car, it would appear that (unless Lear retained a duplicate key) a valid *donatio* has been made of the car. Although the passing of dominion over a chattel is usually effected by physical delivery, delivery of the key both enables Goneril to take possession of the car and (together with the delivery of the vehicle registration document, which evidences Lear's ownership) effectively puts it out of Lear's power to deal with it.

Parting with dominion over a chose in action requires the donor to part with the essential evidence or indicia of title: *Birch* v *Treasury Solicitor* [1951] Ch 298. There, the Court of Appeal held (*inter alia*) that a *donatio mortis causa* of a chose in action represented by a deposit pass book to Barclay's Bank was effected by delivery to the donee of the pass book. In such instances, equity will perfect the imperfect gift by treating the deceased's personal representatives as trustees of the chose in action for the donee: *Duffield* v *Elwes* (1827) 1 Bli NS 497. This principle would therefore apply to Lear's deposit account with the Serpent's Tooth Bank plc.

Lear's country cottage is land and, until recently, it was doubted, on the basis of dicta in *Duffield* v *Elwes*, whether land could ever be the subject-matter of a *donatio mortis causa*. In *Sen* v *Headley*, however, the Court of Appeal held that it could. There was no difference in substance between the principle applicable to choses in action established in *Birch* v *Treasury Solicitor* and the parting with dominion over land by the delivery of the title deeds. Although the doctrine of *donationes mortis causa* is anomalous, it was preferable to avoid creating anomalies of anomalies. *Sen* v *Headley* concerned unregistered land, but the same principle would appear to apply to the delivery of the Land Certificate in registered land.

Although Lear has parted with dominion over the Land Certificate, whether he has parted with dominion over the cottage itself is less clear. He did after all subsequently lease it out. Such a situation was hypothesised in *Sen* v *Headley* by the Court of Appeal, which opined that a retention by the donor of a power to deal with the subject-matter did not invariably preclude a parting with dominion. It was a matter of fact in each case. Although the donor in *Sen* v *Headley* retained a key to the premises, the donee had her own set and was in *de facto* control. The problem does not state how many sets of keys there are, nor who has possession of them. If Regan has the only set of keys to the cottage, that might, in accordance with *Sen* v *Headley*, be a sufficient parting with dominion by Lear. Nevertheless, the legal principle is obscure. Mummery J at first instance could not see how the equitable interest of the donee, which arises only on the death of the donor, can be binding upon a tenant of a lease granted during the donor's lifetime. The Court of Appeal does not seem to provide a satisfactory answer to this.

It is well established that delivery of the donor's own cheque to the intended donee cannot constitute a valid *donatio mortis causa*: *Re Beaumont* [1902] 1 Ch 889,

Re Leaper [1916] 1 Ch 579. A cheque is merely a revocable order to a banker to pay a sum of money. The position may be otherwise if the cheque is presented and the donor's account credited during the donor's lifetime or before the bank has been informed of his death. Subject to these qualifications, Cordelia can derive no benefit from the cheque, which is mere waste paper.

Further reading

Clarke, P., All ER Rev, 2002, p. 229.

Doggett, A. (2003) 62 CLJ 263.

Garton, J. [2003] Conv 364.

Hallach, M. [2003] Conv 192.

Ladds, D. [2003] 17 TLI 35.

Tjio, H. and Yeo, T. [2002] LMCLQ 296.

5

Trusts, powers, and discretionary and protective trusts

Introduction

A thorough understanding of the distinction between trusts and powers is essential. The different types of trusts—fixed and discretionary—have different rules determining their validity. There is also the distinction to be grasped between fiduciary and non-fiduciary powers.

An examination question may call for an analysis of the distinction between a discretionary trust and a power. These can look very similar, and they may be created for a similar purpose. A testator wishing to provide for the members of his family after his death could create a fixed trust under which each beneficiary has a fixed share. The testator may, however, prefer to give his trustees a discretion in the allocation of the beneficial interests, so that account can be taken of the changing needs and circumstances of the objects after the testator's death. The appropriate machinery for this is the discretionary trust.

It is important to distinguish individual and class rights. Under a discretionary trust, each individual object has, before distribution, specific rights in equity—personal rights which fall short of an equitable interest. Such personal rights are known as mere equities. As a class, however, the objects of a discretionary trust may have more extensive rights. If, the objects of a discretionary trust are all of full age and sound mind (*sui iuris*) and together form a closed class, they can compel the trustees to put an end to the trust and hand the trust assets over to them as they (the objects) direct. In other words, the equitable interest lies with the class as a whole. The objects of a discretionary trust of income do not have this right, however, if the trustees have a power to keep the income in the trust, i.e., a power to accumulate.

It is vital to be precise in your use of terminology. Confusion can easily arise because some terms are used by different judges or writers to mean different things; so, unless they define the sense in which they are using the terms, you will have to look to the context in order to determine what the meaning is. The term 'trust-power' is a dangerous one to use without any explanation of its meaning. A trust-power is a combination of a duty (a trust) and a power. For this reason, a discretionary trust is often called a trust-power, since it combines a duty to distribute with a power of selection. Unfortunately, the term trust-power can also be used to mean a fiduciary power, since this too combines a power and a trust obligation, i.e., a power to distribute and a duty to consider exercising it. In this chapter, the term trust-power is used to mean a discretionary trust.

Another problem is with the term 'mere power'. This expression is used in contradistinction to a trust-power (in the sense of a discretionary trust). It is, in other words, a power which the donee or fiduciary is not obliged to exercise. In this sense, the term 'mere power' embraces both fiduciary and non-fiduciary powers. By contrast, a 'bare power' (sometimes called a 'personal power') means a non-fiduciary power.

An individual object of a power (whether fiduciary or non-fiduciary) has a right (a mere equity) to prevent any appointment being made outside the defined class of objects. Only an object of a fiduciary power, however, has equitable rights (mere equities) in relation to the exercise of the power. These rights are broadly similar to those enjoyed by an object of a discretionary trust; but the crucial distinction, which was emphasised by Lord Wilberforce in *McPhail* v *Doulton* [1971] AC 424, is that trustees of a discretionary trust are under a greater duty to survey the class than donees of a fiduciary power. The right of an object to be considered is therefore correspondingly greater if the object is an object of a discretionary trust than if he is an object of a fiduciary power. The object of a non-fiduciary power, by contrast, has no right to be considered; and the donee of the power can appoint spitefully, or capriciously, or even go to sleep and forget about exercising the power at all.

Recent case law has tended to blur the differences between discretionary trusts and fiduciary powers. Thus *McPhail* v *Doulton* held that the test for certainty of objects of powers should be applied as the test for certainty of objects of discretionary trusts. Furthermore, a number of later cases involving pension funds, where the objects supply consideration in the form of contributions from their salaries, have extended the rights of the objects of powers. It is not yet clear, however, whether this latter development is applicable solely to pension fund trusts, or to all trusts under which the objects provide consideration in money or money's worth.

You should try to keep separate in your mind the rules relating to the validity of an instrument (whether as a fixed or discretionary trust or as a power) and the duties and powers of the trustee or donee in relation to the exercise of any power he has. A question concerned with the rights of the objects of a discretionary trust or power is not concerned with the validity of the instrument. Certainty of objects, administrative unworkability and capriciousness (where the definition of objects negatives any sensible intention on the part of the settlor) are concerned with matters of validity. Administrative unworkability invalidates a discretionary trust, but not, apparently, a power.

This chapter also includes a question relating to protective trusts, which are a two-stage combination of a fixed trust and a discretionary trust. Protective trusts in a family context are not as common today as they were in earlier times, so your course may not deal with them very extensively if at all. Protective trusts are, however, of modern importance in relation to pension-fund trusts; see, e.g., *Re Scientific Investment Pension Plan Trusts* [1999] Ch 53. If protective trusts form part of your course, you will need to be familiar with the intricacies of the **Trustee Act 1925, s. 33**, as well as with the sometimes conflicting case law.

Question 1

Adam, who has just died, made the following dispositions in his will:

(a) £50,000 to my trustees on trust to apply the net income of the fund in making, at their absolute discretion, grants to or for the benefit of any of the employees or former employees of Abel & Sons, their spouses or dependants, or any others having a moral claim on me.

(b) £5,000 to my trustees upon trust to be divided equally amongst my friends at the 'Paradise' public house, Edenton.

(c) £100,000 to be applied by my trustees as they see fit for the benefit of the middle classes of my home town, Edenton.

(d) The residue of my estate to my wife, Eve, absolutely, but I direct my trustees to allow such old friends of mine who wish to do so, to acquire any of my collection of stuffed reptiles at fifty per cent of market price.

Advise the trustees of the will as to the validity of these dispositions.

Commentary

There usually appears in examination papers a question on certainty of objects dealing with the ramifications of the House of Lords' decision in *McPhail v Doulton* **[1971] AC 424** and its application by the Court of Appeal in *Re Baden's Deed Trusts (No. 2)* **[1973] Ch 9**. So a careful preparation of the case law will repay the effort!

For a high mark, some discussion of the issues going beyond a simple application of the cases to the problem is desirable. Some further discussion of the issues of conceptual certainty, evidential certainty, ascertainability and administrative workability would be appropriate.

Answer plan

(a) • Test for certainty of objects of a discretionary trust is the individual ascertainability test adopted in *McPhail v Doulton*

- Employees, former employees and their spouses would be conceptually certain and satisfy the test
- The Court of Appeal decision in *Re Baden (No. 2)* is authority that relatives and dependants also satisfy the certainty test
- But persons having a moral claim upon me would fail the test
- **(b)** • This disposition is a fixed trust and the test for certainty is therefore the complete list test (*IRC v Broadway Cottages*)
  - Friends at the Paradise would not satisfy this test and would fail
- **(c)** • This is a discretionary trust and the test for certainty of objects is the *McPhail v Doulton* individual ascertainability test
  - 'Middle classes' would not satisfy this test
  - Also, if this were a very large number of people, it would additionally fail for administrative unworkability, as the trustees of a discretionary trust should survey the whole class
- **(d)** • 'Old friends' as a class gift would fail the individual ascertainability test
  - But in *Re Barlow*, this type of disposition was construed as a series of conditional individual gifts to persons able to prove that they were old friends, and so was valid

Suggested answer

(a) A trust must be for ascertained or ascertainable beneficiaries: *Re Endacott* [1960] Ch 232, CA. The test to determine certainty of objects in a discretionary trust was decided by the House of Lords in *McPhail v Doulton* [1971] AC 424 ('can it be said with certainty that any given individual is or is not a member of the class?').

Since this decision, therefore, it is no longer necessary to prepare a complete list of objects of a discretionary trust as is still required in a fixed trust (*IRC v Broadway Cottages Trust* [1955] Ch 20, CA). In *McPhail v Doulton* (supra) the House of Lords adopted the test for certainty of objects of powers established in *Re Gulbenkian's Settlement Trust (No. 2)* [1975] AC 508, and the two tests are now the same.

It is necessary, therefore, to apply the test to the terms of Adam's will and ask: can it be said with certainty whether any individual is or is not an employee or former employee of Abel & Sons, or their spouse or dependant, or any other having a moral claim on Abel?

Employees or former employees would satisfy the test.

In *Re Baden's Deed Trusts (No. 2)* [1973] Ch 9, CA, the terms 'relatives' and 'dependants' were subjected to the test. It was considered that the terms were conceptually certain and, therefore, sufficient to satisfy the test although all three judges gave different reasons for finding 'relatives' certain.

The term 'spouses' is clearly certain as a concept and this part of the gift would be valid.

However, the gift also includes a category of 'any others having a moral claim on me'. It was said in *McPhail* v *Doulton* that such an expression is conceptually uncertain.

It is not clear whether this would cause the whole gift to fail for uncertainty or whether the courts could sever the offending part, thereby saving the valid parts (*Re Leek* [1969] 1 Ch 563, CA; *Re Gulbenkian's Settlements* [1968] Ch 126 at 138, CA).

(b) The gift upon trust to be divided equally amongst my friends at the 'Paradise' is a fixed trust. The beneficiaries hold equitable interests under the trust in fixed shares. It is necessary to be able to draw up a list of all the beneficiaries in order for the division to be made. The older and stricter rule in *IRC* v *Broadway Cottages Trust* applies. The expression 'friends' is not a term that is sufficiently certain for such a complete list to be drawn up. The expression 'old friends' was held to be certain in *Re Gibbard's Will Trusts* [1967] 1 WLR 42 in relation to a power, but this case used the old test of whether it could be said of any one person that they were within the class (a test favoured by Lord Denning MR in his dissenting judgment in the Court of Appeal in *Re Gulbenkian*). This test was rejected by the House of Lords in *Re Gulbenkian* however, and so is not now good authority for this point. A gift to 'friends' was upheld in *Re Barlow's Will Trusts* [1979] 1 WLR 278, but this was a series of gifts with a condition precedent. The size of the gift to each recipient did not alter according to the numbers answering the description, therefore it is not authority for certainty of the expression 'friends' in a class gift, whether a fixed (or discretionary) trust.

(c) This gift constitutes a purported discretionary trust. It raises questions about certainty of objects and administrative workability.

First, the problem of certainty of objects is raised in respect of the definition of 'middle classes' (*McPhail* v *Doulton*). Again, it is necessary to decide whether such a concept is certain applying the test in *McPhail* v *Doulton*. Although it may be possible to say definitely whether some individuals are or are not members of the middle classes, there may be a number of people who cannot be classified in this way. There was a difference of approach amongst the judges in *Re Baden's Deed Trusts (No. 2)*.

Megaw LJ accepted that there may be a substantial number of persons about whom it could not be proved whether they are in or out. However, this may relate more to the question of evidential uncertainty. Conceptual certainty means that the class must be definable. Evidential certainty is the proof an applicant must supply to establish membership of the class. In the case of a gift to 'middle classes' it is difficult to define criteria for such a concept.

However, even if the gift is conceptually certain, then the question of administrative unworkability arises. In *McPhail* v *Doulton*, it was said that if the definition of 'objects is so hopelessly wide as not to form anything like a class', then the trust would be administratively unworkable. A discretionary trustee has duties to survey the class and this is impossible in a class of great width. This was the position in the case of *R* v *District Auditor, ex parte West Yorkshire Metropolitan County Council* (1986) 26 RVR 24, where a trust for the inhabitants of the county of West Yorkshire was held to be too wide and therefore void for administrative unworkability. If the trust could be construed as a power this rule would not apply: *Re Manisty's Settlement* [1974] Ch 17.

(d) This gift must be distinguished from discretionary trusts. It is not a trust for a class but a number of individual gifts to any person who is able to prove to the trustees that he or she qualifies as 'an old friend'. Such a gift does not require conceptual certainty. The gift will be valid if only one person seeking to take can be identified as an 'old friend' (*Re Allen* [1953] Ch 810, CA). In *Re Barlow's Will Trusts*, the direction to sell a painting at a preferential price to 'any friends of mine who may wish to buy one' was held to be a valid gift. A friend was a social acquaintance of long standing and anyone who satisfied this condition precedent could take the gift.

On the basis of this authority, this final disposition is therefore valid.

Question 2

In January 1982 Simon settled property on Tom and Tam 'on protective trusts' for Betty (who was then aged 25) until she should reach the age of 35 and, if no determining event had by then occurred, upon trust for Betty absolutely; but if a determining event had occurred, then upon protective trusts for Betty until she should attain the age of 45; but, if no determining event had by then occurred, upon trust for her absolutely, and subject thereto, to hold the property in trust for Betty for life with remainder to her children, Romulus and Remus.

In December 1987 Betty asked the trustees to pay her £50,000 for the purpose of setting up a feline beauty parlour. Although such amount exceeded the income of the trust, Tom and Tam duly paid the money. In 1988, having taken legal advice that this constituted a breach of trust, they sought to remedy the breach by withholding a part of Betty's income from the following year. Betty's beauty parlour was not a success. In 1989 it went out of business and Betty went bankrupt. Tom and Tam continued to pay the fees at the local further education college where Betty was studying for a diploma in hairdressing and beauty.

In June 1995, Betty's husband petitioned for divorce on the ground of Betty's unreasonable behaviour. The divorce court awarded him custody of the children and ordered Betty to pay maintenance for the children, to be charged on Betty's interest under the settlement. Betty has refused to pay.

Advise Tom and Tam as to the following:

(a) The legal effect of the aforementioned events on the settlement and the nature of the interests of Betty, Romulus and Remus under the settlement, from 1982 onwards.

(b) Would your advice differ if Betty, as opposed to Simon, had been the settlor?

 Commentary

The facts in the question make it appear long and confusing. However, if you have revised protective trusts, this is the question for you as it is discrete. A rough plan setting out the sequence of events is desirable.

Such a plan might look something like this:

1982 (Betty aged 25)

| Determinable
| interest for Betty
| 1987   advancement (terminating event?)
| 1988   impounding income (terminating event)
| 1989   bankruptcy (terminating event)
↓

1992 (Betty aged 35)

| Second determinable
| interest for Betty
| 1995   court order (terminating event?)
↓

2002   (Betty aged 45)

There are a number of points in the question, each supported by a case, so it is largely a matter of spotting them all. The more you spot, the higher the mark. A diagram of events might prevent you missing any.

The point on the matrimonial order raises two cases which are difficult to reconcile. Grasp the nettle and deal with the conflict, explaining which one is preferred and why. For further discussion on this point see (1963) 27 Conv (NS) 517; F. R. Crane.

The reference to the note by R. E. Megarry in the *Law Quarterly Review* is not essential merely to pass, but demonstrates a breadth of reading which is essential for achieving a higher class.

Answer plan

(a) • There are two protective trusts to which **Trustee Act 1925, s. 33(1)** automatically applies; the first is for ten years until Betty is 35, and the second (if Betty's interest does not become absolute) is for a further ten years until she is 45

• **Section 33(1)(i)** is widely drafted to deprive the tenant of his life interest if he loses any part of the income

• An advancement lawfully made is expressly exempted from the operation of the section

• The trustees impounding the income to make good a breach and Betty's bankruptcy in 1989 are both determining events

• From the determining event to the end of the ten-year period, a discretionary trust for Betty and her children arises under **s. 33(1)(ii)**, and payment of college fees would be a matter for the trustees' discretion

• The period of the second protective trust starts in 1992, and there are conflicting decisions as to whether charging the income with payments due under a court order will cause a forfeiture or not

(b) • The only difference would be as to Betty's bankruptcy

• Bankruptcy will not be a determining event if the bankrupt herself sets up the trust, as this would allow the bankrupt to protect assets from her creditors

Suggested answer

(a) The wording of the disposition invokes Trustee Act 1925, s. 33, which initially creates a determinable interest for Betty, the principal beneficiary. Section 33(1)(i) defines very widely the events which will determine the interest of the principal beneficiary as 'any act or thing ... or event' which deprives her of the right to the whole or any part of the income.

The settlement does, in fact, create a series of protective trusts. The advantage of this is that, if a determining event occurs before Betty is 30, she gets a second chance before her interest is irrevocably reduced to a life interest. This application of the protective trust was recommended by R. E. Megarry as making the best possible use of the existing machinery ((1958) 74 LQR 184).

In December 1987 the trustees make an advance to Betty of £50,000 to set up a feline beauty parlour. Section 33(1) provides that '... an advance under any statutory or express power ... ' is not a determining event. An advance may, therefore, be made if there is an express power in the settlement or, if the life tenant consents, under the provisions in the Trustee Act 1925, s. 32. This section confers upon the trustees power to pay capital for the advancement or benefit of any persons entitled, even if (like Betty), they are entitled merely contingently to the capital. An advancement properly made, therefore, does not constitute a determining event. Setting up a beneficiary in business is an appropriate reason for an advance.

If the advancement was not lawfully made under the terms of the trust however, then it would be of no avail for Betty to argue that she was still enjoying the benefit of the capital taken from the trust as she still had the feline beauty parlour. This argument was made on behalf of a principal beneficiary in *Re Smith's Will Trusts* (1981) 131 NLJ 292, but Megarry J held that in such circumstances, what the beneficiary is enjoying is the benefit of capital which has been taken out of the trust thereby depriving her of part of the income from the trust. However, whether the advance was lawfully made or not, the attempt by the trustees to impound Betty's income to make good the breach which they believed had occurred, is a determining event for the purposes of s. 33 (*Re Balfour's Settlement* [1938] Ch 928).

As soon as a determining event occurs (the advancement if unlawful in 1987, or impounding the income in 1988), then the principal beneficiary's interest ceases and the discretionary trust under s. 33(1)(ii) arises instead. This is a discretionary trust for Betty, her spouse and her children, Romulus and Remus, for the remainder of the ten-year period of the protective trust, i.e., until 1992. Betty's bankruptcy in 1989 would also have been a determining event, but as the interest had already determined, it will be of no effect (*Re Detmold*—see (b) below).

The trustees continue to pay Betty's college fees after the determining events. Once the determinable interest has come to an end, the discretionary trusts arise. The trustees are able to make payments at their absolute discretion to the principal beneficiary, his or her spouse and issue for their maintenance, support or other benefit. Betty, as the principal beneficiary, may, therefore, receive payments at the discretion of the trustees even though she has no proprietary interest in the trust. However, a difficulty arises where the principal beneficiary has been declared bankrupt. If she receives more than what is sufficient for her mere support, then the trustee in bankruptcy may impound any payments made to her. However, it would seem that where payments are made to a third party for services rendered to the principal beneficiary, the trustee in bankruptcy is unable to intercept such payments (*Re Coleman* (1888) 39 ChD 443).

In 1992, a second protective trust arose for a further ten-year period until 2002.

In June 1995 a court order was made charging Betty's interest with a maintenance order. This order is available to the Family Division of the High Court under the **Matrimonial Causes Act 1973**. There are conflicting cases on whether this is an event which will determine her protective interest. In *Re Richardson's Will Trusts* [1958] Ch 504, it was held that such an order caused a forfeiture. However, in *General Accident Fire and Life Assurance Corporation Ltd* v *IRC* [1963] 1 WLR 1207, part of the income was ordered to be paid to an ex-wife and this did not cause a forfeiture. The object of the protective trust is to protect not only the principal beneficiary from financial disasters, but also his initial family who are beneficiaries under the discretionary trust, and Donovan LJ said that the section could give no protection against such a court order. *Re Richardson* was not referred to in the later case and commentators suggest that the *General Accident* case is to be preferred as the protective trust may well have been set up with the very intention of protecting the principal beneficiary's original spouse and family. To replace this with a discretionary trust under s. 33(i)(ii) could operate to deprive them in favour of a later spouse and family. If the *General Accident* case is followed, then the court order will not determine Betty's interest which would continue until 2002 when she would have obtained an absolute interest.

(b) If Betty were the settlor instead of Simon, this would affect the advice about the bankruptcy which occurred in 1989. A settlor may protect another person from the consequences of their bankruptcy. However, settlors may not protect their own property from bankruptcy in this way. In *Re Burroughs-Fowler* [1916] 2 Ch 251, the settlor settled property in trust for himself until a specified event should occur, whereupon the income should be paid to his wife. One of the events was bankruptcy, which did occur. It was held that the trustee in bankruptcy was entitled to the income.

This applies only to bankruptcy, and not to other determining events. So, there would be no difference in the advice in respect of the other events. In 1989, when the bankruptcy occurred, Betty's interest has already determined as a result of the trustees' decision to withhold income (*Re Balfour's Settlement*). As the discretionary trusts have already arisen, the bankruptcy can have no effect (*Re Detmold* (1889) 40 ChD 585).

Question 3

But it is difficult in borderline cases to draw a dividing line between discretionary trusts and powers ... The decision turns on the proper construction of the language of the instrument. The matter is made more difficult by reason of the fact that a discretionary trust may be 'exhaustive' or 'non-exhaustive'. (Hanbury and Martin, *Modern Equity*, 18th edn, Sweet & Maxwell, 2009, at p. 66.)

Discuss.

Commentary

This essay question requires a discussion of the distinction between discretionary trusts and powers with reference to relevant literature; see, for example, (1974) 37 MLR 643, (Y. Grbich). In particular, such reference must be made where an essay of this type is set as an assessed essay.

A straightforward explanation of the difference and the importance of the distinction between discretionary trusts and powers is required. The essay could be grouped under different headings to clarify the different aspects of the problem; for example, the different position of the trustees/donees, and the potential recipients.

Answer plan

- Both a discretionary trust and a power give a person the right to benefit members of a class whom they choose, and are the same in this respect
- A discretionary trust imposes an obligation to select beneficiaries however, whereas a power is merely an enabling provision
- It follows that trustees must exercise their discretion under a trust, and the court will intervene if they do not, whereas the court will not generally intervene to exercise a power
- The donee of a power is not obliged to exercise it, although he should consider its exercise if it is a fiduciary power
- The test for certainty of objects of powers established in **Re Gulbenkian** was adopted in **McPhail v Doulton** for discretionary trusts—can it be said of any given postulant that they are, or are not, within the class of objects?
- Although no individual potential beneficiary under a discretionary trust has any interest in the property, collectively they own the property and the rule in **Saunders v Vautier** applies
- Although the objects of a power generally have no rights, the courts have taken the view in some pension fund cases that, as the objects have given consideration, the courts should have a right to intervene to protect them
- A disposition which contains a gift over if there is no selection will be a power, as selection is clearly not intended to be obligatory

- In the absence of a gift over, the court must decide if the settlor's intention was to benefit the objects in any event (a discretionary trust) or merely to enable someone to benefit them if he so wished (a power)

Suggested answer

At first sight a discretionary trust and a power may achieve the same purpose. A disposition is made which is available for a group of people but the selection of the recipients and the size of their shares is left to the decision of a third party. The purpose of such a disposition is not to benefit each member of the group equally regardless of their need, but instead, a power of selection is given to a trusted third party. That person is to make the selection according to criteria fixed by the settlor or at their absolute discretion. If the settlor wished each member of the group to benefit in any event, then this would have been achieved by creating a fixed trust in equal or other shares.

The person making the selection may be obliged to use up all the property or income in making a selection, as in an exhaustive trust, or there may be power to accumulate income and make no selection as in a non-exhaustive trust.

However, the basic difference that a trust imposes an obligation to distribute, whereas a power is merely an enabling provision, results in important differences in the duties of trustees of a discretionary trust and the donees of a power, and the position of the beneficiaries under each.

Duty of trustees under discretionary trusts

A trustee is under a duty to perform the trust. If the trust is discretionary, the trustees are obliged to consider and exercise their discretion. If they fail to exercise their discretion the court can order them to do so. If the trust is exhaustive, they must make an appointment even though the decision as to the recipient and the size of the distribution is at the trustees' discretion. The court will intervene and make an appointment if the trustees fail to act, or if the trustees predecease the testator—the trust will not fail for want of a trustee. If no appointment is made the property will normally be divided equally between the beneficiaries on the basis that equality is equity, as in the case of *Burrough* v *Philcox* (1840) 5 My & Cr 72.

Duty of donee of a power

There is an initial distinction to be drawn between fiduciary powers and bare powers. A fiduciary power is a power of appointment granted to a trustee or to a person in a fiduciary position (*Re Mills* [1930] 1 Ch 654). Because such persons are in a fiduciary position, they cannot simply ignore the power. In *Re Hay's Settlement Trusts* [1982] 1 WLR 202, it was held that the donee of a fiduciary power must consider the exercise of the power and survey the potential beneficiaries from time to time. The court may intervene if the trustee exercises the power improperly.

However, even where there is a fiduciary power the donee is not required to exercise it. In *Re Gestetner's Settlement* [1953] Ch 672, a power given to trustees to distribute amongst a huge and fluctuating class consisting of employees of a number of companies, was considered valid, even though it was impossible to consider all the potential objects. The test for certainty of powers, as established in *Re Gulbenkian's Settlement* [1970] AC 508, is, in fact, the same for certainty of objects in a discretionary trust. This was held to be the appropriate test for discretionary trusts in *McPhail v Doulton* [1971] AC 424. The test is that it must be possible to say with certainty whether any given individual is or is not a member of the class.

A bare power does not impose on the donee any fiduciary duties. A donee of a bare power may exercise the power at will. If the power is not exercised, the court cannot compel the donee to exercise it or even to consider its exercise. If the donee predeceases the testator, then the power lapses. If no appointment is made under any power (whether fiduciary or not) the property will pass to the person entitled in default of its exercise, so that, if the donor of the power has not specified who is to take over in this event, the property may go back to the settlor or to the testator's estate under a resulting trust.

Position of beneficiaries under a discretionary trust

The beneficiaries under a fixed trust own the property in equity, and, if of full age and sound mind, can call for the trust to be extinguished and the property distributed (*Saunders v Vautier* (1841) 10 LJ Ch 354). Under a discretionary trust, no individual beneficiary owns a particular part of the trust property until an appointment has been made (*Gartside v IRC* [1968] AC 553). However, as a group, all the potential beneficiaries own the trust property and, as in a fixed trust, if adult and of sound mind, they can collectively call for the trust to be brought to an end.

Position of objects of a power

The objects of a power have no interest in the property. They cannot call for a distribution to be made. They only acquire an interest once a distribution is made in their favour. They have no right to seek the intervention of the court if no appointment is made. If no appointment is made, therefore, unless there is a gift over, the property will revert on resulting trust to the settlor or the settlor's estate. The only occasion on which the objects of a bare power can apply to court is to restrain the exercise of a power which is outside the terms of the instrument granting it, as this would be tantamount to a fraud on the power. Objects of a fiduciary power may additionally prevent or have set aside an appointment which is made capriciously, or where improper considerations are taken into account (*Klug v Klug* [1918] 2 Ch 67).

In some cases concerning pension funds however, the courts have taken the view that, as the beneficiaries are not volunteers, a fiduciary obligation attaches to the power and the courts do have a *locus standi* to act, even in the case of a fiduciary power, where there is nobody else to act because, for example, the company with the power has gone into liquidation (*Mettoy Pension Trustees Ltd* v *Evans* [1990] 1 WLR 1587). Moreover, it was said in *Imperial Group Pension Trust* v *Imperial Tobacco* [1991] 1 WLR 589 that if the company with a power to appoint under a pension fund does so, then it must do so bona fide and not in breach of its fiduciary duties to its employees.

Construction of document to distinguish between power and discretionary trust

As indicated in the question, it may be extremely difficult to decide whether a power or a discretionary trust has been created. The language of the gift in a well-drafted document should make it clear. Failing this, the court must decide whether the intention of the instrument is to impose an obligation to benefit the objects, or merely to enable them to be benefited.

First, an obligation cannot be deduced where the settlor provides a gift over in default of appointment. This implicitly acknowledges that no selection might be made and there is no power to force a selection. A power, therefore, has been created and not a discretionary trust (*Re Gestetner*). The reverse does not, unfortunately, always hold true. In *Re Weekes' Settlement* [1897] 1 Ch 289, it was held that there was no intention to create a trust for the objects of the power, even though there was no gift over, as the disposition did not impose any obligation.

In *Burrough* v *Philcox*, property was left by the testator to his two children for their lives. The survivor was given a power to leave the property in her will 'amongst my nephews and nieces or their children, either all to one of them, or to as many of them as my surviving child should think proper'. The court decided that this was effective to create a trust. As no selection was made, the court would intervene and make the gift in equal shares amongst the beneficiaries. Had the conclusion been that the gift was a mere power, then the court would have been powerless to intervene and the property would have resulted back to the settlor's estate. Lord Cottenham in *Burrough* v *Philcox* said that where there is a general intention in favour of a class with a particular intention to select particular individuals from that class then, if the selection fails, the class will benefit as a whole. The significant factor is an intention to benefit the objects of the gift if no selection is made.

So, the distinction is often hard to deduce in cases where the instrument is not clear. The distinction, nevertheless, is important in terms of the differing rights and duties of the trustees and donees and the potential objects of the trust or power.

6

Charitable trusts

Introduction

In our experience the topic of charitable trusts is a favourite one for examiners and students alike. There are complexities in this area, however, and it can be difficult in borderline cases to decide whether a particular trust is charitable or not. Nevertheless, the law itself is probably more easily understood than in some other topics in equity and trusts. The examiners may devote an entire question to charitable trusts. On the other hand, a question on this area may be mixed with another topic. A favourite combination in practice involves a mixing with non-charitable purpose trusts.

The questions in this chapter deal with the areas of charity law that are most commonly covered in courses on Equity and Trusts: namely, the legal meaning of charity and cy-près schemes. The legal definition of charity has changed. The **Charities Act 2006, Part I** which came into force on 1 April 2008, introduced a statutory definition of charity and was intended to strengthen the public benefit requirement (although whether it will have any such effect seems doubtful). At the time of writing, the Charities Bill was progressing through Parliament. This Bill will consolidate the **Charities Act 2006** together with some other statutes on charity law such as the **Recreational Charities Act 1958**. As a consolidating statute it is uncontroversial, and we have, therefore, included reference throughout to the **Charities Act 2011** as the governing statute on the assumption that it will complete its progress through Parliament and be successfully enacted in 2011. Examination questions on charitable trusts might well consider the potential impact of the **Charities Act 2006** (as consolidated in the **Charities Act 2011**) on the meaning of charity and on public benefit. This chapter therefore concludes with a question that explores what the effect of such changes is likely to be.

Question 1

Geoffrey, who died earlier this year, left a will directing his executors and trustees to constitute his residuary estate a trust fund and to hold one-third thereof upon trust for each of the following purposes:

(a) To provide snooker tables and prizes for snooker tournaments for university students.

(b) To assist the vicar and churchwardens of St Peter's, Faversham, in parish work.

(c) To encourage the preservation of the world's rainforests.

Consider whether these dispositions are of a charitable nature.

Commentary

Since you are asked to advise as to the charitable nature of each disposition, it is unnecessary to consider whether any of them might be otherwise valid (e.g., as a trust of imperfect obligation). Had the question, however, demanded that you 'advise as to the validity' of the dispositions, a discussion of other means of upholding them would have been appropriate.

Do not waste time dealing with points which do not cause problems. There is no need, for instance, in part **(b)** of the present question, to write at length about whether the advancement of various esoteric beliefs might nevertheless be charitable.

If you are permitted to take statutes into the examination, you will not gain many marks for merely reciting what they contain. Reference to recreational charities within the **Charities Act 2011** should refer to the relevant section and paragraphs, but quotations should be limited to the key words: e.g., in the answer to part **(a)** of the present question, to the issue of 'need'.

The answer does not conclude definitely whether any of the dispositions are charitable. This is because whether a particular purpose is charitable is a mixed question of law and fact. As a law student you are expected to know the law; but you cannot be decisive about matters of construction. For this reason, it is best merely to indicate what you consider the more likely construction and state the law relevant to it. You might, however, go on to consider the consequences which would flow from any other reasonable constructions.

Answer plan

(a) • Advancement of amateur sport?

  • Means of furthering a charitable purpose?

  • Advancement of education?

  • Recreational charity?

(b) • Advancement of religion?

  • Gift to office-holder, but super-added words

  • Wholly and exclusively charitable?

(c) • Advancement of environmental protection?

  • But political purpose?

  • Political element merely ancillary?

Suggested answer

To be charitable, each of the dispositions must promote a charitable purpose, it must contain a public benefit and the purpose must be wholly and exclusively charitable. It is necessary to consider each disposition separately.

(a) Under the Charities Act 2011, to be charitable a purpose must both fall within the list of purposes that are set out, and also be for the public benefit: s. 2(1).

The list of purposes in s. 3(1) includes the advancement of amateur sport (para. (g)), thereby reversing the pre-Act decision in *Re Nottage* [1895] 2 Ch 649, CA. The provision of equipment for sport can be regarded as promoting sport. However, the Act states that 'sport' means sports or games that promote health by involving physical or mental skill or exertion: s. 2(3)(d). Snooker is a game, but whilst the playing of it involves both physical and mental skills, it is less clear that snooker promotes health. However, in *Hitchin Bridge Club* (28 Feb 2011) the Charity Commission held the club charitable for the promotion of amateur sport because it was satisfied that bridge is a game involving high mental skill and there was evidence that playing bridge reduced dementia and mental illness in later life. Snooker might therefore qualify if similar evidence of health-giving effects can be adduced.

Alternatively, it might be argued that the purpose can be regarded as a means of furthering the education of the university students, the advancement of education being itself a purpose within the statutory list (para. (b)). In *Re Mariette* [1915] 2 Ch 284, for instance, the judge regarded the playing of sport as an integral part of the boys' education, and so held charitable a gift to provide squash courts and prizes for sport in the particular school. It is clear that this principle is not limited to sports but can extend to games. In *Re Dupree's Deed Trusts* [1945] Ch 16, a trust for an annual chess tournament in Portsmouth for boys and young men up to the age of 21 was held charitable, the court accepting expert evidence that chess was educational. In each of these cases it seems that the court was willing to treat the purpose of the trust as the advancement of education because it was limited to young persons. In *IRC v McMullen* [1981] AC 1, the House of Lords held that a trust to provide facilities for pupils at schools and universities to play football was charitable for the advancement of education, even though some university students are well above school age: the fact that the majority are young persons was apparently sufficient. It is however a matter of construction in each case whether the expressed purpose can be treated as a means of furthering a charitable purpose: *IRC v City of Glasgow Police Athletic Association* [1953] AC 380. In the *McMullen* case, the trust deed expressly stated that the facilities were a means of improving the students' minds. Since no such words are expressed here, the provision of snooker tables can fall within para. (b) only if the court is satisfied that the playing of snooker is a means of advancing the university students' education. This is by no means certain: snooker is not as intellectual a game as chess, and (unlike football or squash) it does not involve significant physical exercise.

To be charitable a purpose must also be for the public benefit: Charities Act 2011, s. 2(1)(b), and it is not presumed that a purpose of a particular description is for the public benefit: s. 4(2). Public benefit under the 2011 Act has the same meaning as it had in the law of charities before April 2008: s. 4(3). University students are therefore a sufficient section of the community to benefit for the purposes of paras (b) and (g) within the list of statutory purposes.

This is not, however, the end of the matter. Under the Charities Act 2011, s. 5 it is charitable to provide facilities for recreation or other leisure time occupation in the interests of social welfare. The requirement of social welfare is satisfied if the facilities are provided to improve the conditions of life for the persons for whom they are primarily intended, and either the persons have need of such facilities (for the reasons there specified, including youth) or the facilities are to be available to members of the public at large, or male, or female, members of the public at large. As university students are clearly not the public at large, the element of 'need' would have to be satisfied. Although the majority of the Court of Appeal in *IRC* v *McMullen* [1979] 1 WLR 130 took the view that 'need' imported some element of deprivation, the House of Lords in *Guild* v *IRC* [1992] 2 AC 310 held that this is not so. Assuming, therefore, that there is evidence of a need for snooker tables at universities, the specified purpose is likely to fall within s. 5. To be charitable under s. 5, the trust must also be for the public benefit (s. 5(5)), and (as has been discussed) this requirement would be satisfied.

(b) As office-holders, the vicar and churchwardens promote a charitable purpose, regarding the advancement of religion, which is a purpose listed in s. 3(1) of the Charities Act 2011 (para. (c)). Therefore a gift to these persons described as such, without more, would be regarded as a good charitable gift for the advancement of religion. The problem here, however, is that a purpose is specified: namely, parish work. This means that the persons specified hold the property for such a purpose, and the charitable status of the gift depends upon whether a trust for parish work is wholly and exclusively charitable. In *Re Simson* [1946] Ch 299, a gift to a vicar 'for his work in the parish' was held charitable; whereas in *Farley* v *Westminster Bank Ltd* [1939] AC 430, HL, a gift to a vicar 'for parish work' was not. The difference was that in *Farley* the parish work was not limited to work which fell within the charitable scope of the vicar's office. It could, for example, include a civic reception for a footballer. It is, in each case, a matter of construction; but, unless the court can put a different construction on the present gift from that of the House of Lords in *Farley*, it will fail as not being wholly and exclusively charitable.

(c) The advancement of environmental protection or improvement is a purpose listed in s. 3(1) of the Charities Act 2011 (para. (i)). The public benefit means a benefit to the public in the United Kingdom; but scientific evidence has revealed the importance of the rainforests to the world's climate, and suggests that they contain as yet undiscovered species of plants which may assist in the development of cures for human diseases. The preservation of the animals in the forests may also tend to moral improvement of the human race: *Re Wedgwood* [1915] 1 Ch 113. Thus, subject to the possible qualification which follows, even though no rainforests are in the United Kingdom, this trust would appear to satisfy the public benefit requirement of s. 4 of the Charities Act 2011, and, therefore, to be charitable.

The qualification is that a trust will be denied charitable status if its purpose is considered to be political. Although the High Court of Australia recently held that in Australia political objects are not excluded from charitable purposes (*Aid/Watch Inc.* v *Commissioner of Taxation* [2010] HCA 42), such prohibition is well established in English law. A trust which aims to change the law is political because the court has no means of judging whether a proposed change in the law is or is not for the benefit of the public in the United Kingdom: *McGovern* v *A-G* [1982] Ch 321. It is therefore impossible for the public-benefit test in s. 4 to be satisfied by such a trust. In the *McGovern* case it was thought that there was a risk that the aims of the trust established by Amnesty International might prejudice this country's relations with countries overseas. An additional reason for the denial of charitable status to political trusts is that the Attorney General might be required to enforce trusts whose purposes are against the interests of the state: *Bowman v Secular Society Ltd* [1917] AC 406; *National Anti-Vivisection Society* v *IRC* [1948] AC 31, HL. It might therefore be argued that the purpose specified in the problem could be carried out by seeking to change the law of the United Kingdom or of other countries, and this would make it a political purpose and so vitiate charitable status. It is, perhaps, the word 'encourage' which causes anxiety on this point.

Nevertheless, given the scientific evidence mentioned above, the court might well consider that any potential political element is merely ancillary to the charitable purpose: *IRC* v *Temperance Council* (1926) 136 LT 27. If this is the case, the trust will still be wholly and exclusively charitable. Charities are, after all, permitted a limited amount of political activity, provided there is a reasonable expectation that such activity will further their stated purposes. Since the late 1990s, the Charity Commission has taken an increasingly relaxed attitude to the extent to which charities may engage in political activity: see its guidance, CC9 (March 2008). The borderline, indeed, between education and propaganda is sometimes narrow (see *Re Koeppler Will Trusts* [1986] Ch 423) and the courts will deny charitable status to political propaganda disguised as education (*Southwood* v *A-G*, unreported, 28 June 2000, CA). The court might save the gift for charity by treating the encouragement as limited to means that are not political.

Question 2

To be charitable, a trust must promote a public benefit.

Discuss.

 Commentary

In an essay question it is additionally important to have a structure in mind before you start writing, because such questions (unlike some problem questions) will not always suggest a structure to you. Examiners will be impressed by a well-structured and coherently argued essay. The basic structure to the following suggested answer is the distinction between the two senses in which public benefit is used. Note that, in the first sense, cases are drawn upon from those pertaining to the definition of charity. It is necessary to be selective, mentioning only those relevant to the answer. By preparing a preliminary structure, perhaps by way of a few rough notes, you will obtain a better idea of how much time (and therefore detail) you can afford to give to each aspect of the answer.

The question is short and therefore, perhaps, appealing. The danger with it is that the student may not spot everything which is asked. This is always a potential danger with very short questions. In our experience a large number of students will fail to deal with both aspects of public benefit, but not those who study this suggested answer!

Answer plan

(i) Public benefit in the purpose itself

- Presumed under statutory categories (a) to (l)
- Not presumed at an evidential level
- Impact of **s. 4(2)** on different categories of charity
- Political purposes

(ii) Public benefit as the section of the community to benefit

- Essentially matter of evidence, but nexus test
- Poverty exception
- Relaxation in advancement of religion
- Impact of **s. 4(2)**, including on class-within-a-class prohibition
- Recreational charities: **s. 5**

Suggested answer

The general rule that for a trust to be charitable it must be for the public benefit, has existed for many years in charity law, although it did not emerge as a distinct requirement until after *Pemsel's Case* **[1891] AC 531**. As a distinct requirement, it was clear that the element of public benefit varied across the four heads of charitable purposes in *Pemsel's Case*. Under the present law, contained in the **Charities Act 2011**, a charitable purpose is a purpose that both falls within one of the categories of purposes there listed and is also for the public benefit: **s. 2(1)**. The meaning of public benefit is the same as it was immediately before 1 April 2008. The only apparent modification to the law before that date is that, by virtue of **s. 4(2)**, 'it is not to be presumed that a purpose of a particular description is for the public benefit'. To analyse the requirement of public benefit under the existing law, it is therefore necessary to look at its meaning under the law before 1 April 2008 to ascertain the precise effect of **s. 4(2)**.

The concept of public benefit in the law of charity is used in two different senses.

(i) Public benefit in the purpose itself

First, the concept of public benefit can mean that the purpose itself must be of public benefit. Under the previous law (i.e., before 1 April 2008), this requirement was self-evident under the fourth head of charity in *Pemsel's Case* (other purposes beneficial to the community), so that, when it was sought to bring a new purpose under that head, the public benefit of that purpose would need to be proved. In determining public benefit under the fourth head, the court would weigh the benefits of the proposed purpose against any detriments: *National Anti-Vivisection Society* v *IRC* [1948] AC 31, where a moral benefit was outweighed by a tangible detriment. By contrast, a trust for one of the other three heads, the relief of poverty, the advancement of education and the advancement of religion, was for a purpose that was already regarded as containing this element of public benefit. In other words, it was not necessary for the courts to have to decide on each occasion whether, as a *concept*, the advancement of education (for example) was for the public benefit: that was presumed.

In relation to the first three heads of *Pemsel*, therefore, the difficulty with public benefit in this first sense arose only at an *evidential* level, i.e. if it was not clear whether the particular purpose designated in the trust instrument itself ranked as the relief of poverty, the advancement of education or the advancement of religion. It therefore remains the case that those purposes that previously fell within the first three heads of *Pemsel*, and which now fall within paras (a) to (c) of the list in s. 3(1), are conceptually for the public benefit. The same must also hold for the other purposes listed in paras (d) to (l). After all, if the position were otherwise, the courts could effectively delete any of the statutory categories (a) to (l) by holding that any of those categories is not for the public benefit. That would be nonsense, since it must follow from the fact that such purposes are specified in the statutory list that they are, conceptually, for the public benefit.

What then is the effect of s. 4(2)? As it states that public benefit is not to be presumed in relation to a purpose 'of a particular description', it follows that the sub-section operates only at an evidential level. This applies to each of the specified categories of charity in paras (a) to (l).

It had previously been held that a trust was not necessarily for the advancement of education merely because the settlor believed that the purpose was for the public benefit: *Re Pinion* [1965] Ch 85, CA (where the testator tried to foist upon the public as a museum a 'mass of junk'). In a borderline case, such as *Re Pinion* or *Re Dupree's Deed Trusts* [1945] Ch 16 (chess tournaments for young males in Portsmouth up to the age of 21), the court could derive assistance from expert evidence. In the case of the advancement of education, it therefore seems that s. 4(2) has no impact on public benefit in this first sense, since there was never any evidential presumption of public benefit under that head.

Under the advancement of religion, it had previously been held that the court was willing to presume public benefit; thus a trust to publish religious writings, even if of no religious, literary or other merit, would be treated as charitable for the advancement of religion, provided there was no evidence that such writings were immoral or against all religion: *Thornton* v *Howe* (1862) 31 Beav 14, applied in *Re Watson* [1973] 1 WLR 1472. Section 4(2) may reverse this presumption, but it may not have much practical effect, as the earlier case law shows that the courts were easily satisfied of public benefit in the advancement of religion. Thus in *Re Watson*, the court was satisfied that the writings in question had no intrinsic merit, but might have the effect of confirming existing believers in their faith. However, in the *Gnostic Centre* (16 Dec, 2009) the Charity Commission held that the Centre was not charitable because it could not satisfy the Commission that it had an 'identifiable, positive, beneficial, moral or ethical framework capable of having a beneficial impact on society'.

Under the previous law, a trust which contained political purposes was not charitable, one reason being that the court had no means of judging whether a change in the law was for the public benefit: *National Anti-Vivisection Society* v *IRC* and *McGovern* v *A-G* [1982] Ch 321. Although the Charities Act 2011 does not itself expressly prohibit the charitable status of political purposes, it is clear that the prohibition remains as an aspect of public benefit. Thus a political trust masquerading as the advancement of education (as in *Southwood* v *A-G* [2000] WTLR 1199), or as any of the other categories of charity, will fail to meet the public benefit requirement. There is a counter-argument that some of the purposes listed in s. 3(1) are inherently political, so that the statute has, to a limited extent at least, relaxed the rule prohibiting political purposes. Examples of such purposes might appear to be the prevention of poverty in para. (a), the advancement of human rights and the other purposes mentioned in para. (h) and the advancement of environmental protection or improvement under para. (i). However, the Act, by keeping public benefit as a distinct requirement, maintains the prohibition: *Hanchett-Stamford* v *A-G* [2009] Ch 173. Thus it seems that the decision in *McGovern* v *A-G* would remain the same today. Whilst the advancement of human rights is no longer a political purpose (and was recognised as charitable by the Charity Commissioners even before 1 April 2008), a trust to promote human rights overseas would probably remain political for the reason that Slade J gave in *McGovern*: namely that the carrying out of the trust's purposes overseas might adversely affect this country's relations with other jurisdictions. Public benefit could therefore not be proved.

(ii) Public benefit as the section of the community to benefit

Secondly, public benefit can mean that the community or the section of the community to benefit must be sufficient. Essentially, this is a matter of degree. In one case an appeal for the widows, orphans and dependants of six fishermen drowned at sea was held charitable: *Cross* v *Lloyd-Greame* (1909) 102 LT 163. However, it was later held that where the beneficiaries are defined by reference to a personal nexus, the trust, as a matter of law, cannot be charitable. This test was first established in the context of a blood relationship in *Re Compton* [1945] Ch 123, CA, and was applied by the House of Lords in *Oppenheim* v *Tobacco Securities Trust Co. Ltd* [1951] AC 297 to deny charitable status to a trust to educate the children of employees of a named company. Where, however, the primary class to benefit did constitute a sufficient section of the community, a preference for a private class did not destroy the charitable nature of the trust, provided that the preference did not go to more than 75 per cent of the trust income: *Re Koettgen's Will Trusts* [1954] Ch 252. This qualification did not apply if the private class had a right in priority (*Caffoor* v *ITC* [1961] AC 584). Where no preference for a private class was specified in the trust, a *de facto* application by the trustees to a private class did not constitute an application for exclusively charitable purposes (*IRC v Educational Grants Association Ltd* [1967] Ch 993), and would appear to be a breach of trust. It seems that these decisions are now imported into the public-benefit test in s. 4 of the **Charities Act 2011.** Even the decision in *Koettgen* is unaffected, since s. 4 is concerned with public benefit in relation to purposes, whereas *Koettgen* was concerned, not with purposes, but with a provision relating to the manner in which the trustees were to perform the trust.

Before 1 April 2008, there was an important exception to the personal nexus test, namely, it did not apply to trusts for the relief of poverty. Cases going back to the eighteenth century had held that a trust to relieve poor relations was charitable, and this principle had been extended, for instance in *Re Coulthurst* [1951] Ch 661, CA, to poor employees of a bank. In *Dingle v Turner* [1972] AC 601, the House of Lords affirmed that these earlier cases had not been affected by the ruling in *Oppenheim*. In *Dingle v Turner*, Lord Cross opined that the *Oppenheim* test had been established in order to prevent companies providing tax-free fringe benefits to their employees, and for this reason he thought that a trust to advance religion among the members of a company might be charitable, provided the benefits were purely spiritual. It should be noted, however, that the majority of their Lordships in that case expressly dissociated themselves from Lord Cross's view that, in determining charitable status, the courts ought to take tax benefits into account. Even under the previous law, however, a trust could not be charitable for the relief of poverty if the persons to benefit were individually named: *Re Scarsbrick* [1944] Ch 229 (a principle infringed by the first-instance decision in *Re Segelman* [1996] Ch 171).

It is unclear whether the relief of poverty continues to be exempt from the personal nexus test. If the exception is based on the notion either that no public benefit in this second sense is needed in the case of the relief of poverty or that the public benefit is presumed, it would appear that the anomaly has been swept away by s. 4. If, on the other hand, the exception is based on the notion that, as a matter of law, there is always a public benefit in relieving one's poor relations or employees, then s. 4 may leave it untouched. The Attorney General's reference to the Charity Tribunal on this issue was heard in November 2011, but an appeal is possible.

Although a trust for the advancement of religion is subject to the public-benefit requirement in this second sense, cases under the previous law show that this requirement was generally applied less stringently. Thus, whereas in *Re Compton* (in the context of the advancement of education) the court rejected the notion of indirect public benefit (viz. that there was a benefit to society in having educated people in the population), such a notion was admitted in the context of the advancement of religion in *Neville Estates Ltd v Madden* [1962] Ch 832. This was a trust to advance religion among members of the Catford Synagogue. Although this comprised only a small number of persons, the court held that the public-benefit requirement was satisfied because such persons would mix with others in society and the benefit would thereby rub off. A similar approach was evident in *Re Hetherington, Gibbs v McDonnell* [1990] Ch 1, where a trust for the saying of masses for the soul of the testatrix was held charitable because the masses could be held in public. There was no mixing with the public however in *Gilmour v Coats* [1949] AC 426, where the purposes of a Carmelite convent were held not to be charitable. The nuns were a cloistered and purely contemplative order. Since they never mixed with society, the only public benefit could be that derived from spiritual edification or from intercessory prayer. The House of Lords held that these benefits were not susceptible to judicial proof, and it was not enough that the Roman Catholic Church believed that these things benefited the public. *Gilmour v Coats* was distinguished from *Thornton v Howe* in *Re Watson* on the basis of the dissemination of the works in the earlier case. As the courts needed to be satisfied of public benefit in these cases, it seems that this would be sufficient to satisfy **s. 4**, so it would appear that the less stringent approach to the community to benefit in trusts for the advancement of religion survives into the current law.

Under the law before 1 April 2008, there was an additional vitiating factor in relation to trusts under the fourth head of *Pemsel*. Thus, if the description of persons to benefit comprised a class within a class, the trust could not be charitable under the fourth head: see *IRC v Baddeley* [1955] AC 572, HL. If the class-within-a-class prohibition is treated as an aspect of public benefit—which it presumably is—then it survives into the new law. If it does so survive, it is not clear whether the class-within-a-class prohibition now applies to all categories of purposes listed in **s. 3(1)**. If it does, many trusts that were previously charitable under the first three heads of *Pemsel* are no longer entitled to charitable status. However, as the meaning of public benefit has not changed, it is also possible to argue that the prohibition applies only to categories (d) to (m), or that it applies only to category (m), this being the residual category broadly equivalent to the fourth head of *Pemsel*. **Section 5**, which provides for recreational charities, provides that nothing in the section is to derogate from the principle that for a trust to be charitable it must be for the public benefit: and see *Guild v IRC* [1992] 2 AC 310. On this basis it is arguable that the decision in *Baddeley* would be the same today, as the section of the community to benefit was a class witin aclass.

Question 3

(a)   Consider the legal differences between a charitable trust and a private trust.

AND

(b)   By her will, Jemima (who died recently) left £100,000 'upon trust for charitable and deserving purposes'.

Consider the validity of this disposition.

Commentary

Part (a) involves a broad range of knowledge. The skill here is not merely to show that you know what the differences are, but also to treat them in a balanced way. Given that this is only half of the question, you cannot be expected to go into great detail. The more fundamental differences are considered first, leaving the more technical ones (such as the numbers of trustees) until later. Taxation differences are also mentioned briefly at the end to indicate that the student is aware of them, but they are not elaborated upon since such differences do not relate to the substantive law of trusts. A possible variation of this question is to consider the advantages of charitable trusts over private trusts.

Part (b) illustrates the point that, where more than one construction can reasonably be placed upon a form of words, it is essential to consider all reasonable constructions. As the question asks about 'validity', it is necessary to consider briefly if it could be valid as a non-charitable trust.

Answer plan

(a) • Nature of benefit conferred

  • Enforcement

  • Certainty of objects (private trusts only)

  • Cy-près schemes (charitable trusts only)

  • Perpetuity rules

  • Unanimous/majority trustee decisions

  • Numbers of trustees

  • Tax and rate reliefs

(b) • Wholly and exclusively charitable?

  • Conjunctive or disjunctive construction?

  • Void if not charitable (objects uncertain, unenforceable)

Suggested answer

(a) The primary legal difference is that a charitable trust aims to benefit society at large (or at least a sufficient section of it) whereas a private trust is designed to benefit specified persons or groups of persons, or (in a limited number of anomalous instances) for purposes which the law does not recognise as charitable: see *Latimer* v *IRC* [2004] 1 WLR 1466, PC. It is sometimes difficult to ascertain which has been created. This was illustrated by the uncertainty surrounding the legal status of the main fund raised following the Penlee Lifeboat Disaster. Since then, many public disaster funds (such as the main appeal fund following the Bradford City Fire Disaster) have been specifically drafted as private discretionary trusts in order to give the trustees greater flexibility in the application of the fund. The difficulty in distinguishing between a charitable or a private trust can be particularly acute in the context of a trust for the settlor's poor relations: *Re Segelman* [1996] Ch 171.

Whereas private trusts are enforced by the beneficiaries (the beneficiary principle: *Morice* v *Bishop of Durham* (1804) 9 Ves 399, 32 ER 656), charitable trusts are enforced by the Attorney General on behalf of the Crown. This itself leads to another difference between the two sorts of trusts. Thus, whereas certainty of objects is an essential requirement for a private trust (*Re Astor's Settlement Trusts* [1952] Ch 534), it is not necessary for a charitable trust. Provided the purposes of a trust are wholly and exclusively charitable and the public-benefit element is satisfied, the trust will not fail merely because the purposes are vague. Thus a trust for 'charitable purposes' is a good charitable trust. Similarly, in *Re Smith* [1932] 1 Ch 153, a gift 'unto my country England' was held to be charitable. Where the purposes of a trust are wholly and exclusively charitable but vague, the court or the Charity Commissioners will settle a scheme applying the property to specific purposes. If, however, the expressed purposes are so vague that the property could, consistently with the terms of the trust, be applied to non-charitable purposes, the trust cannot be charitable. Thus a trust for 'the general welfare and benefit' of children in a children's home was held not charitable because it could be applied in the provision of television sets for juvenile delinquents. Such a purpose could not be considered to be charitable: *Re Cole* [1958] Ch 877.

If the objects of a private trust fail, the property (in the absence of any express provision) will usually go on a resulting trust for the settlor or the settlor's estate. By contrast, if the objects of a charitable trust fail, the property can sometimes be saved for charity by the application of a cy-près scheme; if the failure occurs before the property has vested in trust for the charity, a general charitable intention must be shown by the settlor: *Re Wilson* [1913] 1 Ch 314. Cy-près is also applicable to charitable trusts in the instances specified in the Charities Act 2011, s. 62. Funds raised for specific charitable purposes which fail may be applicable cy-près under ss. 63–65.

Whereas private trusts are subject to both rules against perpetuities (the rule against remoteness of vesting and the rule against perpetual trusts), charitable trusts are subject only to the rule against remoteness of vesting. Even this is subject to the qualification that a gift over from one charity to another may validly occur outside the perpetuity period: Perpetuities and Accumulations Act 2009, s. 2(2), and *Christ's Hospital* v *Grainger* (1849) 1 Mac & G 460. There are no restrictions on accumulations of income for private trusts under the Perpetuities and Accumulations Act 2009 (s. 13), but a maximum period of 21 years applies to charitable trusts (s. 14).

Further distinctions arise in regard to the trustees themselves. In the case of a private trust, subject to a contrary provision in the trust instrument, the decisions of the trustees must be unanimous: *Re Mayo* [1943] Ch 302. By contrast, in the case of a charitable trust, except where statute provides otherwise, decisions need only be by a simple majority: *Re Whiteley* [1910] 1 Ch 608. Again, whereas the maximum number of trustees of a private trust of land is four, there is no such limit if the trust is charitable: **Trustee Act 1925, ss. 36(6), 34(3)(a)**.

It might also be mentioned briefly that charitable trusts enjoy certain important fiscal exemptions and reliefs as compared with private trusts: these include limited exemptions from income tax, capital gains tax and inheritance tax. They also enjoy relief from business rates.

(b) To be charitable a trust must be wholly and exclusively charitable: **Charities Act 2011, s. 1(1)(a)**. Although a trust for charitable purposes alone satisfies this requirement, a trust for charitable and deserving purposes may not do so. This is because 'deserving purposes' are not necessarily charitable. Whether the disposition in the problem is charitable depends, therefore, upon whether the word 'and' is construed conjunctively or disjunctively. The former construction means that every purpose to which the property can lawfully be applied must be both charitable and deserving; such a trust will therefore be charitable. The latter construction means that the property could be applied to purposes which are either charitable or deserving (but not necessarily both); such a trust is not wholly and exclusively charitable. In *Re Sutton* (1885) 28 ChD 464, a trust for 'charitable and deserving objects' was construed conjunctively and so held charitable. A similar construction was applied to the words 'charitable and benevolent' in *Re Best* [1904] 2 Ch 354. By contrast, 'charitable or public purposes' were construed disjunctively in *Blair v Duncan* [1902] AC 37, as were the words 'charitable or benevolent' in *Chichester Diocesan Fund v Simpson* [1944] AC 341. Similarly, a trust for 'charitable institutions . . . or any . . . institutions operating for the public good' was held not charitable in *A-G of the Cayman Islands v Wahr-Hansen* [2001] 1 AC 75, PC.

These cases might suggest that 'and' tends to be construed conjunctively, whereas 'or' is usually construed disjunctively. Ultimately, however, it all turns on a construction of the particular gift in the context of the instrument as a whole. Thus in *A-G of the Bahamas v Royal Trust Co.* [1986] 1 WLR 1001, the Privy Council held that a gift for the 'education and welfare' of Bahamian children was to be construed disjunctively. The trust was therefore void because 'welfare' purposes were not wholly and exclusively charitable.

Thus, while Jemima's gift (because it uses the word 'and') appears to be prima facie charitable, whether this is so is essentially a matter of construction. If the gift is held not to be wholly and exclusively charitable, it will probably fail both for uncertainty of objects and for unenforceability: *Morice v Bishop of Durham* (1804) 9 Ves 399, 32 ER 656.

Question 4

(a) Consider how the cy-près doctrine has been extended by statute.

AND

> (b) By his will made in 1975, Tommy gave his entire estate to his executors and trustees upon trust to use the same to build a hostel for the working people of Walkley. Tommy died last year. The value of his estate is insufficient to enable the hostel to be built. Tommy's next-of-kin are claiming his estate.

Discuss.

Commentary

Part (**a**) asks you to consider, not to describe. If you have the statutes in the examination room with you, there should be no problem with mere description, and clearly some description of the scope of the provisions is needed. The examiners, however, will be looking for more than a recitation of the statutory provisions. Simply copying out the statutory provisions will not achieve many marks: it is definitely not to be recommended!

Part (**b**) demands that you consider the charitable status of the gift before going on to consider a possible application cy-près.

Answer plan

(a) • Five circumstances in **CA 2011, s. 62**

  – paras (a)–(e)

  – 'spirit of the gift'

• Modifying objects of small charities

  – **Charities Act 2011, s. 275**

(b) • Charitable purpose?

  – relief of poverty?

• Failure of purpose

  – cy-près scheme: **Charities Act 2011, s. 62**

  – failure *ab initio*: general charitable intention?

Suggested answer

(a) Section 62 of the Charities Act 2011 re-enacts a provision originally contained in the Charities Act 1960 which extended the scope of the cy-près doctrine beyond cases of failure and surplus. The section specifies five circumstances in which the original purposes of a charitable gift can be altered. Paragraphs 1(a) and (b) apply where the purposes have been fulfilled, or cannot be carried out, or where they provide a use for part only of the gift. Paragraph (e)(i) and (ii) apply where the purposes have, since being laid down, been adequately provided for by other means, or have ceased to be charitable in law. This last provision might, for instance, be applicable if the courts were to hold the purposes of gun clubs (which can be charities under the principle in *Re Stephens* (1892) 8 TLR 792) no longer charitable. Essentially, however, these paragraphs merely put pre-existing cy-près circumstances onto a statutory basis.

Paragraph (c), however, was an important extension of the doctrine. It enables property to be applied cy-près where it, and other property applicable for similar purposes, can be more effectively used in conjunction and made applicable to common purposes. Before the Charities Act 1960, in the absence of failure or a surplus, neither the court nor the Charity Commissioners had power to alter the purposes of charities. Thus, whilst a scheme might facilitate the administration of several trusts for broadly similar charitable purposes, such scheme could not make any alteration to the specific purposes of each charitable trust: *Re Faraker* [1912] 2 Ch 488. This would now be possible.

Under para. (d), cy-près is permissible where the original purposes were laid down by reference to an area which has since ceased to be a unit for some other purposes, or by reference to a class of persons or to an area which has since ceased to be suitable or practical. *Peggs v Lamb* [1994] Ch 172 concerned a charitable trust for the freemen of Huntingdon, whose numbers had seriously declined. The court applied para. (d) in order to extend the class of persons who could benefit to everyone living in that borough.

Paragraph (e)(iii) applies where the original purposes have ceased 'in any other way' to provide a suitable and effective method of using the property. It was used in *Varsani v Jesani* [1999] 2 Ch 219, CA, where there was a split over doctrinal matters amongst adherents of a charitable trust which had been set up to promote the faith of a particular Hindu sect. The Court of Appeal directed that the property be applied cy-près between the majority and minority groups.

All the paragraphs except (b) require reference to 'the spirit of the gift'. In *Re Lepton's Charity* [1972] Ch 276 it was stated that this means the basic intention underlying the gift. In that case the court used paras (a)(ii) and (e)(iii) to authorise an increase, to allow for inflation, in the stipend payable to a minister out of the income of an eighteenth-century charitable trust. Paragraphs (c), (d) and (e)(iii) also require consideration to be given to the social and economic circumstance at the time of the proposed alteration: Charities Act 2011, s. 62(2)(b) (originally inserted by the Charities Act 2006). It should also be noted that s. 62(3) apparently preserves the need for a general charitable intention where that was required before the Act, i.e., in cases of initial failure only. A general charitable intention is not therefore needed in any other cy-près circumstances in s. 62.

Powers of trustees of small charities to modify their objects were first introduced in the Charities Act 1985 (since repealed) and were re-enacted and simplified in later Charities Acts. Section 275 of the Charities Act 2011 applies to an unincorporated charity if its gross income does not exceed £10,000, and if it does not hold any land held on trusts that state that it is to be used for the purposes of the charity: s. 275(1). The trustees of such a charity may resolve to modify the trusts by replacing all or any of the charity's purposes with other charitable purposes: s. 275(2), (3). The trustees can do this only if it is expedient in the interests of the charity, and only, so far as reasonably practical, if the new purposes are similar to those replaced: s. 275(4). The resolution must have at least a two-thirds majority, and the trustees must notify the Charity Commission, which can require public notice to be given and can request additional information or explanations: s. 275(5), (6) and s. 276. Unless public notice is required or the Commission objects, the resolution takes effect after 60 days: s. 277.

(b) The specified purpose, a hostel for the working people, may be a charitable purpose within category (a) of the statutory list in s. 3(1) of the Charities Act 2011, namely the prevention or relief of poverty. Poverty is not confined to destitution but includes simply going short. The trust may still be charitable for the relief of poverty if a poverty requirement can be inferred from the instrument—as occurred in *Re Cottam* [1955] 1 WLR 1299—but not from extrinsic evidence alone: *Re Drummond* [1914] 2 Ch 90. In *Re Sanders' Will Trusts* [1954] Ch 265, a trust to provide dwellings for the working classes in Pembroke Dock was held not to be charitable: the judge did not consider the working classes were necessarily poor. By contrast, in *Re Niyazi's Will Trusts* [1978] 1 WLR 910, Megarry V-C held that a trust to build a working men's hostel in Cyprus was charitable: the case was near the borderline, but the two expressions together contained just enough indication that the purpose was to relieve poverty. On this basis, the present trust is likely to be held charitable.

If the trust is held to be charitable, the next issue is the insufficiency of the estate. This ranks as a failure of the purpose, which is a cy-près circumstance within the Charities Act 1993, s. 13. Since the trust fails *ab initio*, however, the court must be satisfied that the testator had a general charitable intention, i.e., an intention to benefit a wider purpose than that specified: *Biscoe* v *Jackson* (1887) 35 ChD 460. The issue is whether the testator intended the avowed purpose to be merely a means of effecting a wider purpose: see *Re Wilson* [1913] 1 Ch 314 and *Re Lysaght* [1966] 1 Ch 191. Whether a general charitable intention is present is ascertained by construing the words used in the context of the instrument as a whole and in the light of admissible extrinsic evidence: *Re Woodhams* [1981] 1 WLR 493. Generally, the more detailed the specified purpose, the more difficult it becomes to find the requisite intention: *Re Good's Will Trusts* [1950] 2 All ER 653 and *Kings* v *Bultitude* [2010] EWHC 1795 (Ch). On the other hand, the fact that a gift is one of residue (or of the testator's entire estate) may indicate a general charitable intention, since no specified amount is provided: cf. *Re Goldschmidt* [1957] 1 WLR 524.

If a general charitable intention is found, the property will be applied cy-près; if not, it will pass to Tommy's next-of-kin.

Question 5

(a) By his will made in 1990, Boris, who died last month, gave one-third of his residuary estate to each of the following institutions: the Rotherham Rabbit Sanctuary; the Dronfield Donkey Home; and the Broomhill Animal Hospital.

The Rotherham Rabbit Sanctuary was an incorporated charity, which closed last week. In accordance with a provision in its constitution, its members have decided to apply its assets to another charity, the South Yorkshire Rabbit Fund. The Dronfield Donkey Home was an unincorporated charitable association which ceased to exist a year before Boris's death because of lack of funds. No institution called the Broomhill Animal Hospital has ever existed.

Advise Boris's executors how they should deal with Boris's residuary estate.
AND

(b) Earlier this year, the residents of the village of Eastwick decided to raise funds to build a cottage hospital. Money was raised for this purpose by means of street collections and the sale of raffle tickets. The appeal fund trustees also received a large number of cheques for various amounts. Unfortunately, the total sums raised proved insufficient to enable the hospital to be built.

Advise the trustees how they should deal with the funds raised.

Commentary

The candidate should note that in part (**a**), the question states that the first two named institutions were charities. There are therefore no marks to be obtained from discussing whether the institutions with these names are charitable.

For an analysis of the statutory predecessor to the **Charities Act 1993, s. 14**, the student is referred to the valuable article by Wilson [1983] Conv 40. There is also a general discussion of the impact of the section in Luxton, *The Law of Charities*, Oxford University Press, 2001, at pp. 583–94. Other sources of fund-raising which a question such as this might require you to deal with are membership subscriptions and deeds of covenant.

Answer plan

(a) • RRS: beneficial gift that vested at Boris's death
 • DDH: trust for purposes of home
  – can purposes be carried out (scheme)?
  – failure *ab initio*? (general charitable intention?)
 • BAH: mere misdescription or failure?
  – if failure, cy-près only if:
   – charitable institution intended
  – general charitable, intention (since *ab initio*)
(b) • Charitable purpose?
  – failure *ab initio*: cy-près? **Charities Act 2011, s. 63**

- donations by cheque

- street collections

- raffle tickets

Suggested answer

(a) A gift to an incorporated charity, such as the Rotherham Rabbit Sanctuary, will be construed as a gift to the particular institution beneficially, unless (which does not appear to be the case here) the words of the will indicate otherwise: *Re Vernon's Will Trusts* [1972] Ch 300n, applied *Re ARMS (Multiple Sclerosis Research) Ltd* [1997] 1 WLR 877. Therefore, as the Sanctuary was in existence at Boris's death, the gift to it would have vested on his death, and will be applied in the same way as its existing assets: *Re Slevin* [1891] 2 Ch 230. In *Re Slevin* itself, the court held that the legacy passed, with the charity's other assets, to the Crown, but this might be explained on the basis that the members of the charity had not made provision for the application of its assets to another similar charitable institution before its dissolution. In the problem, therefore, this share of Boris's residuary estate will pass to the South Yorkshire Rabbit Fund.

As the Dronfield Donkey Home ceased to exist before Boris's death, it might appear that the gift would lapse, in the same way that a gift by will to an individual generally lapses if the legatee predeceases the testator. The Home was, however, an unincorporated charitable association, and it has been held that a gift to such an institution is treated as being made upon trust for its purposes: *Re Vernon's Will Trusts*. If, therefore, those purposes are still capable of being carried out, the gift will be applied to them. The failure of the particular institution, the Home, is regarded as a mere failure of the particular machinery by which those purposes were to be carried into effect, not a failure of the purposes themselves. A scheme will therefore be needed; but as the purposes are the same, this is not a cy-près scheme, so no general charitable intention need be sought.

If the purposes of the Dronfield Donkey Home can no longer be carried out after its closure, however, there will be a failure of the purposes of the gift. As the institution closed before Boris's death, the failure will be failure *ab initio*. This share of residue can therefore be applied cy-près only if a general charitable intention can be found on Boris's part. A general charitable intention means an intention to benefit charity in a broader way than merely benefiting the particular named institution: *Re Finger's Will Trusts* [1972] Ch 286. Where (as here) a specific institution has been named, the finding of a general charitable intention might be difficult (*Re Rymer* [1895] 1 Ch 19; *Re Spence* [1979] Ch 483); but it is not impossible (*Re Finger's Will Trusts*). It is a matter of construction of Boris's will whether a general charitable intention can be found. The fact that the gift is one of residue is slight evidence that a general charitable intention might be present: *Re Goldschmidt* [1957] 1 WLR 524. The fact that a gift is one of several to charity in the same will might also suggest a general charitable intention (*Re Satterthwaite's Will Trusts* [1966] 1 WLR 277); but whether this principle can be applied here depends upon whether the gift to the Broomhill Animal Hospital is charitable (which is considered below). If no general charitable intention can be found, this second share of residue will go (in the absence of any gift over) on resulting trust for Boris's next-of-kin.

As no such institution by the name of the Broomhill Animal Hospital has ever existed, the court will first need to determine if Boris has merely misdescribed an existing institution which does exist: *Bunting* v *Marriott* (1854) 19 Beav 163. If he has, that share of residue will simply pass to that institution (regardless of whether it is a charity or not). In the absence of mere misdescription, the gift will fail *ab initio* unless it can be applied cy-près. The cy-près doctrine is, however, available only to charitable gifts, and it is unclear whether Boris had a charitable institution in mind, or a non-charitable institution, such as an anti-vivisection society. In *Re Jenkins's Will Trust* [1966] Ch 249, it was held that a gift to a non-existent anti-vivisection society was clearly not a charitable gift and so not applicable cy-près.

In the problem, however, the name of the legatee does not necessarily suggest a non-charitable body, and is consistent with a charitable institution. In *Re Satterthwaite's Will Trusts*, the court considered that the fact that the gift to a non-existent animal hospital was one of several made to charity in the will, indicated both that a charitable institution was intended and that the testator had a general charitable intention. In that case, therefore, the court applied the gift to the non-existent institution cy-près. If the court were able to take the same approach to the gift to the Broomhill Animal Hospital, it too would be applicable cy-près. It has also been pointed out that if a gift is made to a non-existent charitable institution, it is easier to find a general charitable intention than if the gift is made to an institution which formerly existed but has closed down: *Re Harwood* [1936] Ch 285. If the gift is found not to be to a charitable institution, or not to be made with a general charitable intention, this share of residue will pass (in the absence of a gift over) to Boris's next-of-kin.

(b) The provision of a cottage hospital is clearly a charitable purpose under para. (d) of s. 3(1) of the Charities Act 2011, namely the advancement of health.

The insufficiency of the funds raised means that the charitable purpose has failed *ab initio*. In such circumstances, equity itself does not permit an application cy-près unless the donors had a general charitable intention. Donors putting money in collecting boxes, however, might be presumed to be giving for a specific purpose and not with a general charitable intention. Thus, in *Re Gillingham Bus Disaster Fund* [1959] Ch 62, CA, anonymous contributions to a non-charitable fund were ordered to be held for such contributors on a resulting trust.

To avoid a similar outcome with failed charitable collections, the Charities Act 2011, s. 63 (which re-enacts with amendments provisions originally contained in the Charities Act 1960) provides that, in certain circumstances, funds given to charity are applicable cy-près, i.e., to other charitable purposes similar to those for which the funds were raised. Section 63 can apply only where (*inter alia*) the property belongs to donors who gave for specific charitable purposes which fail. It has been argued that the section has little impact on anonymous contributions, since these never belong to the donors: Wilson [1983] Conv 40. First, anonymous contributions may be treated as abandoned and so pass as *bona vacantia* to the Crown, which results in an application cy-près: see dicta in *Re Ulverston* [1956] Ch 622. Secondly, they may be treated as having been given out and out: see dicta of Denning LJ in *Re Hillier* [1954] 1 WLR 700. Out and out gifts might be considered to be made with the widest possible general charitable intention: see Sheridan and Delany, *The Cy-près Doctrine*, Sweet & Maxwell, 1959.

If, however, s. 63 applies, some donations made by cheque may be applicable cy-près under s. 14(1): first, where, after prescribed advertisements and inquiries, a donor cannot be identified or found; and, secondly, where a donor has executed a disclaimer in the prescribed form: s. 63(1). Some of the remaining donors by cheque may have given such small amounts that it would be unreasonable to incur expense in returning their money. This is dealt with by s. 64(2), which enables the court or the Charity Commission to treat property as belonging to unidentifiable donors where it would be unreasonable either:

(i) having regard to the amounts likely to be returned to the donors, to incur the expense of returning it; or

(ii) having regard to the nature, circumstances and amount of the gifts, and the lapse of time since they were made, for the donors to expect them to be returned.

A donor who cannot be identified, but whose donation is applied cy-près other than by virtue of s. 64, must claim within six months of the making of the scheme, and the charity trustees are permitted to deduct properly incurred expenses from any repayment: s. 63(4), 63(5). This might enable the trustees to deal, for instance, with a large donation made by a donor who cannot be identified or found.

Under s. 65, special provision is made for the situation where a solicitation for funds was accompanied by a statement that the property given would, in the event of failure of purposes, be applicable cy-près as if given for charitable purposes generally, unless the donor made a declaration that he wished to be given the opportunity to request its return. If the donor made such a declaration at the time of making the gift, then, in the event of failure, the trustees must notify him and inquire whether he wishes it to be returned; and they must return it to him if he so requests within the prescribed period. If the trustees cannot find him, or if he does not request the return of the property, or if he did not make a declaration at the time he made the gift, then the property is applicable cy-près as if it belonged to a donor who had executed a disclaimer within s. 64(1).

The street collections and the money raised by raffles will be dealt with by s. 64(1). Thus the proceeds of cash collections made by means of collecting boxes and (*inter alia*) of any lottery (after allowing for prizes) are deemed (without advertisement or inquiry) to belong to unidentifiable donors. Such money will therefore be applicable cy-près.

Question 6

Consider the extent to which the meaning of charity in English law is affected by the enactment of the **Charities Act 2006** (since consolidated in the **Charities Act 2011**).

 Commentary

With the **Charities Act 2006, Part I,** having come into force on 1 April 2008, and having since been consolidated with most other charity legislation in the **Charities Act 2011**, candidates should be prepared for a question dealing with the changes it made to the meaning of charity in English law. A student dealing with such a question will therefore need to be acquainted with the law both before and after the changes made. Study of an area currently under review, or recently the subject of reform, should be a rewarding one for the candidate, as it is all too easy for students, whose study of any given area of the law tends to be compressed into a few months, to perceive the law as relatively static. Candidates who show knowledge of important recent developments will also impress examiners.

The introduction of the statutory list of charitable purposes presents few difficulties for the candidate. The effect of the legislation on public benefit, however, presents many problems, as doubts were expressed during the passage of the Bill that became the **Charities Act 2006** whether the relevant clauses in the Bill would have the effect that the government intended it to have. Underlying this is the politically charged issue of the charitable status of the independent and public schools.

Before what became the **Charities Act 2006** began its passage through Parliament, a draft Charities Bill was considered by a Joint Committee of both Houses. Evidence was submitted by the Charity Commission (and by a number of lawyers), that the clause that is now contained in the **Charities Act 2011, s. 4(2)** would make little, if any, difference to the public-benefit principles. The Joint Committee report (2004, HL Papers 167–1; HC 660–1) said that 'This interpretation left the draft Bill in the ludicrous position of promising to bite on the public benefit bullet without having any teeth to do so.' It also noted that the Home Office took a different view from the Charity Commission on the effect of this provision—a position that the Joint Committee report described as 'ludicrous', 'deeply unsatisfactory' and 'nothing short of farcical'. In the event, a joint position was agreed between the Home Office and the Charity Commission on how the public-benefit test would be applied, and this led to the introduction of what is now **s. 17** of the **Charities Act 2011** (requiring the Commission to issue public-benefit guidance); but one suspects that the Charity Commission has effectively retreated under government pressure.

The underlying tension between the position of the government and the Charity Commission on the one hand, and many lawyers on the other, is that the government (or at least the Labour Government that left office in May 2010) and the Commission perceive the public-benefit test to be a means of ensuring that charities provide sufficient public benefit in the carrying out of their activities. To this end, charities are required to inform the Commission about how their activities provide such benefit. This aim contrasts markedly with the general principle that, for a trust to be charitable, its purposes must (*inter alia*) be for the public benefit. In the law of charities, in other words, public benefit relates not to activities, but to purposes. The **Charities Act 2011** maintains this vital distinction: see **s. 2(1)**. If a trust is established for wholly and exclusively charitable purposes that contain the necessary element of public benefit, it is a charity, however the trustees apply (or misapply) its income or other assets. Were this not so, the courts and the Commissioners would potentially lose their charitable jurisdiction over such a trust at the very time (e.g. on a breach of trust) when it is most needed. The interpretation of these sections is a highly contentious matter, but there is a strong case for saying that the whole of the Commission's consultation process relating to how a charity can show that its activities are for the public benefit is utterly misconceived. The advice to candidates when dealing with a politically sensitive area is to remember that the question is intended to test your legal knowledge, understanding and reasoning, not your personal political views. The examiners will be looking for a carefully structured answer that is founded on legal analysis. The suggested answer looks at what the government's intention was in securing the enactment of what is now **s. 4(2)** of the **Charities Act 2011**, and considers whether, legally, such intention is likely to be achieved, as well as what the other possible effects will be.

Answer plan

Background to **Charities Act 2006**
(i) • **A statutory list of charitable purposes**
   • Preamble and *Pemsel* classification
   • Perceived defects of previous law
   • Strategy Unit report
   • Paras (a) to (m)
   • Limited change of law
   • Continued development through final category

(ii) • **Public-benefit test**
   • Intended reversal of presumption of public benefit in first three heads?
   • What did government intend by what is now **Charities Act 2011, s. 4(2)**?
   • Status of independent schools
   • Impact on poor relations cases?
   • Impact on the advancement of religion?
   • Impact on other concepts (class within a class, self-help)?
Conclusion

Suggested answer

Sections 1–4 of the Charities Act 2011 were originally introduced in Part I of the Charities Act 2006 (in force from 1 April 2008). These provisions modify the meaning of charity in English law in two ways. First, s. 3 contains a statutory list of charitable purposes; secondly, s. 4(2) affects the requirement of public benefit. The effect of each of these provisions will be considered in turn.

(i) A statutory list of charitable purposes

Before Part I of the 2006 Act came into force, the only statutory list of charitable purposes was that contained in the Preamble to the Statute of Elizabeth 1601, which set out a number of purposes that were regarded as charitable at that time. The list in the Preamble was not, however, exhaustive; and in the following centuries, the courts developed the meaning of charity by admitting as charitable those purposes that were either analogous to purposes stated in the Preamble, or analogous to purposes already held charitable by such means: *Scottish Burial Reform and Cremation Society Ltd* v *Glasgow City Council* [1968] AC 138. A simpler classification was that of Lord Macnaghten in *Special Comrs of Income Tax* v *Pemsel* [1891] AC 531, who identified four heads of charity: the relief of poverty, the advancement of education, the advancement of religion, and other purposes beneficial to the community. The courts soon limited the fourth head in holding that benefit to the community was not itself sufficient, but the purpose also had to fall within either the letter or the spirit of the purposes listed in the Preamble of 1601: *Re Macduff* [1896] 2 Ch 451. The last head had been likened to a portmanteau: *Scottish Burial* case (above), 150 (per Lord Upjohn). The process of developing charity law by analogy was therefore continued under the fourth head, and included numerous purposes as diverse as the promotion of public works (such as the repair of highways, the provision of street lighting and the building of bridges), the defence of the realm, the advancement of public health (*IRC* v *Baddeley* [1955] AC 572) and the welfare of animals (*Re Wedgwood*). This process of development by analogy with the Preamble was unaffected by its repeal in the Charities Act 1960, as the Preamble survived within the case law.

Although the courts were thus able to develop the meaning of charity far beyond the purposes listed in the Preamble, some of the purposes listed in the Preamble had become either effectively obsolete (e.g., 'the marriage of poor maids') or had suffered from a change in the meaning of language (e.g., 'the relief of ... impotent ... persons', or 'the help of ... persons decayed'). Apart from this, many important charitable purposes were not mentioned in the Preamble, either because of political sensitivity in 1601 (e.g., the advancement of religion), because of later scientific and technical progress (e.g., the promotion of industry) or social changes (e.g., the welfare of animals). Furthermore, whilst the promotion of sport was not charitable in itself, a trust or body established for such purpose might often achieve charitable status if the promotion of sport could be treated as a means of furthering a purpose that was avowedly charitable, such as the advancement of education (*Re Mariette* [1915] 2 Ch 284). This process involved a certain amount of mental gymnastics. It had also been said that the 'spirit and intendment' of the Preamble 'have been stretched almost to breaking point': per Lord Upjohn in the *Scottish Burial* case (above), 153.

A report of the Cabinet Office's Strategy Unit, *Private Action, Public Benefit* (2002) suggested that a new statutory list of charitable purposes was desirable explicitly to recognise the range of modern charitable purposes, and to make a number of changes to the pre-existing law: notably, the addition of the prevention of poverty as a charitable purpose, and deeming to be charitable the promotion of amateur sport and the promotion of human rights (this last of which had not at that time been expressly treated as charitable).

The process initiated in the Strategy Unit report culminated in the Charities Act 2006, since consolidated in the Charities Act 2011. Section 3(1) of the Charities Act 2011 lists 13 descriptions of charitable purposes. The first 12 (in paras (a) to (l)) are specific purposes, and the last (in para. (m)) is a general description equivalent to the fourth head of *Pemsel*. Paragraphs (a) to (c) are almost identical to Lord Macnaghten's first three heads respectively, except that para. (a) specifies not merely the relief of poverty, but also its prevention (the ambit of which is not entirely clear). This extension had been recommended some years ago by the Goodman Committee, *Charity Law and Voluntary Organisations*, Bedford Square Press, 1976. For the purposes of para. (c), the advancement of religion, the meaning of religion is explained in s. 3(2)(a). First, it includes a religion which involves belief in more than one god; this clarifies what had been unclear from the case law, especially as dicta of Lord Parker appeared to suggest that religion was limited to monotheistic theism: *Bowman* v *Secular Society* [1917] AC 406. Secondly, it includes a religion which does not involve belief in a god; under the previous law, religion, with the possible exception of Buddhism, connoted belief in a god: *Re South Place Ethical Society* [1980] 1 WLR 1565. It seems that the effect of the reform is to ensure that Buddhism is a religion for this purpose. What is advanced under para. (c) must still be a religion, however, and this excludes most purely philosophical or ethical belief systems (such as humanism), especially if (which is not clarified) the previous requirement of worship survives into the new law.

The remaining nine specific purposes in paras (d) to (l) comprise a longer list than that originally envisaged in the Strategy Unit report, owing in part at least to successful lobbying by the appropriate interest groups. It therefore includes purposes not originally set out in separate paragraphs, e.g., the welfare of animals, and the saving of lives—the latter of which is intended to encompass the provision of lifeboats and the like. The advancement of amateur sport is now charitable (under para. (g)), so reversing the effects of *Re Nottage* [1895] 2 Ch 649, provided that the sport or game promotes health by involving physical or mental skill or exertion (s. 3(2)(d)). Sports which do not, and which can therefore be expected to fall outside para. (g), include activities such as ballooning, sky-diving and motor-racing.

For two reasons, the statutory list itself makes only minor changes to the meaning of charity in English law. First, most of the purposes listed in the specific categories (paras (d) to (l)) had already been recognised as charitable (whether by the courts or by the Charity Commissioners) either under the former heads of *Pemsel* or as recreational charities (under what is now s. 5 of the **Charities Act 2011**); and under the **Charities Act 2011**, charitable purposes include all purposes (not within **paras (a)** to **(l)**) that were charitable immediately before 1 April 2008: s. 3(1)(m) and s. 3(4). There was some doubt whether, even after the **Human Rights Act 1998**, the promotion of human rights was a charitable purpose, as the decision whether to legislate to remove a declaration of incompatibility is left to the legislature; but the Charity Commissioners shortly afterwards took the view that the promotion of human rights was capable of being charitable: CC RR12—*The Promotion of Human Rights* (April 2003). Similarly, the Commissioners had already recognised environmental protection (including sustainable development) as charitable: see *The Environment Foundation* (2003) (CC). Secondly, even if a purpose falls within one of the listed categories, it will still be charitable only if it satisfies the 'public benefit' test contained in s. 4 (discussed further below), so that it might still be argued that the promotion of human rights in a country overseas that is not a signatory to any human rights treaty might result in damage to the economy of the United Kingdom, and so lacks the public benefit required by s. 4, as in *McGovern v A-G* [1982] Ch 321.

The ability of charity law to develop is preserved by the final category, **para. (m)**. All purposes previously recognised as charitable or which are recreational charities under s. 5 fall within this final category. But this paragraph is equivalent to the fourth head of *Pemsel* in that it also preserves the ability of the courts to develop charity law. Thus **para. (m)** also enables new charitable purposes to emerge by analogy with, or within the spirit of, any of the purposes listed in **paras (a)** to **(l)**, or with purposes already held to be charitable. Although this paragraph makes no reference to it, the courts will still be able to refer to the Preamble in determining what is analogous, since the Preamble is preserved in the case law. The other limiting factor in the old fourth head, that the purpose be beneficial to the community, is not mentioned in s. 3, but it is now apparently subsumed within the broader 'public benefit' test contained in s. 4.

(ii) Public-benefit test

More difficult to assess is the likely impact of the legislation on the public-benefit requirement. Under the **Charities Act 2011** (as under the law before 1 April 2008), every purpose to be charitable must be for the public benefit: s. 2(1)(b). Furthermore, public benefit has the same meaning as under the previous law: s. 4(3). Section 17 provides for the Commission to issue guidance on the public-benefit requirement; but such guidance can only explain, not change, the legal meaning of public benefit. The problem is with s. 4(2), which states that, in determining whether the public-benefit requirement is satisfied, 'it is not to be presumed that a purpose of a particular description is for the public benefit'.

Section 4(2) is evidently based on what Lord Wright had said in *National Anti-Vivisection Society Ltd v IRC* [1948] AC 31: 'The test of benefit to the community goes through the whole of Lord Macnaghten's classification, though, as regards the first three heads, it may be prima facie assumed unless the contrary appears.' It would therefore appear that the predecessor of **s. 4(2)** (namely the **Charities Act 2006, s. 3(2)**) was intended to change the law by reversing the presumption of public benefit in the first three heads. This was what had been suggested in the NCVO report, *For the Public Benefit* (2001), and its proposal was later taken up by the Cabinet Office Strategy Unit report of 2002. From the Strategy Unit report, it seems that the aim of what is now **s. 4(2)** of the **Charities Act 2011** is to ensure that a body will satisfy the public-benefit requirement only if it can show that there is open access, or that in some other way it reaches out, to the community. If a body charges high fees, which thereby effectively exclude the majority of the public from being able to use it, this requirement will not be met. The report says 'that the Charity Commission would identify charities likely to charge high fees and undertake a rolling programme to check that provision was made for wider access' (para. 4.28). The report expressly referred to the charitable status of the independent schools, commenting that, under its proposals, instead of being presumed to be for the public benefit, such schools would have to show that they were carrying on for the public benefit (although it added that most of them probably already were). The report is vague on precisely what degree of open access would be sufficient: whether it is enough for fee-paying schools to make their sports fields available periodically to local state schools, or whether they would have to provide a reasonable number of free, or assisted, places.

Unfortunately, **s. 4(2)** has created uncertainty and confusion in charity law. It seems that it has little impact on the previous law, since all purposes that had been held to be charitable under the previous law have been already held to be for the public benefit. In these instances, public benefit is not based on any presumption, but has been established as a matter of law, so no apparent reversal of any presumption by **s. 4(2)** will make any difference. New purposes under **para. (m)** will have to be shown to be for the public benefit, but this is the same as the previous position under the fourth head of *Pemsel*.

At first sight, it might appear that charitable trusts for poor relations, poor employees or poor members of a club constitute an exception on the ground that they are charitable without there being any public benefit, and so might have difficulty retaining their charitable status in the light of **s. 4(2)**. It is true that such 'poverty' trusts had been treated as anomalous, since under other heads of *Pemsel*, a personal or contractual nexus precluded charitable status; but this does not mean that the 'poverty' trusts are anomalous in not being for the public benefit, since it might be considered that there is always at least an indirect public benefit in relieving the poor. On this basis, **s. 4(2)** does not affect the charitable status of these 'poverty' cases. It does not seem that the intention of the Strategy Unit report, or that of Parliament, was to remove the charitable status of this line of cases; but it is unfortunate that the legislation should have been drafted as to leave their charitable status in doubt. In 2011, the Attorney General referred the issue to the Charity Tribunal for clarification.

Even under the previous law, the court did not accept that a purpose was for the public benefit merely because the testator considered it so: *Re Hummeltenberg* [1923] 1 Ch 237. To this extent, the effect of **s. 4(2)** is at least very limited, since it seems merely to put into statutory form what Russell J had said in *Re Hummeltenberg* (above, 240–1), namely that under whatever of the four classes in *Pemsel* a gift may prima facie fall, it is still necessary to show that it will be for the public benefit. Russell J's judgment in *Re Hummeltenberg* was expressly approved by Lord Simonds in the *National Anti-Vivisection Society* case. Thus, even under the second head of *Pemsel*, the court needed to be satisfied that what the testator was proposing was for the advancement of education. In satisfying itself of this, the court was necessarily assessing whether the purpose was for the public benefit. In many instances, the public benefit was self-evident, and no evidence needed to be produced: *Re Shaw's Will Trusts* [1952] Ch 163 (Vaisey J). In other cases, the court would form an opinion upon the evidence before it: *Re Hummeltenberg* (above, at 242). In *Re Dupree* [1945] Ch 16, for instance, the court accepted that the promotion of a chess tournament for boys and young men in Portsmouth was charitable because it accepted the evidence of a schoolmaster that chess was educational. In *Re Pinion* [1965] Ch 85, a gift by will to establish a museum for the public was held not to be charitable, because expert evidence showed that none of the objects was of any real merit. Harman LJ said that he declined to foist onto the public 'this mass of junk'.

There was a partial qualification to the need to show public benefit under the third head of *Pemsel*, the advancement of religion. The courts did not distinguish between one religion and another, and so did not try to weigh up the merits of any particular religious doctrines or writings. Thus it had been held that a trust to publish religious writings was charitable, even though such writings lacked any merit, unless they were immoral or against all religion: *Thornton* v *Howe* (1862) 31 Beav 14, applied in *Re Watson* [1973] 1 WLR 1472. Similarly, the promotion of faith-healing in a religious context was held charitable in *Re Le Cren Clarke* [1996] 1 WLR 288 under the third head without the need for evidence that the faith-healing worked. This was the reverse of the position under the second head, the advancement of education, where (as already explained) the court needed evidence that the particular purpose specified was meritorious. On this analysis, *Gilmour* v *Coats*, where the House of Lords held not charitable a trust for the purposes of a Carmelite convent, can be explained on the basis that there was evidence in that case rebutting the presumption of public benefit: see Browne-Wilkinson J in *Re Hetherington* [1990] Ch 1.

However, even if s. 4(2) does reverse the presumption of public benefit in this context, it may be of little practical effect, since it might still be argued that the degree of public benefit required is less than that needed for the advancement of education. Evidence of public benefit might be inferred from the religious nature of the purpose itself: *Re Watson* (above). This might be sufficient evidence of public benefit to rebut the presumption in s. 4(2). In any event, it does not appear that the Strategy Unit report intended its proposals to reverse the impact of *Thornton* v *Howe*. Nevertheless, the Charity Commission declined to register the Gnostic Centre as a charity apparently because it could not establish public benefit: *The Gnostic Centre* (16 Dec, 2009)—a decision that may infringe Art. 9 of the ECHR.

The reason most independent fee-paying schools were charitable before Part I of the Charities Act 2006 came into force was that they existed for charitable purposes (the advancement of education). There are judicial statements to the effect that a charity cannot exclude the poor, notably Lord Camden's comments in *Jones* v *Williams* [1767] **Ambl 651, 652,** that a charitable gift is 'a gift to a general public use which extends to the poor as well as to the rich'. However, the charitable fee-paying schools do not in terms exclude the poor; and even if this is considered to be the effect of fee-charging, public benefit was satisfied before the Act because such schools provide either (i) sufficient free or subsidised places; or (ii) an indirect benefit, in relieving the pressure on the state sector (a ground relied on by Lord Wilberforce in *Re Resch's Will Trusts* [1969] **1 AC 514** to explain the charitable status of an endowment for a private fee-paying hospital). Since public benefit has the same legal meaning under the **Charities Act 2011** as it had immediately before 1 April 2008 (s. 4(3)), s. 4(2) will not affect the charitable status of such schools. The matter was considered by the Upper Tribunal in *Independent Schools Council* v *Charity Commission and National Council for Voluntary Organisations* [2011] **UKUT 421 (TCC),** but an appeal is unlikely, and the issue may well reach the Supreme Court in due course for a definitive ruling.

There are other problems with public benefit to which the **Charities Act 2011** gives rise. Under the fourth head of *Pemsel,* there could not be a charitable trust if those to benefit were a class within a class: *IRC* v *Baddeley* [1955] AC 572. This restriction did not apply under the first three heads; but what is unclear is to what extent it might apply to the descriptions of purposes listed in **paras (d)** to **(l).** It is also not clear whether the concept of 'self-help' survives as a vitiating factor (*Re Hobourn* [1946] Ch 194, 201, **CA)** either independently or as an aspect of public benefit.

In conclusion, it can be said that the changes originally contained in **Part I** of the **Charities Act 2006** are unlikely to achieve the aims that are suggested in the Strategy Unit report, and will probably have little impact on the meaning of charity in English law. They might, however, have consequences that the government did not intend, and case law will be needed to establish beyond doubt their precise effect.

Further reading

Dunn, A., 'Shoots among the Grassroots: Political Activity and the Independence of the Voluntary Sector', in *The Voluntary Sector, the State and the Law* (A. Dunn, ed.), Hart Publishing, 2000, chapter 10.

Hackney, J., 'Charities and Public Benefit' (2008) 124 LQR 347.

Luxton, P., 'Public Benefit and Charities: the Impact of the Charities Act 2006 on Independent Schools and Private Hospitals', in *Contemporary Aspects of Property, Equity and Trusts Law* (M. Dixon and G. Griffiths, eds), Oxford University Press, 2007, chapter 10.

Luxton, P., *Making Law? Parliament v The Charity Commission*, Politeia, Policy Series No. 64 (June 2009).

Luxton, P. and Evans, N., 'Cogent and cohesive? Two Charity Commission decisions on the advancement of religion' [2011] Conv 144.

Mitchell, C., 'Redefining Charity in English Law' (1999) 13 TLI 21.

Mitchell, C., 'Reviewing the Register', in *Foundations of Charity* (C. Mitchell and S. Moody, eds), Hart Publishing, 2000, chapter 7.

Rahmatian, A., 'The continued relevance of the "poor relations" and the "poor employee" cases under the Charities Act 2006' [2009] Conv 12.

Wilson, D., 'Section 14 of the Charities Act 1960: a Dead Letter?' [1983] Conv 40.

Trusts of imperfect obligation

Introduction

This is a brief topic upon which it is possible to find discrete questions, but it may also be incorporated into questions on other topics such as certainties or charities. For an example of this, see Chapter 6, question 3(a) the answer to which requires at least a mention of the 'beneficiary principle'. It is an important topic in that it deals with one of the fundamental principles of trusts. Comparatively recently, the courts have devised convenient interpretations of the rules to save dispositions which might otherwise fail as purpose trusts. These cases (referred to in the suggested answers) are important and a familiarity with them is essential to a study of this subject. Although the Perpetuities and Accumulations Act 2009 is now in force, it does not apply to non-charitable purpose trusts (s. 18). Its operation is prospective and only applicable to instruments taking effect after 5 April 2010 (except for wills which must have been executed after that date).

Question 1

Daniel, who died last month, made the following dispositions in his will which was executed on 1 January 2010:

(a) £50,000 to the Seaview District Council for the erection and maintenance of a statue on the promenade in memory of my late wife.

(b) £5,000 for the care of my cat Tortoiseshell and any kittens she may have.

(c) £20,000 for the fostering of cordial relations and understanding between countries.

(d) The residue of my estate to the Cranford Cricket Club for the purpose of building a new pavilion and changing rooms.

The Cranford Cricket Club is a non-charitable unincorporated association.

Advise Daniel's executors as to the validity of these dispositions.

Commentary

This is a typical problem question on this area of the law, where the examiner chooses from the cases examples of trusts which may or may not fail for certainty of objects or perpetuity. Although it is a fairly compact area of law, you need to know the cases on it and the reasoning applied in them to answer the question well.

It is possible that such a question might also include a charitable disposition. For example, in part **(a)**, if the disposition had been for the erection and maintenance of a shelter on the promenade, it might have been valid as a charitable disposition under the fourth head of charity (trusts for other purposes beneficial to the community).

To obtain good marks on such a question, you would probably have to demonstrate not merely a knowledge of any authorities which may be relevant to the precise terms of the gifts, but also a broader understanding of the underlying principles, for example, a knowledge of the cases on monuments in part **(a)** and of Cross J's analysis of gifts to unincorporated associations in part **(d)**.

This area of the law being fairly self-contained should, however, be an area on which well-prepared students should be able to acquit themselves well.

Answer plan

(a) • This is a non-charitable purpose trust and therefore risks failing for certainty of objects and perpetuity. By virtue of **s. 18**, the **Perpetuities and Accumulations Act 2009** does not apply to non-charitable purpose trusts

• If the statue can be regarded as a monument (should have some funeral connection) then it might be valid as one of the anomalous exceptions to the rule as to certainty of objects, but it would only be valid for its erection and not maintenance as this has not been limited to the perpetuity period

(b) • A trust for the care of individual animals is not charitable but is an anomalous exception to the rule as to certainty of objects

• It has not been limited to the perpetuity period however and so would be void

• As kittens are included, it could not possibly fall within such cases as *Re Haines* and *Re Dean*, where the judges appear to have taken judicial notice that the animal could not live for longer than 21 years

(c) • Unlikely to be charitable; no ascertainable objects and not limited to perpetuity period

• Therefore fails as a non-charitable purpose trust (similar to *Re Astor*)

(d) • Although expressed as a purpose trust, it is possible to say that the members of the club are the indirect beneficiaries

• It will not infringe the perpetuity rule if it can be construed as a gift to the members beneficially, which is how such a gift was construed in *Re Lipinski*

Suggested answer

(a) To be valid, a trust must comply with the requirement for certainty of objects, that is, there must be ascertainable persons able to enforce the trust. In *Morice* v *Bishop of Durham* (1804) 9 Ves 399, 32 ER 656 a trust for 'such objects of benevolence and liberality as the Bishop of Durham in his own discretion shall most approve of' was held to be void. Grant MR said that such 'an uncontrollable power of disposition would be ownership and not trust'.

To be valid a trust must also comply with the rule against perpetual trusts, unless it is a charitable trust. This rule is not affected by the Perpetuities and Accumulations Act 2009. In any event, this Act does not apply to wills executed before the date (6 April 2010) on which the Act came into force (s. 16(5A)(a), Perpetuities and Accumulations Act 1964).

The gift in this clause is essentially a trust for a purpose and there are no particular objects that are able to enforce it. It cannot be brought within any of the four heads of charity in *Pemsel's Case* [1891] AC 531 and is therefore a non-charitable purpose trust. It is not dissimilar to the disposition in *Re Endacott* [1960] Ch 232, where a testator left his residuary estate to the North Tawton parish council 'for the purpose of providing some useful memorial to myself'. The gift could not take effect as an outright gift to the parish council as the purpose attached to it created a trust. It was not charitable, and was too wide and uncertain to fall within the anomalous cases 'when Homer has nodded' (per Harman LJ), namely, the maintenance of tombs. A valid trust within this category should probably have some funerary association and should not be excessive in amount (*Re Endacott*). £50,000 might well be regarded as excessive.

The courts have made a concession for such trusts for the maintenance of tombs and monuments and of individual animals (such trusts having been described by Roxburgh J in *Re Astor's Settlement Trusts* [1952] Ch 534 at p. 547 as 'concessions to human weakness or sentiment'), but only as regards lack of objects and not perpetuity, so that a trust for the erection and maintenance of a monument limited to 21 years might be valid. The gift here is for the maintenance of the statue as well as its erection, and therefore will be void additionally as infringing the perpetuity rule.

If the statue could be regarded as a monument then a donation for its erection, but not its maintenance, might be valid under this exception to the general rule (*Mussett* v *Bingle* (1876) WN 171).

(b) Although a trust for the care of animals generally (*Re Wedgwood* [1915] 1 Ch 113) and the care of cats in particular (*Re Moss* [1949] 1 All ER 495) can be a charitable trust, a trust for the care of individual animals is not. Nevertheless, a trust for the care of individual animals can be valid as a private trust, this being another anomalous exception to the rule requiring certainty of objects. Again, however, any such trust must not infringe the rule against perpetuities.

Although there are cases such as *Re Haines, The Times,* 7 November 1952 and *Re Dean* (1889) 41 ChD 552, where the judges appear to have taken judicial notice of the fact that the particular animals concerned would be unlikely to live beyond the perpetuity period (a cat in *Re Haines* and horses and hounds in *Re Dean*), it would seem that such judicial indulgence is misguided. The rule against perpetual trusts, which was expressly preserved by the **Perpetuities and Accumulations Act 1964, s. 15(4)** (and which is not affected by the **Perpetuities and Accumulations Act 2009**), must be applied at the time the trust is created and it must be possible to say at that time that the trust will not continue for longer than the perpetuity period, which in the present case is 21 years. Moreover, the rule against perpetuities has never recognised animal lives as lives in being for the purposes of calculating the perpetuity period (*Re Kelly* [1932] IR 255).

One must therefore conclude that the disposition to Tortoiseshell and her kittens is void, although had it been limited to 21 years or 'for so long as the law allows' then it could have been valid for 21 years. It could also have been limited to the life or lives in being of a person or persons living plus 21 years as in *Re Howard, The Times,* 30 October 1908, where the lifetime of the survivor of two specified servants was used from which to measure the perpetuity period for the maintenance of a parrot.

(c) This disposition would again be a purpose trust without objects able to enforce it and would therefore fail unless it could be brought under one of the heads of charitable trusts. However, a disposition with laudable objects is not necessarily charitable and it is unlikely that this one would be. Although similar objects were held to be charitable within the head of education in *Re Koeppler's Will Trusts* [1986] Ch 423, the disposition there was to 'Wilton Hall', a recognised series of lectures which the testator had organised during his lifetime. This is much more vague however in its application.

In *Re Astor's Settlement Trusts* a trust for (*inter alia*) the maintenance of good understanding between nations and the preservation of the independence and integrity of the newspapers was considered too vague and uncertain as to its application for the court to administer and was void.

(d) A gift to a non-charitable unincorporated association may also fail for lack of certainty of objects and for perpetuity (note as above that the rule against perpetual trusts is not affected by the **Perpetuities and Accumulations Act 2009**).

There have been cases where the courts have interpreted gifts to associations as being gifts to the current members beneficially as in *Re Clarke* [1901] 2 Ch 110, where a gift to the 'Corps. of Commissionaires' was held to be a valid gift to the members beneficially for the time being.

In *Re Lipinski's Will Trusts* [1976] Ch 235 however, Oliver J followed the principle of *Re Denley's Trust Deed* [1968] 1 Ch 373 by finding that although a trust for the erection of buildings for the Hull Judeans (Maccabi) Association was expressed as a purpose trust, it was in fact for the benefit of ascertainable individuals, namely, the members of the club, and he therefore held the trust to be valid. It was argued that because the testator had made the gift in memory of his late wife, this tended to a perpetuity and precluded the association members for the time being from enjoying the gift beneficially: this argument was rejected by Oliver J. Applying the principle of *Re Lipinski's Will Trusts* to this disposition therefore, it might well not fail for certainty of objects.

The further requirement of compliance with the rule against perpetuities must also be satisfied as regards a disposition to an unincorporated association. Gifts to members of an unincorporated association were considered in detail by Cross J in *Neville Estates Ltd v Madden* [1962] Ch 832. He identified two categories of gifts to unincorporated associations which would not infringe the perpetuity rule, namely, where the gift is to the members themselves as joint tenants beneficially, or to the members as members of the association, but there is nothing in the rules of the association to preclude the members from deciding, if they so choose, to divide the gift up between themselves. In both these cases the possibility of immediate division of the gift makes it inoffensive to the rule against perpetuities. Cross J's third category however is where there is some factor, such as the rules of the association (see *Re Grant's Will Trusts* [1980] 1 WLR 360), or the nature of the gift (see *Leahy v A-G (NSW)* [1959] AC 457), which precludes any immediate division of it between the members of the association for the time being. Such gifts will be void. This analysis by Cross J was adopted by Brightman J in *Re Recher* [1972] 1 Ch 526 where he was prepared to accept as valid a gift to the members of an association on a contractual basis according to the terms of the association's rules, which did not preclude the members from dividing up the gift between themselves if they so decided.

Assuming that there is nothing in the rules of the Cranford Cricket Club which would preclude the members for the time being from dividing the gift between themselves if they decided to do so, the gift would not fail for perpetuity and could therefore be a valid trust.

Question 2

There can be no trust over the exercise of which this court will not assume control ... (Grant MR in *Morice v Bishop of Durham* (1804) 9 Ves 399, 32 ER 656.)

Keeton and Sheridan, *The Law of Trusts*, 10th edn, Professional Books Ltd, 1974, wrote:

Modern cases regard (Grant MR) as saying that a trust must have definite human or corporate objects or be charitable. Construing his judgment in this sense has impeded the development of purpose trusts.

Explain the rationale for Grant MR's dictum and discuss the solutions which the courts have found to some of the problems raised by the rule.

Commentary

This is a fairly typical essay question on trusts of imperfect obligation which requires you to demonstrate an understanding of the rationale for such a rule. You should also be aware of the criticisms of the rule and the ways in which the courts have mitigated the harshness of it in some of the more recent cases.

Answer plan

- Every trust must have objects as otherwise there would be nobody able to enforce the trust obligation and the trust property would be left unfettered in the hands of the trustees
- The courts must be able to control a trust and to administer it if necessary, but it would be impossible to do this if the objects were too wide or uncertain
- Purpose trusts may also infringe the perpetuity rule unless they are expressly limited to the perpetuity period. The rule against perpetual trusts is not affected by the **Perpetuities and Accumulations Act 2009 (s. 18)**
- There are anomalous exceptions for certain non-charitable purpose trusts—the erection of tombs and monuments and the maintenance of individual animals
- Gifts to unincorporated associations present problems as to certainty of objects (the members are a fluctuating body which will also include future members) and perpetuity (no limited time for their existence)
- Gifts to unincorporated associations will be valid if they can be construed as gifts beneficially to the members for the time being, or there is nothing in the rules of the association to prevent the members from deciding to treat them as such, or if the gift can be construed as one to be held by the members under a contract (*Re Recher*)
- The courts have been able to construe some purpose trusts as having indirect beneficiaries (*Re Denley*, *Re Lipinski*)

Suggested answer

One of the three requirements for certainty for a trust is certainty of objects. The reason expressed for this by Grant MR was that there must be a person or persons able to enforce the obligations of the trust against the trustees, as otherwise property would be left in their hands entirely without obligation attaching to it. This would abnegate the essential nature of a trust of division of legal and equitable ownership and would be equivalent to unfettered ownership.

Trusts for charitable purposes are enforced by the Attorney General so that this problem does not arise. However, trusts for non-charitable purposes clearly do present a problem in this respect.

A further objection to enforcing a non-charitable purpose trust is the difficulty of interpreting and applying the purpose. This was illustrated in *Re Astor's Settlement Trusts* [1952] Ch 534. The court must be able to control and administer a trust itself if necessary. Any uncertainty or ambiguity as to the purpose to be carried out will make this impossible and is a further reason for the invalidity of such trusts.

A further problem with non-charitable purpose trusts is the unlimited scope of purposes which the courts might be called upon to recognise as valid. Although many non-charitable purpose trusts might be useful and beneficial to some persons, other such purported trusts may benefit nobody. The case of *Brown v Burdett* (1882) 21 ChD 667, where a house was left in trust to be shut up for 20 years, illustrates the undesirable purposes for which eccentric testators might create trusts. Such capricious trusts will not be recognised. However, any decision on the desirability or otherwise of any particular purpose necessarily involves a difficult value judgment. From a practical point of view, Roxburgh J said in *Re Astor's Settlement Trusts* 'it is not possible to contemplate with equanimity the creation of large funds devoted to non-charitable purposes which no court and no department of State can control, or in the case of maladministration, reform'.

Non-charitable purpose trusts must also comply with the perpetuity rule. An application of this rule invalidates any non-charitable purpose trust which might subsist for more than a life or lives in being plus 21 years, or if no lives are specified, then for more than 21 years. This rule is not affected by the **Perpetuities and Accumulations Act 2009** which establishes a new perpetuity period for other trusts (other than those which are for charitable purposes). Purpose trusts infringe this rule if they provide for the tying up of capital for more than the permitted period. If all the capital can be spent at once, this problem does not arise: *Re Lipinski's Will Trusts* [1976] Ch 235.

Nevertheless, it must be conceded that many purpose trusts may be valuable and for the law automatically to deny validity to them is harsh. There are certain exceptions to the rule therefore which have always been recognised, and more recently the courts have been prepared to interpret purpose trusts more generously where possible to recognise 'indirect' objects and so validate them.

The clearly recognised anomalous exceptions are trusts for the maintenance of tombs and monuments and of individual animals. All such trusts must, however, comply with the perpetuity rule.

A gift to an unincorporated association may necessarily involve problems as to both certainty of objects and perpetuity, as the association is a fluctuating body of people which may include future members, and may have purposes which are perpetual. This problem was addressed by Cross J in *Neville Estates Ltd v Madden* [1962] Ch 832, who was able to find that a disposition to the members for the time being beneficially (either as joint tenants or tenants in common) is unobjectionable. They themselves are the object of the gift and so they may, if they wish, divide the gift between themselves at any time. Such a disposition is also unobjectionable as regards perpetuity.

A second possibility is that the gift is one to the members as members of the association, in which case they take beneficially, but subject to the contractual rules of the association. Provided that there is nothing in the rules to prevent the members from agreeing to change them if necessary in order to take the gift beneficially, then the gift will again be unobjectionable on grounds of certainty of objects or perpetuity. If however, there is something in the nature or terms of the gift, or the rules of the association, which precludes the members from taking beneficially, then the gift will be for the purposes of the association and will offend the certainty of objects rule and possibly also the perpetuity rule. In *Re Grant's Will Trusts* [1980] 1 WLR 260 the rules of the local Chertsey and Walton Constituency Labour Party were subject to the rules of the National Labour Party and could not be altered by the local party. The members could not alter the rules to make the gift one which they had control over and it therefore failed.

In *Re Recher's Will Trusts* [1972] Ch 526 Brightman J found that a gift to an anti-vivisection society would have been valid as within Cross J's second category, although it might have surprised the testatrix to know that this was the legal position! (In this case, a gift to an amalgamated association which was incorporated after the testatrix's death was void, as it contemplated a different contractual situation from that subsisting at death.)

In *Re Denley's Trust Deed* [1968] 1 Ch 373 land was left on trust for use as a recreation ground for the employees of a company. Goff J upheld the trust as he was able to find that the employees were the *de facto* beneficiaries, even though the trust was expressed as a purpose trust, and so had *locus standi* to enforce the trust. This was followed in *Re Lipinski's Will Trusts* where a trust 'solely' for the erection and improvement of new buildings for the Hull Judeans (Maccabi) Association was held to be valid on two separate grounds, one of them being that the members of the association could be treated as the *de facto* objects of the trust. The other ground was on the contract-holding construction described in *Re Recher's Will Trusts*. Oliver J held in *Re Lipinski* that the expressed purpose of the gift being 'in memory of my late wife' did not imply an intention to create a permanent endowment but was merely a tribute to the testator's wife and therefore did not necessarily tend to a perpetuity.

Clearly legal recognition afforded only to trusts with objects able to enforce them is open to criticism on the grounds of harshness and inflexibility and creates difficulties with endowments for unincorporated associations. Whilst any general abrogation of the rule would be undesirable, the modifications made by the courts where there are discernible 'indirect' objects are to be welcomed.

Further reading

Luxton, P., 'Gifts to clubs: contract-holding is trumps' [2007] Conv 274.

8

Implied and resulting trusts

Introduction

There has been much academic discussion of the theoretical basis for resulting and implied trusts in recent years, and so question 1 compares them with constructive trusts.

Question 2 deals with implied and resulting trusts (and a few related concepts) on voluntary transfers of property. The question demands a knowledge of the recent judicial discussion of the correct interpretation of the **Law of Property Act 1925, s. 60(3)**. Another part of this question involves a discussion of the so-called '*Quistclose* trust', so named after *Barclays Bank Ltd* v *Quistclose Investments Ltd* [1970] AC 567. A few years ago, Sir Peter Millett, writing extra-judicially, put forward a resulting-trust analysis of the *Quistclose* trust, and he put forward the same view in his speech more recently in *Twinsectra Ltd* v *Yardley* [2002] 2 AC 164. The decision in *Twinsectra* is likely to stimulate further interest in this area, so if your lecturer spends a lot of time on the *Quistclose* trust, then be prepared for a question on it.

Question 3 is a fairly traditional question on the distribution of the assets on the dissolution of an unincorporated association.

Question 1

Distinguish a resulting trust from an implied trust and a constructive trust.

Commentary

This question raises difficult, but absorbing, issues. Students deeply interested should read P. Birks, *An Introduction to the Law of Restitution*, Oxford University Press, 1989, which places many different areas of law, including the law of trusts and the rules relating to tracing, in a restitutionary framework. Also very valuable is Chambers, *Resulting Trusts*, Oxford University Press, 1997.

Answer plan

- Resulting and implied trusts compared
  - ambiguity in phrase 'resulting trust'
  - distinction from implied trust
  - automatic and presumed resulting trusts
- Comparing each with constructive trusts
  - basis for imposition
  - substantive institution or remedy?
  - common intention constructive trust

Suggested answer

The Law of Property Act 1925, s. 53(2) excludes from the scope of s. 53(1) the creation or operation of 'resulting, implied or constructive trusts'. This might suggest that these are different examples within a single classification; but this is not so. These are, in fact, examples drawn from different methods of classification, and the terms are not therefore necessarily mutually exclusive.

The term 'resulting trust', is ambiguous. As Professor Birks has indicated, it appears to be used in two distinct senses: Birks, *An Introduction to the Law of Restitution*, pp. 57–64. First, it is used merely descriptively, i.e., to denote a trust under which a transferor or settlor retains a beneficial interest. Birks calls such a trust 'resulting in pattern'. In this sense, a beneficial interest, retained by a settlor under even an express trust, can be described as resulting: e.g., where S transfers property to T in trust for B for life, remainder for S himself. Secondly, the term is used to denote, additionally, that the settlor's interest under such a trust arises only by implication—which therefore makes it a particular species of implied (or presumed) trust. Birks calls such a trust 'resulting in origin'.

An implied trust is a trust which arises from the presumed intention of the transferor. Thus if A transfers property into the name of B, who is in law a stranger, there is an equitable presumption (except in the case of land) that B holds the legal title in trust for A: *Re Vinogradoff* [1935] WN 68. The presumption (which can easily be rebutted by evidence of a contrary intention) is therefore one of resulting trust. Where an implied trust leaves the beneficial interest with the settlor, it is also (in both senses) a resulting trust.

Because of this closeness of identity, resulting trusts have sometimes been treated as synonymous with implied trusts. This, however, disregards the fact that some trusts classifiable as implied (e.g., those arising under mutual wills) are not resulting. It is equally wrong to treat resulting trusts solely as a sub-species of implied trust because, as Megarry J lucidly explained at first instance in *Re Vandervell's Trusts (No. 2)* [1974] Ch 269, not all resulting trusts are implied. Megarry J there distinguished between 'presumed resulting trusts', which arise from the implied intention of the transferor, and 'automatic resulting trusts', which do not depend upon intentions or presumptions, but are an automatic consequence of the transferor's failure to dispose of what is vested in him. An automatic resulting trust therefore arises where, for instance, S transfers property to T upon trust for B for life, but does not state what is to happen to the property on B's death. In this instance, the resulting trust arises, not from S's implied intention, but merely from S's failure to dispose of the entire beneficial interest in the property transferred to T.

The distinction between the two types of resulting trust emerged in the litigation involving the Vandervell family. In *Vandervell* v *IRC* [1967] 2 AC 291, the House of Lords held that Mr Vandervell was liable to pay tax on dividends declared on shares which he had transferred to a charity. One reason was that he had failed to dispose of his interest under a resulting trust of an option to repurchase the shares. The retention of an interest under a resulting trust was probably the last thing Mr Vandervell intended, since it deprived the scheme of the very tax advantages which it was designed to secure. As Megarry J pointed out in *Re Vandervell's Trusts (No. 2)*, however, Mr Vandervell's interest under a resulting trust was automatic, and not based upon his presumed intention.

A different view was taken in *Davis* v *Richards & Wallington Industries Ltd* [1990] 1 WLR 1551, where Scott J inferred from the circumstances that the members of a pension scheme should not be taken to have intended to retain any interest in a surplus by way of resulting trust. Similarly, in *Westdeutsche Landesbank Girocentrale* v *Islington LBC* [1996] AC 669, at p. 708, Lord Browne-Wilkinson doubted that there was such a thing as an automatic resulting trust; in his view, all resulting trusts are based on intention. More recently, however, Lord Millett, giving the advice of the Privy Council in *Air Jamaica Ltd* v *Charlton* [1999] 1 WLR 1399, at p. 1412, whilst expressing the view that a resulting trust gives effect to intention, said that a resulting trust can arise even when the transferor positively wishes to part with the beneficial interest, and he expressed the view that, on this point, *Davis* v *Richards & Wallington Industries Ltd* was wrongly decided. Lord Millett's observations effectively support the automatic resulting trust, since, in the light of his comments, it is difficult to see how evidence of intention could ever rebut a resulting trust of this sort: see Harpum [2000] Conv 170, at p. 178.

It has been said that both resulting and constructive trusts arise by operation of law, although only the former give effect to intention: *Air Jamaica Ltd* v *Charlton*, at p. 1412 (Lord Millett). Indeed, a constructive trust frequently arises regardless of intention. In English law, a constructive trust is not founded on a single principle, but it might be broadly stated that it is a trust imposed by equity in specific circumstances to promote justice and good conscience. In some circumstances these objectives might involve the imposition of a constructive trust in order to ensure that effect is given to the intention of a settlor (as under the rule in *Re Rose* [1952] Ch 499) or of parties to an agreement. Examples within the latter category are the trusts which arise under mutual wills, or the common intention constructive trust in relation to a family home (as illustrated in *Grant* v *Edwards* [1986] Ch 638). Since these sorts of constructive trust are based upon the intention of the parties, they might also be classified as implied trusts. Such constructive trusts are also closely akin to the doctrine of proprietary estoppel: *Yaxley* v *Gotts* [2000] Ch 162, CA.

A resulting trust is always a substantive trust, and therefore arises from the moment the defendant has the property in his hands. A constructive trust, by contrast, although generally treated as a substantive institution, does sometimes have remedial overtones (as in the case of the trust which arises under mutual wills). In the *Westdeutsche Landesbank* case, Lord Browne-Wilkinson opined that there might be merit in developing the concept of a remedial constructive trust in English law as part of the broader development of the law of restitution. The advantage of a remedial constructive trust (which is recognised in the USA) would be that it would arise only when imposed by the court instead of when the property was acquired by the defendant, and so would not interfere unjustly with the property rights of third parties.

An area in which the distinction between a resulting and a constructive trust has not always been made clear is in the determination of beneficial interests in a family home where the parties have failed to specify what their interests should be. The original source of the confusion is to be found in dicta of Lord Diplock in *Gissing* v *Gissing* [1971] AC 886, HL. In various cases in the Court of Appeal, Lord Denning MR attempted to develop the concept of a new model constructive trust of a remedial nature. This approach was subsequently rejected in *Burns* v *Burns* [1984] Ch 317, CA, and in *Lloyds Bank plc* v *Rosset* [1991] AC 107, HL.

Some recent cases have, however, renewed the confusion between resulting and constructive trusts in relation to the family home. Under a resulting trust the size of the claimant's share is determined by the amount of his or her contribution: *Re Densham* [1975] 1 WLR 1519. By contrast, under a common intention constructive trust the size of the share depends upon the agreement of the parties. In *Midland Bank plc* v *Cooke* [1995] 4 All ER 562, however, the Court of Appeal held that a wife who had contributed less than 7 per cent of the purchase price was nevertheless entitled to a half share in the matrimonial home. The fact that she had contributed financially indicated that she was to have a beneficial interest; and the court inferred from the circumstances that the parties intended her to have an interest, even though there was no evidence that they had ever discussed this matter. Furthermore, in calculating the size of that interest, the court considered that it could have regard to the parties' overall conduct, whether such conduct related to the acquisition of a beneficial interest or not. The decision seems to revive the confusion between resulting and constructive trusts which it was thought that *Lloyds Bank plc* v *Rosset* had finally expunged. Similar criticisms can also be made of *Drake* v *Whipp* [1996] 1 FLR 826, CA.

Question 2

In 1997, Rook bought shares which he transferred into the name of his nephew, Pawn, then aged 17. Pawn, however, delivered the share certificate to Rook, and always paid the dividends he received in respect of the shares into Rook's own bank account.

In 1999 Rook voluntarily, and without any expression of intention, conveyed his freehold land known as 'Castle' into Pawn's name.

Last year Rook handed Pawn a cheque in the sum of £5,000 which he had made out in Pawn's favour. At the same time Rook declared: 'This is to enable you to pay your creditors'. In fact Pawn's debts at the time amounted to only £3,000. Having paid off his creditors, Pawn gave the balance of £2,000 to his girlfriend, Queenie.

Rook died recently. In his will he gave all his property to Knight.

Advise Knight whether he has any claim to the shares, to 'Castle', or to the money received by Queenie.

Commentary

This question is clearly in three parts, each dealing with a different item of property, and the examiner will probably appreciate it if the candidate deals with each part in turn. To aid clarity, it can be helpful (as in the suggested answer) to discuss each part under a separate heading. All three parts involve a discussion of resulting trusts, although the last part (involving the cheque to enable Pawn to pay his creditors) also requires a more wide-ranging discussion of other concepts. As all the issues turn on matters of construction and evidence, it is not possible to reach any definite conclusion upon the facts. At the time of writing, **s. 199** of the **Equality Act 2010**, which will abolish the presumption of advancement, had not been implemented.

Answer plan

The shares
- Presumption of resulting trust or advancement?
- Significance of Pawn's acts after the transfer

'Castle'
- **LPA 1925, s. 60(3)**
- Possible interpretations
- Attitude of courts

Money received by Queenie
- Trust for creditors?
- *Quistclose* (resulting) trust?
- Gift subject to equitable charge?

- Contract?
- Conditional gift?

Suggested answer

As the sole beneficiary under Rook's will, Knight will have a claim to these items of property if he can establish that Rook retained a beneficial interest in them by way of a resulting trust. Let us deal with each item in turn.

The shares

In certain cases, where a person puts his property into the name of another, it is presumed (in the absence of evidence to the contrary) that he intended the legal title to carry with it the beneficial interest. This is known as the presumption of advancement. It arises in three instances: transfers from husband to wife; transfers from a father to his legitimate child; and transfers from a person *in loco parentis* to his quasi-child. Transfers which do not fall within these three categories are known as transfers to strangers. Here the presumption is reversed, i.e., there is a presumption of resulting trust. It is presumed that the transferor did not intend the legal title to carry with it the beneficial interest. These presumptions are weak and are easily rebutted by evidence of the transferor's intention. Even evidence of a close relationship between the parties may be sufficient: *Fowkes* v *Pascoe* (1875) LR 10 Ch App 343; contrast *Re Vinogradoff* [1935] WN 68.

There is nothing in the question to indicate that, at the time he transferred the shares into the name of his nephew, Pawn, Rook stood *in loco parentis* to Pawn. In the absence of contrary evidence, therefore, the presumption is that Pawn holds the shares on a resulting trust for Rook. It is necessary to consider the impact upon this presumption of Pawn's acts subsequent to the transfer. The payment of the dividends to Rook is somewhat equivocal: it could indicate that Pawn considers himself merely a trustee for Rook, who (under a resulting trust) would have the entire equitable interest under the trust and thus (*inter alia*) a right to the dividends received. On the other hand, the payment to Rook of the dividends could be characterised as merely a series of independent gifts to Rook, of property which is now Pawn's both at law and in equity: see the judgment of Lord Denning MR in *Re Vandervell's Trusts (No. 2)* [1974] Ch 269, CA.

Pawn's delivery of the share certificate to Rook per se is evidence of a resulting trust, since it effectively puts it out of Pawn's power to deal with the shares. Unless this can be explained on some other basis—that the certificate was returned, for instance, to Rook for safe-keeping—it points away from Pawn having the beneficial interest in the shares. However, were Rook found to be *in loco parentis* to Pawn in 1993, the mere delivery to Rook of the share certificate might not be sufficient to rebut the presumption of advancement: see *Scawin* v *Scawin* (1841) 1 Y & CCC 65. Some additional evidence may be needed: in *Warren* v *Gurney* [1944] 2 All ER 472, CA, this was supplied by a contemporaneous declaration by the father that no gift was intended. In the present case, the additional factor may be the gift of the dividends. Such evidence is not as cogent, however, as that in *Re Gooch* (1890) 62 LT 384. There, a father bought shares in a company in the name of his son, but the latter always paid the dividends to his father and even handed him the share certificate. Additionally, it was shown that the shares were transferred to the son in order that he could qualify as a director of the company. The presumption of advancement was rebutted.

'Castle'

Although the normal presumption upon a transfer to a stranger is one of resulting trust, it was for many years uncertain whether this presumption applied to a voluntary transfer of land. The uncertainty arose because the Law of Property Act 1925, s. 60(3), states: 'In a voluntary conveyance a resulting trust for the grantor shall not be implied merely by reason that the property is not expressed to be conveyed for the use or benefit of the grantee.' Section 60(3) could be interpreted to mean that in a voluntary conveyance of land there is always a presumption that the equitable interest passes to the grantee even if the conveyance does not state that it is for his use or benefit. Another interpretation, however, is that s. 60(3) is merely intended to ensure that, with the repeal of the Statute of Uses 1535, a beneficial interest can pass post-1925 if intended to pass even where the words 'use or benefit' are not contained in the conveyance. In *Hodgson* v *Marks* [1971] Ch 892, the court found evidence of the transferor's intention and therefore found it unnecessary to consider the effect of s. 60(3), which Russell LJ considered to be debatable, as did Lord Browne-Wilkinson in *Tinsley* v *Milligan* [1994] 1 AC 340.

The former interpretation was preferred at first instance in *Lohia* v *Lohia* [2001] WTLR 101 (left open on appeal at [2001] EWCA Civ 1691, CA), and has since been accepted as the correct interpretation by the Court of Appeal: *Ali* v *Khan* (2002) 5 ITELR 232. In neither of those cases, however, did the result ultimately depend on the interpretation of s. 60(3). In *Lohia* v *Lohia*, any statutory presumption of resulting trust would in any event have been rebutted by evidence that the transferor intended to pass his beneficial interest. In *Ali* v *Khan*, where a father had transferred a house into the names of his daughters, it was held that there was a resulting trust. This decision was, however, based on evidence of the father's intention to retain his interest, such evidence being sufficient to rebut the presumption of advancement.

In the light of these recent decisions, therefore, it appears that a resulting trust is not presumed *merely* because the conveyance is voluntary. This interpretation of s. 60(3) does not, however, rule out the possibility that a resulting trust might be inferred from *other* circumstances. A relevant circumstance might be the relationship between the parties, so that, where the voluntary transferee is in law a stranger to the transferor, that fact alone might be sufficient for the court to infer a resulting trust: see Chambers, *Resulting Trusts*, Oxford University Press, 1997, at pp. 18–19. On this basis, in the absence of direct evidence of Rook's intention, the court might infer a resulting trust if

Pawn was a stranger to him, but infer an intention that the beneficial interest should pass if Rook was *in loco parentis* to Pawn (i.e., the presumption of advancement).

Money received by Queenie

In order to determine whether Knight has a claim to the surplus, it is necessary to construe Rook's intention when he handed Pawn the cheque.

First, if certainty of intention can be found, his words might be interpreted as creating a trust in favour of Pawn's creditors, so that the creditors became beneficiaries (and thereby acquired proprietary rights in equity) from the outset. If this is so, the normal principle is that once the trust has been performed, the surplus is held on a resulting trust for the settlor—in this case, Rook. Other outcomes are, however, possible, depending upon a construction of Rook's intention. Thus, it might be found that he intended that, once the trust had been performed, any surplus should belong to the trustee (Pawn) beneficially: *Re Foord* [1922] 2 Ch 519. This might be presumed if Rook stands *in loco parentis* to Pawn. Yet again, it might be found, as in *Smith* v *Cooke* [1891] AC 297, that Rook intended that the beneficiaries (in this case the creditors) should take any surplus.

Secondly, the transaction might be treated as giving rise to what has become known as a '*Quistclose* trust': *Barclays Bank Ltd* v *Quistclose Investments Ltd* [1970] AC 567. Applying the analysis of such a trust suggested by Lord Millett in *Twinsectra Ltd* v *Yardley* [2002] 2 AC 164, the beneficial interest in the £5,000 would have remained with Rook under a resulting trust, subject to Pawn's having a mandate to apply it in payment of his creditors. Such payment would have reduced Rook's beneficial interest under the resulting trust to an interest in the remaining £2,000.

Thirdly, Rook's words could be held to indicate a gift of the money subject to an equitable charge in favour of the creditors. Upon this construction, it is presumed that the recipient of the fund (in this case Pawn) takes the beneficial interest in it subject only to the payment of the creditors.

Fourthly, the matter could be construed as a contract, whereby Rook pays Pawn £5,000 in consideration for Pawn's paying off his own creditors. On this basis, Pawn has performed his part of the agreement. Strictly, there is no surplus because no debts are charged upon the £5,000, but, in effect, the remaining £2,000 is Pawn's own.

Fifthly, it might be possible to treat Rook as making Pawn a conditional gift of £5,000, i.e., a gift subject to a condition that Pawn pays his own creditors.

In each of these last three constructions, neither Rook nor Knight, as the beneficiary under Rook's will, has any claim to the money paid to Queenie. Knight will therefore have a claim to trace the money into the hands of Queenie only if the first or second construction is adopted, with a resulting trust of the surplus.

Question 3

Three years ago, a bowling club was set up in Plymouth as an unincorporated non-charitable association. Under the rules of the club, members were required to pay an annual subscription of £20, which entitled them to play bowls at the club throughout the year, to use its tea room and other facilities, and to be considered for inclusion in the team for matches with other clubs. Non-members could also play bowls at the club, subject to the payment of £2 per game. Additional funds to support the club were raised through street collections in Plymouth.

The opening of a massive new sports complex in Plymouth has caused interest in the bowling club to decline, and the club's committee has now decided to disband the club. At present, some £20,000 remains in the club's 'Common Fund', into which all payments and donations had been placed.

Advise the club's committee how they should deal with this fund.

Commentary

This is the sort of question frequently found in examinations. Sometimes it will involve a members' club, sometimes more outward-looking types of association. Make sure you deal with the allocation of each part of the fund. Note that the question-setters have been kind, and have expressly told you that the club is a non-charitable unincorporated association. Do not look this gift horse in the mouth. For additional discussion in essays, the student will find valuable analyses by Rickett (1980) 39 CLJ 88, and by Green (1980) 43 MLR 626.

Answer plan

- Resulting trust analysis?
  - resulting trust for identifiable contributors?
  - not appropriate for unidentifiable donors
- Contractual analysis?
  - *bona vacantia*? (members' subscriptions and non-member payments)
  - contrast contract-holding approach (everything belongs to present members)
- Out and out gift analysis?
  - anonymous donations (street collections)

Suggested answer

A number of different legal approaches has been applied to resolve the issue of entitlement to the surplus funds of an unincorporated association upon its dissolution.

One approach is to treat the contributors to the fund as entitled to the surplus by way of a resulting trust. Such a trust arises because the court will presume, in the absence of an expression of intention on the part of the contributors, that they did not intend to part with their contributions out and out. This principle was applied in *Re Hobourn Air Raid Distress Fund* [1946] Ch 194, where factory employees raised a fund to provide for those amongst them who suffered in air raids. The Court of Appeal held that the surplus was held on a resulting trust for the contributors in proportion to the amount each had paid in.

This approach can cause administrative problems, however, where there are many contributors and where the fund has existed for a long time. In such circumstances, two alternative outcomes are possible without abandoning the concept of the resulting trust.

First, it might be presumed that each contributor initially retained an interest in his contribution under a resulting trust until his contribution is spent. On this basis, withdrawals from the fund could be treated as being made according to the rule in *Clayton's Case* (1816) 1 Mer 572, i.e., first in, first out. This would clearly favour later contributors over earlier ones. No reported decision, however, has applied *Clayton's Case* in this context.

Secondly, in *Re Printers* [1899] 2 Ch 184, upon dissolution of a trade union, the surplus of the funds (which had been raised by weekly contributions from members) was held by way of resulting trust for existing members only, rateably according to their contributions. As was pointed out in *Re St Andrews Allotment Association* [1969] 1 WLR 229, however, it is difficult to see how the existing members could take by way of resulting trust a surplus partly derived from the contributions of past members.

An alternative approach is to treat the matter, not as one of trust, but as one of contract. Thus in *Cunnack v Edwards* [1896] 2 Ch 679, a surplus remained in a friendly society's funds after the death of the last widow annuitant. The Court of Appeal held that the members had contributed on the basis of contract, i.e., each payment was made in consideration for the payment of an annuity to the subscriber's widow. Each member had therefore enjoyed their full contractual entitlement from the fund. Thus the surplus went *bona vacantia* to the Crown. This contractual approach was also used in *Re West Sussex Constabulary's Widows, Children and Benevolent (1930) Fund Trusts* [1971] Ch 1, to deal with parts of the surplus remaining on the dissolution of a police benevolent fund. Goff J held that members' contributions, together with funds raised by way of entertainments and raffles, had all been given on a contractual basis, and should therefore go *bona vacantia* to the Crown. There, in contrast to *Re Gillingham Bus Disaster Fund* [1958] Ch 300, the judge said that anonymous contributors must be taken to have given out and out, so that this part of the surplus also went to the Crown.

That part which represented the contributions of identifiable donors, however, was held for such donors on a resulting trust.

A different line of reasoning, however, emerges from a more recent line of authorities. Thus in *Re Recher's Will Trusts* [1972] Ch 526, Brightman J considered that the property of an unincorporated association was held for the members beneficially for the time being subject to the contract which exists between them, i.e., the association's rules. On this basis, unless the rules provide otherwise, the assets are held for the members at the date of dissolution equally, not on any principle of resulting trust, but simply because it is their property.

Problems with the contract-holding approach remain to be addressed: how, for instance, interests can be acquired and lost by new and old members respectively without written assignments complying with the **Law of Property Act 1925, s. 53(1)(c)**. Nevertheless, for the time being at least, this approach has found favour with the courts, e.g., in *Re Sick and Funeral Society of St John's Sunday School, Golcar* [1973] Ch 51, *Re GKN Bolts Nuts Ltd (Automotive Division) Birmingham Works Sports and Social Club* [1982] 1 WLR 774, *Re Horley Town Football Club* [2006] EWHC 2386, and it could also explain *Re St Andrews Allotment Association*. The contract-holding approach was applied to a friendly society in *Re Bucks Constabulary Friendly Society (No. 2)* [1979] 1 WLR 936. Walton J considered that the judge in *Re West Sussex* was wrong to rely on *Cunnack* v *Edwards*. In Walton J's view, *Cunnack* v *Edwards* turned on the friendly society statutes then in force which forbade distribution of surplus to the members.

In the context of outward-looking associations and those which benefit members' widows and orphans, the authorities are therefore in some disarray. Furthermore, pension funds may be a special case, where contractual principles are not necessarily incompatible with a resulting trust: *Davis* v *Richards & Wallington Industries Ltd* [1990] 1 WLR 1511. In the context of members' clubs, however, such as the bowling club in the problem, where the benefits are confined to the members alone, there is now a fair body of opinion favouring the contract-holding approach of *Re Recher*. Thus, subject to a contrary indication in the bowling club's rules, that part of the surplus representing members' subscriptions belongs to the members at the date of dissolution.

The members' club cases, however, have not substantially had to deal with outside contributions. Assuming the criticisms of *Re West Sussex* made in *Re Bucks* are sound, the receipts from non-members for use of the green are paid under a contract and therefore form part of the general assets of the club. The contributions from street collections will probably be treated as absolute gifts, whether or not for the reasons stated in *Re West Sussex*. Greater difficulties might arise in the case of donations from identifiable donors. Dicta in *Re Bucks* suggest that even these would belong to the present members.

In conclusion then, in the absence of anything to the contrary in the club's rules, it is probable that the whole 'Common Fund' belongs equally to those who were members at the date of dissolution.

Further reading

Andrews, G., 'The Presumption of Advancement: Equity, Equality and Human Rights' [2007] Conv 340.

Chambers, R., *Resulting Trusts*, Clarendon Press, 1997.

Glister, J., 'The presumption of advancement to adult children' [2007] Conv 370.

Harpum, C., 'Perpetuities, Pensions and Resulting Trusts' [2000] Conv 170.

Luxton, P., 'Gifts to clubs: contract-holding is trumps' [2007] Conv 274.

Waters, D., 'The Protector: New Wine in Old Bottles?', in *Trends in Contemporary Trust Law* (A. J. Oakley, ed.), Oxford University Press, 1996.

Constructive trusts

Introduction

Constructive trusts lend themselves to both problem and essay questions. The knowledge and understanding obtained from a study of constructive trusts may also make a useful contribution to general essay questions on equity, such as 'Does equity vary with the length of the Chancellor's foot?', or 'Is equity past the age of childbearing?'

A study of constructive trusts demands an understanding of basic concepts such as unconscionable behaviour, unjust enrichment and fiduciary duties. These should not prove too difficult to grasp; but a few of the specific areas in which the courts have sometimes invoked constructive trust concepts—such as mutual wills and the liability of third parties involved in a breach of trust—often present difficulties of their own. Many of the cases in which the courts have been concerned with the personal liability of third parties who deal with, or who receive, property in breach of trust involve very complex frauds. The plots (and the length) of some of these would compare favourably with those of many novels!

Questions 4 and 5 in this chapter deal with secret trusts, which most textbooks now treat as express trusts. Question 5 requires a consideration of the categorisation of secret trusts, which (for reasons pointed out) could be crucial to a beneficiary.

Constructive trusts cover some of the 'high growth' areas of equity. For example the 'new model constructive trust' of property owned by cohabitees was developed by Lord Denning MR in the 1960s and 1970s. Although the post-Denning Court of Appeal rejected his new model, a crucial idea underpinning it—that a constructive trust might be treated as a remedy—was approved by Lord Browne-Wilkinson in *Westdeutsche Landesbank Girozentrale v Islington LBC* [1996] AC 669, and so could be the subject of future development.

Further development occurred in the House of Lords' decision in *Stack v Dowden* [2007] UKHL 17, [2007] 2 WLR 831, which also considered the Law Commission papers on the principles relating to the property rights of cohabitees in a shared home. (See: *Cohabitation: the Financial Consequences of Relationship Breakdown—A Consultation Paper* (Law Com Consultation Paper No. 179, Part 2, 2006) and *Sharing Homes: A Discussion Paper* (Law Com No. 278, 2002).) Further decisions include the

Privy Council decision in *Abbott* v *Abbott* [2008] 1 FLR 1451, and the Court of Appeal decision in *Kernott* v *Jones* [2010] EWCA Civ 578, which (at the time of writing) is awaiting judgment in the Supreme Court.

Since the decision in *Stack* v *Dowden*, the Law Commission in July 2007 issued a report which is being presented to Parliament: *Cohabitation: The Financial Consequences of Relationship Breakdown* (Law Com No. 307, 2007). This report proposes a statutory scheme for cohabitees provided they satisfy certain eligibility criteria. The criteria relate to the length of the cohabitation and the existence of children of the cohabitees. It remains to be seen whether Parliament will see fit to adopt this scheme which represents a radical approach to the determination of property issues between cohabitees in the light of similar development in other jurisdictions.

There has been much litigation in the last decade over the liability of agents and other third parties who assist in a breach of trust or who receive trust property in breach of trust. In the case of assistance, it is now clear that the test for imposing liability on the third party is dishonesty, and this was explained in the important case of *Twinsectra Ltd* v *Yardley* [2002] 2 AC 164 in the House of Lords. The criterion for imposing personal liability on a third party who receives trust property in breach of trust (other than a bona fide purchaser for value without notice) remains, however, unclear. This is an area where you should be looking out for new cases that further refine the principles for the imposition of this type of liability.

The topic of constructive trusts is expanding its scope in some directions, but in the area of imposing personal liability on third parties, it seems to be in retreat. It is now clear that the old language that the courts used to impose personal liability on a third party, that of 'liability to account as a constructive trustee', is inappropriate and misleading where the third party does not hold (and sometimes has never held) the property that is the subject-matter of the trust. Lord Millett made some important observations on this in the House of Lords in *Dubai Aluminium Co. Ltd* v *Salaam* [2003] 1 All ER 97. Nevertheless, because both proprietary and personal actions are sometimes available in the same circumstances, it is convenient to deal with dishonest assistance and with knowing receipt in this chapter on constructive trusts.

Because the law relating to constructive trusts seems to be permanently in flux, there are many new articles dealing with this topic, particularly in journals such as *The Conveyancer*, *Trust Law International* and *The Law Quarterly Review*. For assessed essays you will need to refer to them, and reference to some articles is contained in the Commentaries. The articles may also be helpful in shedding light on particularly difficult topics or in discussion of recent cases. There is also a particularly full and clear analysis of constructive trusts in Parker and Mellows, *The Modern Law of Trusts* (A. J. Oakley, ed.), 9th edn, Sweet & Maxwell, 2008.

The emphasis given to constructive trusts in courses on Equity and Trusts varies, although all courses will include constructive trusts in the syllabus to some extent. In gauging the emphasis that you should give to this subject in preparing for your examination, you should therefore be guided by your lecturer and tutor. If an aspect of constructive trusts is hardly mentioned in the lectures or seminars, it is unlikely to be examined in any depth in the examination. You might therefore do better to devote your in-depth reading to those topics to which your lecturers and tutors devote most attention.

The general advice for all examinations holds good for constructive trusts. Think hard about the question before you start to write. If you have a two-part question, allocate your time roughly equally between the two parts, unless the examination paper indicates, or common sense suggests (as in question 8), that one part is worth more marks than the other.

Question 1

English law provides no clear and all-embracing definition of a constructive trust. Its boundaries have been left perhaps deliberately vague . . . (Edmund Davies LJ in *Carl Zeiss Stiftung* v *Herbert Smith & Co. (a firm) (No. 2)* [1969] 2 Ch 276.)

Discuss with reference to decided cases.

Commentary

This is a very general essay question on the nature of constructive trusts—the sort of question for which you might achieve a pass if you had not actually revised constructive trusts too specifically but had a general overall knowledge of the subject. However, to do well on it, you would need to have a good knowledge of the cases and the recent developments.

The material in this essay answer might well be adapted to similar essays on constructive trusts, such as a discussion of Lord Denning's statement in *Hussey* v *Palmer* [1972] 1 WLR 1286, CA, that 'a constructive trust is one imposed by equity whenever justice and good conscience require it'. However, do always remember that no matter how similar two essay questions may be, you should always slant your answer to the particular question asked.

Answer plan

- A constructive trust is imposed by the court on the person with the legal title to property requiring him to hold the whole or part of the beneficial interest for another
- Unconscionable behaviour and unjust enrichment of the legal owner are usually the grounds for imposing a constructive trust
- The wide and evolving nature of constructive trusts has led to the view that it is remedial in nature, but some lawyers regard it as institutional and think its application should be restricted
- The conflict between these two views can be seen by tracing the changing attitudes to the application of a constructive trust to co-ownership disputes

- Its application to the equitable maxim 'equity will not allow a statute to be used as an instrument of fraud' has led to the enforcement of transactions which would otherwise be void, e.g. secret trusts, contracts not complying with **Law of Property (Miscellaneous Provisions) Act 1989, s. 2**
- A constructive trust will be applied to any profit which a fiduciary derives from his fiduciary relationship. This is a very wide and strict application
- A more dubious application is where an agent or receiver of property which is subject to a fiduciary obligation is made accountable for its loss

Suggested answer

A constructive trust is one imposed by the court on a person in whom the legal title to property is vested. It has the effect of divesting such person of the whole, or part, of the equitable beneficial interest which they then hold as trustee for someone else.

The underlying rationale for the imposition of most constructive trusts is the unjust enrichment of the legal owner, which would result if they were allowed to retain the whole of the beneficial interest, and a constructive trust usually involves some fraudulent or unconscionable behaviour on the part of the legal owner. This is the application of a very general equitable principle and it is hardly surprising that the circumstances in which the courts have been prepared to impose a constructive trust are wide and varied. Moreover, it is an ever evolving area of equity where the courts are constantly re-defining and reviewing the principles on which a constructive trust will be imposed in new cases, often applying the maxims of equity to do so.

There are three well-established categories of constructive trusts. These are where someone obtains an advantage from fraudulent or unconscionable behaviour, where a fiduciary derives a profit from the fiduciary relationship and where a third party receives and holds property in breach of a trust or fiduciary obligation with notice of the breach. Other, less certain classifications are secret trusts (now usually treated as express trusts) and mutual wills, and trusts arising on the incomplete transfer of a legal title and on a specifically enforceable contract for sale.

The application of such a wide equitable jurisdiction as the constructive trust has inevitably led to different approaches by the judges. Lord Denning was always a judge with a strongly developed sense of justice, and he said in *Hussey* v *Palmer* [1972] 1 WLR 1286, CA, that a constructive trust 'is a trust imposed by law whenever justice and good conscience require it. It is a liberal process, founded on large principles of equity, to be applied in cases where the defendant cannot conscientiously keep the property for himself alone, but ought to allow another to have the property or a share of it.' This suggests very much that a constructive trust is really another equitable remedy, as it is in American law, but A. J. Oakley argues that it should not be so regarded and that it is institutional in nature, as it imposes heavy duties of accountability on the trustee and affects property rights. The view that the constructive trust should be constrained in its application is put by Bagnall J in *Cowcher* v *Cowcher* [1972] 1 WLR 425, where he says that it should only be imposed on 'sure and settled principles' as otherwise 'no lawyer could safely advise on his client's title and every quarrel would lead to a law suit'. However, Lord Denning's more liberal approach has received further support from the speech of Lord Browne-Wilkinson in *Westdeutsche Landesbank Girocentrale* v *Islington LBC* [1996] AC 669, at p. 716 where he said:

> The court might by way of remedy impose a constructive trust on a defendant who knowingly retains the property of which the plaintiff has been deprived. Since the remedy can be tailored to the circumstances of the particular case, innocent third parties would not be prejudiced and restitutionary defences, such as change of position, are capable of being given effect.

The reality is probably somewhere between the two views, in that the courts do apply settled principles but the principles themselves are frequently reviewed and modified or extended.

A good illustration of the development of constructive trusts in the context of a desire to effect justice on the one hand, and a desire to keep within well-defined boundaries on the other hand, are the cases involving co-ownership of property where the legal title is vested in one co-owner only. In *Gissing* v *Gissing* [1971] AC 886, the House of Lords laid down the requirements for a party whose name was not on the legal title to property to acquire a beneficial interest. These were that there should be an agreement between the two co-owners, or a common intention, that the co-owner whose name is not on the title should have a beneficial share and that that co-owner should act upon this to his detriment with regard to the property. However, some subsequent cases, such as *Cooke* v *Head* [1972] 1 WLR 518, CA, and Lord Denning MR in *Eves* v *Eves* [1975] 1 WLR 1338, CA, adopted a more liberal view in order to achieve justice in the instant case. This approach was, however, disapproved by the Court of Appeal in *Burns* v *Burns* [1984] Ch 317, which returned to the principles laid down by the House of Lords in *Gissing* v *Gissing*. The principles received confirmation and some refinement by Lord Bridge in *Lloyds Bank Ltd* v *Rosset* [1991] AC 107, but in *Midland Bank* v *Cooke* [1995] 4 All ER 562, the Court of Appeal resiled from Lord Bridge's definitive requirements for inferring a common intention, and was prepared to consider 'the whole course of dealing between the parties relevant to their ownership and occupation of the property' (per Waite LJ).

This position has been subsequently confirmed by the Court of Appeal in *Oxley* v *Hiscock* [2004] 2 FLR 669 and by the House of Lords in *Stack* v *Dowden* [2007] UKHL 17, [2007] 2 WLR 831, although the emphasis in these two latter decisions was that the course of conduct must be in relation to the property—not a general review of the relationship between the parties. It was further reinforced by the Privy Council decision in *Abbott* v *Abbott* [2008] 1 FLR 1451 and the Court of Appeal in *Kernott* v *Jones* [2010] EWCA Civ 578.

Rights of cohabitees and their proprietary rights in a shared home have been the subject of some Law Commission reports and consultations, in particular *Cohabitation: the Financial Consequences of Relationship Breakdown—A Consultation Paper* (Law Com Consultation Paper No. 179, Part 2, 2006) and *Sharing Homes: A Discussion Paper* (Law Com No. 278, 2002).

Further to this consultation, the Law Commission submitted its report (Law Com No. 307) to Parliament in July 2007. The report contains proposals that would introduce a statutory scheme for dealing with property and financial issues between cohabitees on the breakdown of their relationship.

Constructive trusts have been used in widely differing situations to give effect to the maxim of equity, applied in *Rochefoucauld* v *Bousted* [1897] 1 Ch 196, that 'Equity will not allow a statute to be used as an instrument of fraud'. Evidence of secret trusts is admissible in contravention of the Wills Act 1837, as to refuse to admit evidence of the trust could result in the perpetration of a fraud on the intended beneficiary or the testator. In *Bannister* v *Bannister* [1948] 2 All ER 133, CA, evidence was accepted of an oral agreement between the plaintiff and the defendant that the defendant should be allowed to occupy the cottage which she had sold to the plaintiff at below the market price. This did not comply with the Law of Property Act 1925, s. 40 (then the relevant statutory provision governing the formality requirements for a contract for the disposition of land), but to disallow evidence of the oral agreement meant the plaintiff would otherwise have obtained an unfair advantage by fraud. More recently, in *Lyus* v *Prowsa Developments Ltd* [1982] 1 WLR 1044, the court accepted that a purchaser who took property expressly subject to the right of another was bound by that right even if it was not registered under the Land Registration Act 1925, as it could have been. In *Yaxley* v *Gotts* [2000] Ch 162, there was an oral agreement not complying with the Law of Property (Miscellaneous Provisions) Act 1989, s. 2(1), that a builder should have a flat in return for doing conversion work on a building. His carrying out the work was held to raise an estoppel, which was satisfied by a constructive trust (under which he was granted a lease), a constructive trust being exempted from s. 2(1) by s. 2(7).

The courts have shown themselves ready to apply a constructive trust to the profits derived by a fiduciary from his fiduciary relationship in a number of differing circumstances, and in *Boardman* v *Phipps* [1967] 2 AC 46 the House of Lords decided (Lord Upjohn dissenting) that a profit made as a result of information acquired from the fiduciary relationship was within the principle. In *Reading* v *A-G* [1951] AC 507, HL, the concept of fiduciary relationship was extended to that of an army officer and the Crown. The principle means that a trustee may not profit from his position and the courts have applied this to widely differing circumstances. For example, in *Keech* v *Sandford* (1726) Sel Cas Ch 61, a trustee in whose name a lease was renewed was held to be a constructive trustee of it for the trust, and in *Re Macadam* [1946] Ch 73, a trustee who was able to use his position as trustee to appoint himself as director of a company was held to be a constructive trustee for the trust of his director's fees.

In the past, the language of constructive trust was often used when imposing personal liability on a third party who either assisted in a breach of trust, or who received trust property in breach of trust. Where equity imposed liability upon such persons, it usually did so by holding them 'liable to account as constructive trustees', as for instance in *Barnes* v *Addy* (1874) LR 9 Ch App 244. The problem with this terminology, however, was that it suggested that the defendant was holding property on trust, whereas a defendant who merely assisted in a breach of trust might never have received any trust property at any stage. In *Paragon Finance plc* v *D. B. Thakerar & Co.* [1999] 1 All ER 400, at pp. 408–9, Millett LJ pointed out the different situations involved when using the expressions 'constructive trust' and 'constructive trustee'. It seems that equity might have attached the appellation 'constructive trustee' to a defendant who had never received trust property both because the language of trust came naturally to the Court of Chancery and because of some uncertainty whether a personal action would lie in equity against someone other than a trustee. There was, however, no underlying trust, and the expression was 'nothing more than a formula for equitable relief' (*Selangor United Rubber Estates Ltd* v *Cradock (No. 3)* [1968] 1 WLR 1555, at p. 1582, per Ungoed-Thomas J).

In modern times, the label of constructive trust in cases such as these seems positively misleading, and in *Dubai Aluminium Co. Ltd* v *Salaam* [2003] 1 All ER 97, at p. 131, Lord Millett said that it created a trap. His Lordship suggested that the courts should now discard the words 'accountable as a constructive trustee' in this context and substitute the words 'accountable in equity'. On this basis, it is now clear that personal liability for dishonest assistance and knowing receipt is not based on a constructive trust, and so falls outside the definition contained in the quotation that prefaces the question.

Persons who purport to act as trustees without having been appointed have traditionally been called trustees *de son tort*. Such persons can appropriately be considered to be holding the property on trust, and whilst they have sometimes been called constructive trustees (e.g., in *Mara* v *Browne* [1896] 1 Ch 199), their liability to the beneficiaries is the same as if they were express trustees. In the *Dubai Aluminium* case, at p. 130, Lord Millett said that it might now be preferable to term such persons *de facto* trustees.

It is clear from the widely differing situations in which a constructive trust has been applied that it is a versatile and flexible weapon of equity, capable of apparently unlimited adaptability to changing social and commercial circumstances. It justifies the statement by Lord Denning MR in *Eves* v *Eves* that 'Equity is not past the age of childbearing'. However, its adaptability necessarily requires that its boundaries should not be too rigidly defined.

Question 2

Angela was the Council tenant of a house when Bertram, a married man, went to live with her there ten years ago. A year later, the Council offered to sell the house to Angela at a discounted price, being 40 per cent less than the market price of £50,000, and Angela discussed this with

Bertram. They agreed that the house should be conveyed into Angela's name alone as she was the tenant with the right to buy and Bertram was involved in divorce proceedings and property claims from his wife. Of the £30,000 discounted price, £5,000 was contributed by Bertram and the remaining £25,000 was raised by a mortgage in Angela's name which was guaranteed by Bertram.

Angela and Bertram contributed equally to the mortgage repayments until Angela had a baby about a year later, after which Bertram paid them. Angela and Bertram decided to modernise the kitchen and the bathroom, and Bertram, being a qualified carpenter, made all the fitments and did most of the work. Three years ago, they decided to build an extension and Angela took a further mortgage with the Quicklend Bank plc for £30,000 to pay for this. Repayments on this mortgage were also made by Bertram.

Six months ago Bertram left Angela and is now claiming a share of the house. Angela has defaulted on the mortgage instalments to the Quicklend Bank plc who are claiming possession.

Advise Bertram and the Quicklend Bank plc.

Commentary

This is the type of question which could arise in land law, family law or trusts, although each might have a particular slant. There has been much litigation surrounding the area of constructive trusts of which the House of Lords' decision in *Stack* v *Dowden* [2007] UKHL 17, [2007] 2 WLR 831 is the latest. A resulting trust or proprietary estoppel may also arise in these cohabitee situations, and you should also be prepared to consider these.

It is an area which has developed since its early recognition in *Gissing* v *Gissing* [1971] AC 886, where Lord Diplock said (at p. 905) 'A resulting, implied or constructive trust—and it is unnecessary for present purposes to distinguish between these three classes of trust … '. Hayton (in his article referred to below) puts forward some sound reasons for distinguishing a resulting trust from a constructive trust. The distinction received judicial approval in the judgment of Peter Gibson LJ in the case of *Drake* v *Whipp* [1996] 1 FLR 826. In any answer to this type of question on a trusts paper, you should make the same distinction. The Court of Appeal decision, *Oxley* v *Hiscock* [2004] 2 FLR 669 reviewed the various decisions on constructive trusts and confirmed that in determining an interest under a constructive trust or proprietary estoppel the court should have regard to the whole course of dealing between the parties with regard to the property.

The House of Lords' decision in *Stack* v *Dowden* [2007] UKHL 17, [2007] 2 WLR 831, confirmed that the presumption was that where a property was bought in joint names a legal and beneficial joint tenancy arose. This is in accordance with the maxim of equity that 'equity follows the law'. The onus of disproving this presumption would fall on the person who was alleging that the beneficial shares should be unequal. Where property was bought in the name of one person alone then it was for the person claiming that a beneficial interest arose behind a trust to establish that case. In a constructive trust, the test for determining the question of whether the beneficial interests were held in different proportions to the legal interests (or whether a beneficial interest arose at all in the case of a sole name legal interest) is to be answered by considering the parties' intentions in relation to the property which will vary according to the context of the case.

It may be possible to calculate a party's interest under a resulting trust when the property is first bought, as a proportion of the total purchase price. The imposition of a constructive trust may increase that share, but examiners are not likely to expect you to attempt complicated calculations to ascertain an exact amount! All you can be expected to do is to know the circumstances which have been taken into account in increasing a party's share under a constructive trust.

The parties in this question are not married, but you should of course remember that in the case of married couples there is legislation governing the distribution of matrimonial property, notably the **Matrimonial Proceedings and Property Act 1970, s. 37** and (on divorce) the **Matrimonial Causes Act 1973,** but you would not be expected to deal with these in any depth in a trusts examination. Lord Denning MR has said that **s. 37** is merely declaratory of the existing law as to constructive trusts, but there could be a different result in that the section applies 'subject to any agreement to the contrary'. For a presumed agreement to share beneficial ownership equally readily attributed to a married couple, see *Midland Bank plc* v *Cooke* **[1995] 4 All ER 562**.

Answer plan

- The discount on the price may be regarded as a contribution by Angela to the purchase price, which means that the contributions are £20,000 Angela, £5,000 Bertram and £25,000 Angela and Bertram jointly
- Bertram's contribution would mean that a proportionate share of the equitable interest would belong to him under a resulting trust
- A person whose name is not on the legal title to the property may acquire an interest also under a constructive trust where (a) there is an agreement or common intention, which may be express or inferred, that he is to have a beneficial interest and (b) he has acted to his detriment on this understanding
- It might well be inferred from the agreement between Angela and Bertram that Bertram was intended to have a share of the beneficial interest
- Bertram's contributions to the mortgage payments and his improvements to the property would be sufficient acts to his detriment
- Whilst a beneficial interest under a resulting trust is calculated arithmetically according to the proportion of the purchase price a person contributed initially, their interest under a constructive trust should be determined by 'what the parties must, in the light of their conduct, be taken to have intended' (per Baroness Hale in *Stack* v *Dowden* **[2007] UKHL 17, [2007] 2 WLR 831**)
- A resulting trust is more likely to be binding on a third party such as the Quicklend Bank as it arises at the date of purchase and so precedes in time such a third party's interest, and it is for value; a constructive trust will not arise until there are detrimental acts, and also has a flavour of voluntary disposition (*Re Densham*)

- As Bertram was in occupation at the time of the mortgage, he might well have an interest which is binding on the Quicklend Bank

Suggested answer

If the original purchase price of £30,000 represented a discount of 40 per cent, then the market price was £50,000 and £20,000 was allowed to Angela as a Council tenant exercising her right to buy. Of the original purchase price, therefore, £20,000 may be regarded as having been contributed by Angela, £5,000 by Bertram and £25,000 by a mortgage to which they originally contributed equally but latterly Bertram has paid. In *Springette* v *Defoe* (1992) 65 P & CR 1, CA, the discount on the market price on a sale to a council tenant was credited to the tenant who was entitled to buy it under the legislation and this was followed in *Oxley* v *Hiscock* [2004] 2 FLR 669.

Where a person contributes to the purchase price of property and there is no evidence of an intention of gift and no circumstances from which a presumption of advancement arises, there will be a resulting trust for that person of a proportionate part of the equitable interest according to their contribution. There would therefore be a resulting trust for Bertram of one-tenth of the equitable interest and some part of the one half for which they both contributed to the mortgage.

A person whose name is not on the register of title may also acquire an equitable interest in property under a constructive trust if they comply with the requirements laid down in *Gissing* v *Gissing* [1971] AC 886, HL. There must be evidence of an agreement (express or inferred) or a common intention that that person is to have a beneficial interest in the property at the time of its acquisition. In *Drake* v *Whipp* [1996] 1 FLR 826, there was undisputed evidence of a common intention that the parties were to share beneficially. Additionally, the equitable owner must have acted on this understanding to their detriment. In *Lloyds Bank Ltd* v *Rosset* [1991] AC 107, HL, Lord Bridge expressed the view that the detriment could be some material alteration in a party's position in the case of an express agreement, but that in the case of an inferred agreement some direct contributions to the purchase price of the property, either initially or by way of contribution to the mortgage instalments, would be necessary. Baroness Hale in *Stack* v *Dowden* ([2007] UKHL 17 at 63, [2007] 2 WLR 831) suggests that Lord Bridge may have set that hurdle rather too high in certain respects and she cites in support a similar statement in the Law Commission paper, *Sharing Homes: A Discussion Paper* (Law Com No. 278, 2002, at para. 4.23). However, her remarks on this point are obiter dicta.

It is possible to infer such a common intention from what was said when the property was purchased, and a party who has impliedly agreed to this may be estopped from denying it later. In *Eves* v *Eves* [1975] 1 WLR 1338, CA, the man said that the woman's name could not be included on the legal title because she was under age, and in *Grant* v *Edwards* [1986] Ch 638 it could not be included because it would prejudice any settlement in the woman's divorce proceedings. In both cases, the reasons given for omitting the woman's name implied that her name would otherwise have been included on the legal title, from which it could be concluded that she was intended to have a share of the beneficial interest in the property.

The parties' agreement in this case as to why Bertram's name should be left off the legal title might similarly be evidence of a common intention that he should have a share of the beneficial interest. His initial contribution of £5,000 and his guarantee of the mortgage (as in *Falconer* v *Falconer* [1970] 1 WLR 1333, CA) would be conduct from which a common intention could be inferred. The Court of Appeal in *Midland Bank* v *Cooke* [1995] 4 All ER 562, adopted a more liberal approach than Lord Bridge in *Rosset* as to circumstances which might give rise to an inference of common intention, and indicated that the court may consider all the dealings between the parties with regard to the property. In *Oxley* v *Hiscock*, the Court of Appeal suggested that it would make no difference to the outcome of such cases as to whether the analysis of detrimental reliance were applied in proprietary estoppel or constructive trusts.

Assuming there is sufficient evidence of a common intention, Bertram would then have to show that he subsequently acted to his detriment in reliance upon this. He has contributed substantially to the mortgage repayments and carried out improvements to the property, and these might both be regarded as sufficient conduct to his detriment to enable him to acquire an interest under a constructive trust, thereby increasing his original equitable interest under a resulting trust.

The extension appears to have been a joint venture, in that the mortgage to finance it was in Angela's name but Bertram has made the repayments. In *Hussey* v *Palmer* [1972] 1 WLR 1286, CA, a mother-in-law's payment for an extension to her son-in-law's house was held to give rise to a constructive trust in her favour. Similarly here, Bertram could again have an increased share of the equitable interest in the increased value of the property under a constructive trust.

The next question which arises after the existence of a beneficial interest under a constructive trust has been established, is the extent of this interest. It was said in *Oxley* v *Hiscock* that the court should have regard to the whole course of dealing between the parties in relation to the property in deciding their respective shares. This view was largely confirmed by the House of Lords in *Stack* v *Dowden* [2007] UKHL 17, [2007] 2 WLR 831, although Baroness Hale emphasised (at 61) that 'the search is still for the result which reflects what the parties must, in the light of their conduct, be taken to have intended' and 'that did not enable the court to abandon that search in favour of the result which the court itself considers fair'. Conduct may, of course, include financial contributions as well as discussions as to their intentions. Baroness Hale (at 69) in emphasising that 'context is everything' set out a non-exhaustive list of other factors which may lead to evidence of intention such as: the nature of the parties' relationship; the responsibility for children; the arrangement of finances; the discharge of outgoings and household expenses. The intention of the parties may also be deduced from their individual characters and personalities.

Thus, at the outset, a relevant factor in determining the respective shares under a constructive trust would include the fact that Angela and Bertram contributed equally to the mortgage repayments at first. But the parties' intentions might change, and it is arguable that the birth of the baby one year after the purchase of the property plus the change in their financial arrangements whereby Bertram assumes responsibility for the mortgage payments (including later the additional mortgage payment for the extension) could affect the relative shares. Bertram's work on the modernisation of the bathroom, if substantial, might also be an indicator as to their intentions.

The Quicklend Bank plc have made a further loan to Angela and it is necessary to consider whether they are bound by any equitable interest in the property which Bertram has. In his article 'Equitable rights of cohabitees' [1990] Conv 370, D. J. Hayton suggests that, as regards third parties, an interest acquired under a resulting trust is more likely to be binding than one acquired under a constructive trust. An interest under a resulting trust is acquired for money or money's worth at the time when the property is purchased, whereas an interest under a constructive trust may have an element of voluntary settlement, and in any event will not be acquired until the party has acted to his detriment, which will necessarily be subsequent to the purchase. In *Re Densham* [1975] 1 WLR 1519, the original contribution of half the deposit on a house which the wife made towards the purchase price was held to give her a one-ninth share in the equitable interest under a resulting trust which was good subsequently against the husband's trustee in bankruptcy, but any increased share which she might have acquired under a constructive trust was void under bankruptcy law as there was an element of voluntary settlement in it which a trustee in bankruptcy can set aside.

On this basis, it would appear that the mortgage with Quicklend Bank plc will be subject to Bertram's initial interest under the resulting trust. A mortgagee will not have the advantage of a trustee in bankruptcy of being able to set aside a voluntary disposition, however, and it would appear that the mortgage with Quicklend Bank plc will be subject to Bertram's interest under a resulting trust, and probably also subject to any increased interest which Bertram may have acquired under a constructive trust. This was the decision in *Midland Bank* v *Cooke*, and this would seem to be consistent with the general principles of property law where third parties are deemed to have notice of the possible proprietary rights of occupiers in unregistered land (*Kingsnorth Finance Co. Ltd* v *Tizard* [1986] 1 WLR 783), and an occupier's proprietary rights are an overriding interest in land with registered title (*Williams & Glyn's Bank Ltd* v *Boland* [1981] AC 487).

Question 3

James and Lucy Smith, an elderly couple who married three years ago, decided to make mutual wills leaving their entire estates to each other absolutely, and then to James's three children by his first marriage, Amy, Bert and Charles. The wills, made in identical mirror terms on the same day, included an undertaking that the survivor would not revoke their will. At that time, James and Lucy owned a house 'Dunroamin' as joint tenants.

James died last year and Charles died six months later. Lucy sold 'Dunroamin' and, with £30,000 of the sale proceeds, built a granny annexe to Amy's house and moved into it. The annexe has added substantially to the value of Amy's house.

Lucy, a football fan, recently won £50,000 on the football pools.

Lucy died last week. It has now been discovered that she made another will a month ago leaving her entire estate to Amy.

Advise Bert and the personal representatives of Charles.

Commentary

This question raises some of the problems which arise on mutual wills which are at present largely unresolved. It also raises a new problem considered in the case of **Healey v Brown [2002] EWHC 1405**. There have been quite a number of cases on mutual wills over the last few years including the Court of Appeal decision in **Olins v Walters** and this may well be because second marriages are much more common now that people are living longer. One could add to that the fact that divorce is also much more common! The attraction is presumably that the survivor has use of the capital as well as the income of property which they receive. A less contentious alternative to mutual wills would be to leave a survivor a life interest (having first severed any joint tenancy on jointly owned property!) with a power to require an advance of capital for any reasonable requirements.

The subject is discursive and problematic, but there is not a large body of case law (as, for instance, in estoppel) and a knowledge of the few cases on it should enable you to cope with it. Should the subject be set as assessed coursework, there are some articles which, despite their age, could be helpful. These are J. D. B. Mitchell, 'Some aspects of mutual wills' (1951) 14 MLR 136, R. Burgess, 'A fresh look at mutual wills' (1970) 34 Conv 230 and G. Boughen Graham, 'Mutual Wills' (1951) 15 Conv (NS) 28.

Answer plan

- Is there a sufficient agreement for mutual wills?
- Charles acquires a vested interest on the death of James and his estate is therefore entitled to his share
- Is the disposition of 'Dunroamin' in their estates caught by **Law of Property (Miscellaneous Provisions) Act 1989, s. 2(1)**? In any event, the agreement would be enforceable under a constructive trust, and Amy would therefore hold Lucy's estate on trust for herself, Bert and Charles's estate
- What property of Lucy's is subject to the trust arising under the mutual wills? Does it matter that 'Dunroamin' passes to Lucy by the right of survivorship instead of under the mutual will?
- Is Lucy's expenditure of capital on an annexe a breach of trust or not? Are Lucy's winnings of £50,000 also subject to the trust?

Suggested answer

Mutual wills derive from a contract between the parties to make wills in a similar form and not to revoke them (*Olins* v *Walters* [2009] Ch 212). The wills usually benefit the survivor of them as here (although this is not necessary: see *Re Dale* [1993] 4 All ER 129) and then an agreed third party or parties. Identical wills in mirror form made at the same time are not sufficient (*Re Goodchild* [1997] 3 All ER 63) and there must additionally be an agreement not to revoke the wills. In *Olins* v *Walters* [2009], the Court of Appeal held that it was a 'legally necessary condition' that there was clear and satisfactory evidence of a contract between the two testators. The undertakings given in the wills here would constitute such an agreement.

As Charles survived James, he acquired a vested interest under the trust arising under the wills on James's death (*Re Hagger* [1930] 2 Ch 190). The interest cannot vest in possession until Lucy dies, but is vested in interest, rather like a remainder or a reversion. Any share to which Charles is entitled should therefore go to his estate.

The decision in *Healey* v *Brown* (2002) 19 EG 147, raised a problem with regard to land disposed of by mutual wills. David Donaldson QC, sitting as a judge of the High Court, considered that as the agreement necessary for mutual wills contemplated a disposition of land, it was caught by the **Law of Property (Miscellaneous Provisions) Act 1989, s. 2(1)**. In that case, a flat was specifically disposed of ('3, Phoenix Court'), but it is unclear whether a will which incidentally disposes of land, as here, would also be caught by the section. Another potential problem with regard to the application of s. 2(1) is whether the section would apply to the situation where the parties do not own any land at all when the wills are made, but subsequently acquire land which would have been covered by the section.

In *Healey* v *Brown*, the judge decided that the agreement was void as it did not comply with s. 2(1) in that there was not *one* agreement signed by *both* parties. Nevertheless a constructive trust arose, which was enforceable as this was exempt from the formality requirement of s. 2(1) by s. 2(7). There was unconscionable behaviour by Mr Brown, the survivor, who after Mrs Brown's death had transferred flat 3, Phoenix Court to himself and his son Paul as joint tenants, thereby avoiding its passing under his mutual will to Mrs Brown's niece. This resulted in the unjust enrichment of his son Paul, so that all the requirements for a constructive trust were present. He found similarities between the case and that of *Yaxley* v *Gotts*, where there was an agreement between the parties and the only problem was, again, that it was void because it did not comply with s. 2(1). Even if the agreement were void under s. 2(1) therefore, a constructive trust could be imposed on Amy to hold two-thirds of the estate for her brother Bert and Charles's estate.

Another problem which has beset mutual wills is what property owned by the survivor is actually subject to the trust created by the agreement and wills? In *Re Green* [1951] Ch 148 it was held that it was only the property which the survivor received from the first to die, but the case is not a good authority as it was clear from the agreement between the parties that it was only intended to be property received from the other. In *Re Hagger*, the mutual will was held to apply to all the property of both parties. In *Healey v Brown*, having found that the agreement between the parties was in fact enforceable under a constructive trust, the judge then said that it only applied to the property which Mr Brown received from Mrs Brown, although it is by no means clear why this should have been so as the agreement and the wills clearly contemplated the ultimate disposition of all their property (3, Phoenix Court to Mrs Brown's niece and the remainder of their estates to Mr Brown's son). In fact, 3, Phoenix Court was held by Mr and Mrs Brown as joint tenants, and so passed to Mr Brown by the right of survivorship and not under the mutual will. The judge held however that this made no difference, and applying this to the question, it would not matter that Lucy acquired James's share of 'Dunroamin' by survivorship rather than under the will.

Another question with regard to mutual wills is what should happen if the survivor indulges in profligate spending, or conversely, whether a windfall acquisition by the survivor is also subject to the agreement. In the Australian case of *Birmingham v Renfrew* (1936) 57 CLR 666, Dixon J said 'the object of the transaction is to put the survivor in a position to enjoy for his own benefit the full ownership so that, for instance, he may convert and expend the proceeds if he choose. But when he dies he is to bequeath what is left in the manner agreed upon. It is only by the special doctrines of equity that such a floating obligation, suspended, so to speak, during the lifetime of the survivor, can descend upon the assets at his death and crystallise into a trust.' The intention of the mutual wills is probably that the survivor can use the capital for any reasonable needs they have, and Lucy's granny annexe might well be regarded as this. It is nevertheless giving Amy a benefit which she was not intended to have under the agreement and the wills, and it is perhaps possible therefore that she might be required to take this into account in calculating her share of Lucy's estate. There is no case as yet on an unforeseen windfall, and this would presumably depend upon whether the agreement covered the whole of the survivor's property or just that received from the first to die.

Question 4

By his will Peter bequeathed 50 casks of brandy to Smee absolutely. Shortly after the will was made, Peter handed Smee a sealed envelope marked 'Not to be opened until after my death'. He asked Smee to hold the brandy on the terms contained therein, and Smee agreed. The sealed instructions state that Smee can drink as much of the brandy as he likes during his life, but that he must, by his will, bequeath whatever is left to Peter's mistress Tinkerbell.

Peter and Tinkerbell were in a flying accident last month. Tinkerbell was killed instantly and Peter died the next day. Tinkerbell had witnessed Peter's will. Smee says he intends to sell the brandy and spend the proceeds on a world cruise.

Advise Tinkerbell's executors.

Commentary

This is a particularly difficult problem question which you might want to avoid even if you have revised secret trusts and mutual wills very well! If you fail to appreciate all its different aspects, however, you should nevertheless be able to pick up some marks fairly easily for knowing some of the points involved, such as what happens if the secret beneficiary witnesses the will or predeceases the testator.

Definitely a question to think hard about, though, before you set pen to paper!

For further reading on mutual wills, see the Commentary on question 3, and for further reading on secret trusts, see the Commentary on question 5.

Answer plan

- A bequest of the brandy to Smee without any indication on the face of the will that he is to hold part of it for someone else will be a fully secret trust
- This must be accepted by the trustee Smee at any time before death, but there is no objection to the communication being in a sealed envelope handed over with instructions not to open it until after the testator's death
- Tinkerbell's witnessing the will probably will not invalidate it (**Re Young**, a case on half secret trusts)
- If **Re Gardner (No. 2)** were followed, Tinkerbell's estate could benefit from the trust even though she had predeceased the testator, but the case has been much criticised
- The arrangement may fail as a secret trust for uncertainty of subject-matter
- The disposition has some similarities to a mutual will however, where uncertainty as to subject-matter is accepted (**Birmingham v Renfrew**)

Suggested answer

As the brandy is bequeathed to Smee absolutely with no indication on the face of the will that it is to be held by him on trust, this purports to create a fully secret trust.

For a fully secret trust to be valid, it must be accepted by the trustee at any time before the death of the testator. Provided that the trust itself has been accepted, it is probably sufficient if the exact terms are contained in a sealed envelope which is not to be opened until after the testator's death (Lord Wright MR obiter in *Re Keen* [1937] Ch 236, CA). Although *Re Keen* was concerned with a half secret trust, there would seem to be no reason why the principle should not be applicable also to a fully secret trust. It is possible that in the case of a half secret trust, communication has to be by handing over the sealed envelope before the execution of the will (*Re Bateman's Will Trusts* [1970] 1 WLR 1463), but in the case of a fully secret trust, it could be handed over at any time before death.

Assuming that these circumstances create a valid secret trust for Tinkerbell, it will not matter that Tinkerbell, who was a beneficiary under the trust, witnessed Peter's will: *Re Young* [1951] Ch 344, where it was held that a beneficiary under a half secret trust who had witnessed the will was nevertheless able to take under it. The reason is that the beneficiary took under the secret trust and not under the will, so that the **Wills Act 1837, s. 15** (which invalidates a gift to the witness) did not apply. There would seem to be no reason why this principle should not apply also to a fully secret trust.

It is more questionable, however, whether Tinkerbell's predeceasing Peter will render the trust void. In *Re Gardner (No. 2)* [1923] 2 Ch 230, where the secret beneficiary predeceased the testatrix, Romer J held that there was a valid trust for her estate, but this decision has been criticised. Normally a gift to a beneficiary who predeceases the testator will lapse. Even if the doctrine of lapse is avoided by construing the secret trust as one which arises at the moment it is accepted by the secret trustee during the lifetime of the testator, it cannot be fully constituted until his death, and it must be fully constituted to be valid. Nevertheless, if the decision in *Re Gardner (No. 2)* is applied, Tinkerbell's estate would be able to benefit.

A more serious problem in construing Peter's arrangement as a secret trust is that of certainty of subject-matter. In *Sprange v Barnard* (1789) 2 Bro CC 585, where a testatrix left property to her husband for his sole use and at his death 'the remaining part of what is left' was to be divided between a brother and sister, the trust failed for uncertainty of subject-matter. So a secret trust of whatever brandy Smee does not drink may well similarly fail for uncertainty of subject-matter.

However, it might be possible to argue that the arrangement resembles the type of agreement necessary for mutual wills. Smee agrees to hold the brandy on the terms contained in the envelope and he is thereby (although he does not realise it) agreeing to dispose of it in a certain way by his will. In *Ottaway v Norman* [1972] Ch 698, a similar sort of arrangement was successfully enforced by the secret beneficiary, but the case was pleaded as a secret trust and not as mutual wills. As such it was only valid as regards that property which was certain, namely a bungalow and not as regards a sum of money (£1,500) which Brightman J held to be too uncertain. However, mutual wills may be valid even if they involve just the type of uncertainty of subject-matter as here (see Dixon J in an Australian case *Birmingham v Renfrew* (1937) 57 CLR 666, as to the nature of enjoyment and obligation under such an arrangement, namely, rights of virtually full ownership during the survivor's lifetime and an obligation as regards the property which crystallises on his death).

The usual type of agreement for mutual wills is that the parties to it agree to benefit each other and then an agreed third party, but there would seem to be no reason why one party who accepts a benefit should not do so on terms which require him to confer a benefit on a third party, as indeed was the case in *Ottaway v Norman*. In *Re Dale* [1994] Ch 31, it was not even considered necessary for the survivor to receive a personal benefit. It would be necessary however to establish a clear agreement, and it would be arguable that it could not be a binding agreement if Smee did not know the full terms of what he was agreeing to. In *Olins v Walters* [2009] Ch 212, it was held that it was a legally necessary condition of mutual wills that there is clear and satisfactory evidence of a contract between the testators.

This disposition like *Ottaway* v *Norman*, is a mixture of a secret trust and a mutual will! Therefore it is just possible, if a clear agreement could be established between the testators, that an action by Tinkerbell's executors might succeed if pleaded as a mutual will.

Question 5

(a) '. . . the whole basis of secret trusts . . . is that they operate outside the will'. (Megarry V-C in *Re Snowden (deceased)* [1979] Ch 528.)

Discuss.

(b) Meg, a wealthy but eccentric elderly spinster, wished to leave a large sum of money to the Battersea Dogs' Home but did not want her family to know. She therefore asked her old friend James if he and his son Sam would hold £50,000 which she intended to leave to them in her will in trust for the Home. James agreed. Meg made a will the following week leaving £50,000 to James and Sam. James did not tell Sam of Meg's wishes and Meg also forgot to mention anything about it to Sam. Subsequently, Meg decided to increase the legacy to £100,000 and executed a codicil to this effect. She told neither James nor Sam about the codicil, however.

Advise Meg's executors as to what extent the secret trust is effective. Would your answer differ if the legacy had been left to James and Sam 'as tenants in common for purposes I have made known to them'?

Commentary

The two parts of this question make it a fairly lengthy one. You should not be deterred by this as it means that there are a lot of points for you to pick up. However, it does mean that your answer to the essay part must be fairly concise and you must avoid going into too much detail on it at the expense of the time required to answer the problem part.

Part (a) of the question may also lend itself to a discursive essay which could be set perhaps as assessed coursework. In that case, you would obviously need to do some more in-depth reading of the judgments in *Blackwell* v *Blackwell* [1929] AC 318 and the cases such as *Re Young* [1951] Ch 344 which throw up a conflict between the rules of probate and the principles of equity. You will also find articles written on the subject in *The Conveyancer* and other legal periodicals (two by Bryn Perrins: 'Can you keep half a secret?' (1972) 88 LQR 225 and 'Secret Trusts: the key to au dehors' [1985] Conv 248, 'Secret and semi-secret trusts: justifying distinctions between the two' by David Wilde [1995] Conv 366 and one by Patricia

Critchley (1999) 115 LQR 631, 'Instruments of fraud, testamentary dispositions, and the doctrine of secret trusts'). For a piece of empirical research among practitioners as to the extent of use of secret trusts, see 'Secret trusts do they have a future?' by Rowena Meager (2003) 67 Conv 203. As pointed out in the answer to this question, the classification of secret trusts could be highly significant if the secret trust were one of land because of **LPA 1925, s. 53**.

Answer plan

(a) • Secret trusts are only enforceable if evidence is accepted of a testator's intentions not contained in his or her will, contrary to the **Wills Act 1837, s. 9**

  • Part of the rationale for admitting such evidence is to avoid a fraud on the secret beneficiary and the testator; if this is correct, they may be regarded as constructive trusts

  • Later cases take the view however that a secret trust derives not so much from the will itself as from the agreement between the testator and the secret trustee during the testator's lifetime, and this view is supported by cases such as *Re Gardner (No. 2)* and *Re Young*

  • If this is so, they may be regarded as express trusts to which **LPA 1925, s. 53(1)(b)** would apply, although it would not apply if they are constructive trusts (**s. 53(2)**)

(b) • Communication of the secret trust to only one of two secret trustees will never bind the other if they are tenants in common. If they are joint tenants, a communication will bind both if it was made before the will was executed, but not if it was made afterwards (*Re Stead*)

  • James and Sam are joint tenants as there are no words of severance in the disposition to them

  • Communication to James before the will was made therefore binds both of them

  • Neither of them accepted the trust of the increased legacy in the codicil and so neither of them is bound by it

  • They therefore hold the £50,000 trust accepted by James for the Battersea Dogs' Home, but take the additional £50,000 in equal shares beneficially as this is a fully secret trust

  • If the disposition had been to James and Sam as tenants in common on a half secret trust, then only James would have been bound by the secret trust as to half of the £50,000 in the will

  • The half not accepted by Sam and the disposition in the codicil could not be taken by them beneficially and they would hold it for the residuary legatee under the will

Suggested answer

(a) Equity's enforcement of secret trusts necessarily involves accepting evidence of a testator's intentions which were not embodied in his will and which do not therefore comply with the Wills Act 1837, s. 9.

To be valid, a secret trust must be accepted by the secret trustee, although the time of acceptance varies according to whether the trust is a fully secret trust or a half-secret trust. To allow the secret trustee to renege on this agreement would amount to a fraud on the beneficiaries of the trust and on the testator, in that he would not have left property to the secret trustee if the latter had not agreed to the trust. Such rationale may also explain equity's intervention in half-secret trusts, under which the trustee himself cannot derive any benefit as legatee or devisee. Fraud on the beneficiary was the rationale accepted for secret trusts in *McCormick* v *Grogan* (1869) LR 4 HL 82, but this applied only to fully secret trusts. In *Blackwell* v *Blackwell* [1929] AC 318, however, Viscount Sumner took the view that a secret trust is created and becomes binding as a result of the communication of it by the testator to the secret trustee and his acceptance of it during the testator's lifetime, and that the trust which consequently arises is therefore governed by the law relating to trusts and is outside the scope of the Wills Act 1837.

Although this is a better explanation for the operation of secret trusts, it is not entirely satisfactory because the secret trust depends upon the proving of the will for its constitution. This dependence has thrown up some unhappy conflicts in cases where strict adherence to the Wills Act 1837 would have invalidated a secret trust, but the courts have nevertheless been prepared to recognise its existence.

It is debatable, for example, to what extent a secret trust will be enforceable if the secret trustee predeceases the testator or disclaims the gift under the will, and this may vary according to whether the secret trust is fully secret or half-secret. In the case of a half-secret trust the principle that equity will not allow a trust to fail for want of a trustee would probably apply to save the trust. However, Cozens-Hardy LJ in *Re Maddock* [1902] 2 Ch 220, CA, expressed the opinion that a fully secret trust would fail if the secret trustee renounced or disclaimed the gift or died in the lifetime of the testator.

In *Re Gardner (No. 2)* [1923] 2 Ch 230, the beneficiary under a half-secret trust had predeceased the testatrix. This should have resulted in the gift to her lapsing, but Romer LJ held that it went to her personal representatives. Note, however, that this decision has been criticised. In *Re Young* [1951] Ch 344, one of the beneficiaries of a half-secret trust witnessed the testator's will which would have invalidated any gift to him in the will itself. The court held that the legacy was nevertheless valid because the beneficiary took under the trust and not under the will. Many of the decisions therefore illustrate the courts' willingness to modify the strict requirements of the Wills Act 1837 where necessary to give effect to a secret trust. This suggests that the tendency is indeed to regard secret trusts as being governed by the law relating to trusts, deriving from the agreement between the testator and the trustee. This would mean that they are more properly classified as express trusts rather than constructive trusts (A. J. Oakley's opinion—see question 1). This is not an entirely academic question when it is recalled that s. 53(1)(b) applies to the creation of an express trust of land. A constructive trust of land is exempt by s. 53(2).

(b) In *Re Stead* [1900] 1 Ch 237, Farwell J had to consider the situation where a fully secret trust was communicated to one joint tenant trustee but not the other. He stated the rules applicable in a technical way, distinguishing between secret trustees who were joint tenants and secret trustees who were tenants in common. In the case of tenants in common, an acceptance of the secret trust by one only will never bind his co-trustee, as tenants in common take a distinct and separate share in property left to them. In the case of joint tenants, however, communication to one of them before the will is made binds all of them, but communication after the will binds only those to whom communication is made.

In his article 'Can you keep half a secret?' (1972) 88 LQR 225, Bryn Perrins suggests that the distinction between joint tenants and tenants in common arises from a misinterpretation of early cases, notably *Huguenin v Baseley* (1807) 14 Ves 273, in which the rationale for deciding whether a co-trustee, with whom there was no communication, was bound or not, was whether the testator was induced by the promise of the secret trustee to make (or to leave unrevoked) the gift to him in the will. As the relationship between joint tenants is closer than that between tenants in common, a testator is more likely to assume that a joint tenant will readily accept an obligation imposed on a fellow joint tenant and this could therefore induce the gift to them jointly in the will. Thus communication to one of them before the will is made should bind both of them. It is probably more difficult, however, to prove that a gift previously made was left unrevoked by a subsequent promise, so that even a joint tenant trustee where communication is after the will would not generally be bound. A gift to tenants in common gives each of them a distinct and separate share and it is clearly inappropriate to expect that communication to one of them should bind the others whether before or after the execution of the will.

Applying these rules to the question, the secret trustees are joint tenants as there are no words of severance used in the gift. Communication was made to one of them before the will was made and, following the 'inducement' rationale behind the technical statement of the rules in *Re Stead*, the communication will bind both of them. Both James and Sam are bound by the secret trust for £50,000.

However, the subsequent codicil has to be communicated to the secret trustee and accepted in the same way or it will not bind the trustees: *Re Colin Cooper* [1939] Ch 811. Meg's failure to inform either James or Sam will mean that neither of them is bound by the trust as regards the increased legacy and the trust will not affect the further £50,000 which they will take beneficially as joint tenants.

If the legacy had been left to James and Sam as tenants in common, then only James would have been bound by the secret trust of the first gift of £50,000 in Meg's will, as tenants in common are presumed to take distinct and separate shares and a communication to one will never bind another. James therefore holds £25,000 in trust for the Home. As it is clear from the face of the will that there is a trust, however, Sam will not be able to take beneficially and will hold his share on trust for the residuary legatee. As far as the codicil is concerned, neither of them is bound, and each of them will hold the additional sum given by the codicil on trust for the residuary legatee.

Question 6

Alf is a trustee of the Beta Trust which has a 30 per cent shareholding in Gamma Ltd, a pharmaceutical company developing a new drug to stimulate memory, primarily for students taking examinations. In his position as trustee, Alf learned that tests on the drug were indicative of a successful outcome, and he therefore purchased a 25 per cent shareholding in the company himself. He was subsequently elected as a director of the company and has received considerable sums in director's fees.

Shortly after Alf became a director, the company's lease on its factory premises expired and its landlord wanted to sell the reversion for £100,000. The company could not afford this, so Alf and the company's solicitor, Delta, put up £50,000 each and purchased the reversion themselves jointly. They then granted a new lease to the company at a lower rent than under the previous lease.

The company were also interested in a new drug for improving concentration which had been patented. It was agreed between Alf and Delta that Alf would negotiate to buy the patent and, if successful, would receive for his efforts 1 per cent of the purchase price. He negotiated a purchase for £20,000.

Alf began to have doubts about the company's future and decided to sell his shareholding and retire from the directorship. Having retired as a trustee from the Beta Trust six months previously, he sold his shares in Gamma Ltd to the trust for £5,000 below the market value.

The new drugs which the company were developing have recently failed pharmaceutical tests and the company's shares are now almost worthless.

Alf and Delta have received an offer of £150,000 for the freehold of the factory premises and would like to sell it.

Discuss Alf's liability as a fiduciary in the various circumstances.

Commentary

This is a fairly lengthy question involving different fiduciary relationships and different breaches of fiduciary duties. It is the type of question which you should therefore spend some time thinking through, jotting down different points and any relevant cases before embarking on the answer. The risk is, if you do not do this, that you will get to the end and find that there are some points or cases which you have omitted. The question is wide in its scope and requires a fair knowledge of the subject to produce a reasonable answer.

Answer plan

- The rule that a fiduciary must not profit from his or her position has been very strictly applied, even where the fiduciary's acts benefit his or her principal as well as himself and there is no real possibility of conflict of interests

- A trustee who uses his or her position to obtain his or her appointment as a director is accountable for any profit, such as his or her director's fees, unless the appointment is authorised by the trust deed or the dictum of Harman J in *Re Gee* applies
- As a director, Alf is in a fiduciary position to the company and would therefore be accountable for one half of the profit on sale of the premises; it is irrelevant that the company could not have purchased the premises without Alf's contribution
- It is doubtful if Delta can authorise the payment of commission to Alf; in any event, there is a clear conflict of interest, and Alf cannot claim any commission
- If Alf's knowledge of the good prospects for Gamma Ltd can be said to derive from his trusteeship, then he is liable to account to the trust for any profit since knowledge can be regarded as trust property (majority decision of HL in *Boardman* v *Phipps*)
- The sale by Alf to the trust is a breach of the self-dealing rule, which can apply even when he is no longer a trustee, and the transaction will be voidable by the trust

Suggested answer

Equity has consistently demonstrated a harsh attitude to the rule that a fiduciary may not benefit from his position. The rule has been applied even where there is no conflict of interest between the fiduciary and the principal and no evidence of an actual consequent injury to the principal. Indeed, in the House of Lords' case of *Boardman* v *Phipps* [1967] 2 AC 46, the trust, as well as the fiduciary, benefited from the fiduciary's activities, but the strict accountability rule was nevertheless applied. Even in these circumstances, a fiduciary will still be accountable for a profit derived from his fiduciary relationship. The only modification of this strict approach is the Privy Council case of *Queensland Mines* v *Hudson* (1978) 18 ALR 1, which appears to be a decision on the particular merits of the case.

Moreover, a fiduciary relationship is broadly defined and is not restricted to trustee and beneficiary. A director is in a fiduciary position to his company, an agent to his principal, and an employee may also be in a fiduciary relationship to his employer (*Agip (Africa) Ltd* v *Jackson* [1991] Ch 547, CA) although this depends on the nature of the work and the terms of the employment contract (*Nottingham University* v *Fischel* [2000] IRLR 471). In *Reading* v *A-G* [1951] AC 507 it was held that an army officer was in a fiduciary position to the Crown.

A trustee who uses his position to appoint himself as a director of a company is prima facie accountable to the trust for any remuneration he receives as a director: *Re Macadam* [1946] Ch 73. In order to be able to keep his director's fees, Alf would have to show that his appointment as a director would have been made even if the votes attaching to the trust's shares had been used against him (per Harman J in *Re Gee* [1948] Ch 284). So if Alf can show that he would still have been elected as a director, notwithstanding that the voting rights of the Beta Trust's shares had been used to vote against him, then he will be able to keep his director's fees. Otherwise, he will be prima facie accountable to the Trust for them. He would also be able to retain his director's fees if authorised in the trust instrument: *Re Llewellin* [1949] Ch 225.

If the trust property includes a lease, a trustee to whom the lease is renewed (*Keech* v *Sandford* (1726) Sel Cas Ch 61), or who purchases a reversion on the lease (*Protheroe* v *Protheroe* [1968] 1 WLR 519, CA), will become a constructive trustee of the lease or reversion for the beneficiaries. In *Protheroe*, a husband and wife were co-owners of a leasehold interest in their matrimonial home. They separated and the husband subsequently purchased the reversion on the lease. It was held that this became trust property in which his wife also had an interest. As a director of Gamma Ltd, Alf is in a fiduciary position to the company and would therefore hold one-half of the reversion on the lease as a constructive trustee for the company. He would similarly be accountable for one-half of any profit made on its sale. It is irrelevant that the company itself could not have purchased the reversion, or that the company itself benefited from the transaction. In *Regal (Hastings) Ltd* v *Gulliver* [1942] 1 All ER 378, HL, directors purchased shares, which the company could not afford to purchase, in order to enable the company to take a lease of a cinema and subsequently to sell it with other property owned by the company at a profit. They were nevertheless held accountable for their profits as they had acquired their shares through their fiduciary position. Delta, as the company's solicitor, would also be in a fiduciary position and similarly accountable.

In *Guinness plc* v *Saunders* [1990] 2 AC 663 a director who received an unauthorised fee of 0.2 per cent of the value of a takeover bid was held by the House of Lords to be a constructive trustee of this for the company. Neither was he able to claim payment for his services on a *quantum meruit* as he had created a conflict of interest between himself (in whose interest it was to pay a high price) and the company. Assuming that Delta was not authorised to award director's remuneration, the agreement between Delta and Alf would not be binding on the company, and any commission would be a profit derived from Alf's fiduciary position as a director. He would therefore not be able to claim any such commission. As in *Guinness plc* v *Saunders*, any such agreement would also create a conflict of interest between Alf and the company in that Alf has an interest in purchasing for a high price and the company in purchasing for a low price. He would similarly not have any claim for work undertaken in this connection on a *quantum meruit*.

The case of *Boardman* v *Phipps* [1967] 2 AC 46, HL, indicates that a trustee or fiduciary who uses information obtained as a result of his fiduciary position to make a profit will be a constructive trustee of that profit for the trust. If Alf's knowledge were the reason for his acquisition of his 25 per cent shareholding and this resulted in profits, he might be accountable for these. If it could be shown that Alf had serious doubts about the company's future when he sold the shares to the Trust, this would amount to a breach of his fiduciary duty and he might be made liable for the subsequent loss to the Trust.

The rule in *Ex parte Lacey* (1802) 6 Ves 625, which is strictly applied, precludes a trustee from purchasing trust property, and this applies even after a trustee has retired: *Wright* v *Morgan* [1926] AC 788. A trustee's liability does not necessarily cease on his retirement: he or his estate will remain liable for breaches of trust committed during his trusteeship. The rule in *Ex parte Lacey* applies to any dealing between the trustee in his personal capacity and in his capacity as trustee. In *Bentley* v *Craven* (1853) 18 Beav 75, it was held that an agent employed to purchase sugar for a company could not sell to the company sugar he had purchased himself, even at the market price, unless his interest was declared and accepted by the company. In that case, Romilly MR said (obiter) that the same principle would apply to other fiduciary relationships, including a dealing by a trustee with a trust. The transaction necessarily puts the agent in a position of conflict with his principal as to price. Unless there is a full disclosure as to the agent's interest, which is accepted by the principal, the principal may either repudiate the transaction or claim any profit which the agent makes on it. It is quite possible here, therefore, that the Trust could repudiate the sale to them and claim back the purchase price. It is irrelevant that it was an advantageous sale to the Trust at the time when it was made.

Question 7

The issue on this appeal concerns only the accessory liability principle. Different considerations apply to the two heads of liability. Recipient liability is restitution-based, accessory liability is not. (Lord Nicholls in *Royal Brunei Airlines Sdn Bhd* v *Tan* [1995] 2 AC 378, HL.)

Explain and discuss the basis of liability of a third party who deals with, or receives, property in breach of a fiduciary obligation.

Commentary

As indicated in the introduction to this chapter, the criteria for imposing personal liability on third parties who are involved in a breach of trust or breach of fiduciary duty (accessory liability), or who receive property in breach of trust (recipient liability), is one of the more complex areas of equity. As if this were not bad enough, the cases on third party liability often involve complicated frauds, so that the principles are often extremely difficult to apply.

In *Royal Brunei Airlines Sdn Bhd* v *Tan* [1995] 2 AC 378, the Privy Council established that the basis of accessory liability is dishonesty. More recently, the meaning of dishonesty in this context has been clarified by the House of Lords in *Twinsectra Ltd* v *Yardley* [2002] 2 AC 164, which also puts it beyond doubt that the *Brunei* case represents English law.

The basis for recipient liability, however, remains unclear, and a specific decision of the Supreme Court is urgently needed to resolve the different approaches of the lower courts.

The case law still predominantly favours a knowledge-based liability (hence the usual description of 'knowing receipt'), but dishonesty or unconscionability has each been proposed instead. There are indications in Lord Millett's speech in the *Twinsectra* case that the courts might not be averse to an application of restitutionary principles, so that there would be strict liability for beneficial receipt but the recipient would have a change-of-position defence. Dicta of Lord Nicholls in *Criterion Properties plc v Stratford UK Properties LLC* **[2004] 1 WLR 1846, HL** (which did not itself involve knowing receipt) support a restitutionary approach, but cannot as yet be regarded as decisive. It should also be noted that, even though the claim for knowing receipt is a personal one, the process of tracing may need to be applied to establish that there was a receipt by the defendant. Tracing is required where it is alleged, not that the receipt was of the claimant's property itself, but of its traceable product.

For further reading, see Ewan McKendrick in 55 MLR 377, and a case note by Desmond Ryan on *Barlow Clowes International Ltd v Eurotrust International Ltd* (2006) 70 Conv 188.

Answer plan

- Accessory liability
  - law laid down in *Brunei* (PC) and clarified in *Twinsectra* (HL)
  - must be a breach of trust or breach of fiduciary duty
  - third party must have assisted
  - third party must be dishonest (test in *Twinsectra* clarified in *Eurotrust* (PC))
- Recipient liability
  - must be a breach of trust or breach of fiduciary duty
  - must be *beneficial* receipt
  - competing tests:
    - knowledge (and what categories within *Baden Delvaux*?)
    - dishonesty (*Dubai Aluminium*, CA)
    - unconscionability (*Akindele*, CA)
    - restitutionary (favoured in *Brunei*, and obiter in *Twinsectra* and *Criterion* (HL))

Suggested answer

As the quotation from the *Royal Brunei* case makes clear, the basis for imposing personal liability on a third party to a breach of trust differs according to whether the third party merely assisted in the breach (accessory liability), or received trust property in breach (recipient liability). It is appropriate to consider each of them in turn.

Accessory liability

Delivering the advice of the Privy Council in the *Brunei* case, Lord Nicholls clarified the ingredients required for accessory liability. Although as a decision of the Privy Council the advice of the Board in the *Brunei* case was not strictly binding in English law, Lord Nicholls's statement of the law has since been accepted, and further explained, by the House of Lords in *Twinsectra Ltd* v *Yardley* [2002] 2 AC 164. The present law relating to accessory liability is therefore to be found principally in these two cases.

The first requirement for accessory liability is that there should be a breach of trust. The trust may include a resulting trust (*Twinsectra Ltd* v *Yardley* [2002] 2 AC 164), or a constructive trust (*Competitive Insurance Co.* v *Davies Investments* [1975] 1 WLR 1240). It is now recognised that a thief becomes a constructive trustee of the property stolen: *Westdeutsche Landesbank Girozentrale* v *Islington* LBC [1996] AC 669, at p. 705. The term 'trust' is also here used in a broad sense, so that it suffices if property is held subject to a fiduciary duty, such as where a principal's property is held by an agent, or where a director misapplies the company's assets (e.g., *Polly Peck International* v *Nadir (No. 2)* [1992] 4 All ER 769).

The breach of trust does not have to involve dishonesty on the part of the trustee or fiduciary: *Brunei*, at p. 392. Lord Selbourne's classic statement in *Barnes* v *Addy* (1874) 9 Ch App 244, that there needed to be a 'dishonest and fraudulent design on the part of the trustees' was therefore overruled on this point. In *Eaves* v *Hickson* (1861) 30 Beav 136, for instance, personal liability was imposed on a third party who had procured a breach of trust, even though the trustees had acted honestly.

Secondly, the defendant must assist in the breach of trust or breach of fiduciary duty. Assistance could involve actually inducing the breach, as in *Eaves* v *Hickson*, where a father induced the trustees to pay the trust property to his children by producing to them a forged marriage certificate that indicated that the children were legitimate. In many cases, however, the assistance is rendered by the trustees' or fiduciaries' agents or employees. In the *Brunei* case itself, the managing director was held to have satisfied this ingredient by misapplying the money of the company which he controlled. However, this ingredient was not satisfied by a spouse who merely sat next to her husband on several car journeys which he made to Switzerland carrying stolen property: *Brinks Ltd* v *Abu-Saleh (No. 3)* [1996] CLC 133.

Thirdly, there must be dishonesty on the defendant's part. In his classic nineteenth-century formulation in *Barnes* v *Addy*, Lord Selbourne has referred to assisting 'with knowledge', and there had been many subsequent attempts to elaborate on what was meant by knowledge, culminating in a five-fold classification suggested by Peter Gibson J in *Baden Delvaux* v *Société Générale* [1993] 1 WLR 509, at pp. 575–6. In the *Brunei* case, however, Lord Nicholls expressly rejected knowledge as the substantive ingredient for accessory liability, and he said that the courts ought to disregard the categories of knowledge in *Baden Delvaux*. Instead, his Lordship said that the requisite ingredient was dishonesty.

Whilst the *Brunei* case has clarified the law on what is now called 'dishonest assistance', the courts have since had to deal with the problem of what precisely is meant by dishonesty. In *Twinsectra Ltd* v *Yardley*, Lord Hutton mentioned three possible standards that can be applied to determine whether a person has acted dishonestly. First, there is a purely subjective standard ('the Robin Hood test'), whereby a person is only regarded as dishonest if he transgresses his own standard of honesty, even if that standard is contrary to that of a reasonable and honest person. This standard has been rejected by the courts: see, e.g., *Walker* v *Stones* [2001] QB 902, CA, at p. 939 (Sir Christopher Slade). Secondly, Lord Hutton said there is a purely objective standard (the objective test), 'whereby a person acts dishonestly if his conduct is dishonest by the ordinary standards of reasonable and honest people, even if he does not realise this'. Thirdly, there is a standard that combines an objective test and a subjective test (the combined test), 'which requires that ... it be established that the defendant's conduct was dishonest by the ordinary standards of reasonable and honest people, and that he himself realised that by those standards his conduct was dishonest.'

Lord Hutton rejected the first test, as it would enable a man to set his own standard of honesty. He also rejected the second test as being inconsistent with what had been said in *Brunei*; and he further noted that a finding of dishonesty, even in a civil case, is a grave finding, especially against a professional person, such as a solicitor. It would be unsatisfactory if a person could be treated as dishonest when he was not actually aware that what he was doing would be regarded by honest men as dishonest. Lord Hutton decided that the correct test was the combined test, and all their other Lordships supported this view, apart from Lord Millett who dissented on this aspect of the case, preferring the objective test. Delivering the advice of the Privy Council in *Barlow Clowes International Ltd* v *Eurotrust International Ltd* [2006] 1 All ER 333, Lord Hoffmann explained that Lord Hutton's combined test did not require that the defendant should have had reflections about what normally accepted standards of behaviour were; Lord Hutton meant only that the defendant's knowledge of the transaction had to be such as to render his participation contrary to acceptable standards of honest conduct.

In *Twinsectra*, Lord Hutton said that the combined test was similar to that for dishonesty in criminal law in *R* v *Ghosh* [1982] QB 1053. A finding of dishonesty is essentially a finding of fact, and in *United Mizrahi Bank Ltd* v *Doherty* [1998] 2 All ER 230 on an appeal to the Privy Council, the Privy Council set aside the finding of no dishonesty by the Court of Appeal and reinstated the trial judge's finding on the basis that the trial judge had heard the witnesses and was more able to make a finding of fact.

It would probably be too hopeful to consider that *Twinsectra* is going to be the last word on the ingredient of dishonesty. The pervasive difficulty is that, since it is impossible for the court to look into the defendant's mind, and defendants not only rarely admit dishonesty but usually seek to cover it up, the subjective element of dishonesty in the combined test is in the vast majority of cases an inference that the court draws from what are often very complex sets of circumstances. This may explain why, although knowledge was rejected as a substantive ingredient in *Brunei*, an examination of the defendant's knowledge proved so attractive in many of the earlier decisions: if the defendant knew the essential facts of what was going on, then it might easily be inferred that he must have realised what was going on. Even after *Brunei* and *Twinsectra*, the finding of the judge on the matter of subjective dishonesty (as part of the combined test) may still often turn on inferences drawn from what the defendant knew.

Recipient liability

Under general equitable principles, property disposed of in breach of trust remains trust property in the hands of every recipient except one who can establish the defence of a bona fide purchaser for value without notice. If, however, the recipient has in the meantime disposed of the property, the beneficiaries may seek to impose on the recipient a personal liability for the value of the property he received. Even if the recipient still retains the property, if it has fallen in value since its receipt, the beneficiaries may, having recovered the property itself, seek to make the recipient personally liable for the difference in value. Equity has for long recognised that a personal action lies against the recipient in such cases, but the precise basis for liability remains unclear.

First, there must be a receipt by the defendant of property disposed of in breach of trust or in breach of fiduciary duty, and it is not necessary for such breach to be dishonest or fraudulent. The defendant must however receive the property beneficially. The effect of this is that persons who receive property merely as agents cannot be made liable under this category of liability, but only for dishonest assistance. The rationale for this distinction would seem to rest on the notion that a receipt-based action is essentially restitution-based, as Lord Nicholls indicated in the *Brunei* case: the defendant has been unjustly enriched by the receipt and so should have to make good its value to the claimant. On this reasoning, an agent who receives property for transmission to a third party cannot be considered to have been unjustly enriched merely because the property at some stage passed through his or her hands.

Many of the cases after *Brunei*, however, show that, whilst paying lip service to the notion that recipient liability is restitution-based, the courts have mostly continued to treat the liability as essentially fault-based. There is substantial authority for the view that liability depends on the defendant's knowledge of the breach, and for this reason the liability is often expressed to be that for 'knowing receipt'. In *Baden Delvaux*, Peter Gibson J referred to five categories of knowledge: (i) actual knowledge; (ii) wilfully shutting one's eyes to the obvious ('Nelsonian knowledge'); (iii) wilfully and recklessly failing to make such inquiries as an honest and reasonable person would make (what Hayton calls 'naughty knowledge'); (iv) knowledge of circumstances that would indicate the facts to an honest and reasonable persons; and (v) knowledge of circumstances that would put an honest and reasonable man on inquiry.

It seems to be clear that knowledge within the first three categories is sufficient; but there is disagreement whether liability can be imposed where the defendant's knowledge falls only within category (iv) or (v). In *Cowan de Groot Properties* v *Eagle Trust* [1992] 4 All ER 700, Knox J treated any of these five types of knowledge as sufficient to establish knowing receipt; and there were dicta to this effect in the earlier case of *Belmont Finance Corp.* v *Williams Furniture (No. 2)* [1980] 1 All ER 393, CA.

In *Re Montagu's Settlement* [1987] Ch 264, however, Megarry V-C considered that only knowledge within categories (i)–(iii) sufficed. In that case he held that a beneficial recipient of certain chattels was not personally liable for knowing receipt: even if he had at one time been aware of the terms of the trusts, he had since forgotten what the position was, and had received and disposed of them as the result of 'an honest muddle'. Merely being aware of the possibility of a claim that might well be disputed was held not to amount to knowledge in *Carl Zeiss Stiftung* v *Herbert Smith (No. 2)* [1969] 2 Ch 276.

These alternative positions were explained in *Eagle Trust* v *SBS Securities* [1993] 1 WLR 484, where Vinelott J held that liability could be established under any of the five heads where the receipt occurred (as in *Re Montagu*) in a non-commercial transaction. If, however, the receipt occurred in a commercial transaction (as where an agent used part of the funds received to pay his own bill for services) the recipient liability required proof of knowledge under categories (i)–(iii) only.

The first three categories of knowledge in *Baden Delvaux*, involving as they do a consciousness of wrongdoing on the defendant's part, involve some want of probity or culpability, and the Court of Appeal in *Dubai Aluminium Co. Ltd* v *Salaam* [2000] 3 WLR 910, considered that the substantive ingredient for knowing receipt, like that for assistance, was no longer knowledge but dishonesty. At about the same time, in *BCCI (Overseas) Ltd* v *Akindele* [2000] 3 WLR 1423, Nourse LJ in the Court of Appeal expressed the view that there was no single test of knowledge; the test was rather whether the recipient's state of knowledge was such as to make it unconscionable for him to retain the benefit of the receipt. Unconscionability, however, is an ill-defined concept to form the basis for liability for knowing receipt, and would surely open the floodgates for litigation.

The appeal to the House of Lords in *Twinsectra* did not involve knowing receipt, but Lord Millett treated constructive notice (which would seem to include heads (iv) and (v) of *Baden Delvaux*) as sufficient, although his Lordship opined that even that might not be necessary if liability were the same as in other cases of restitution, i.e., strict, but subject to a change of position defence. This view is consistent with what Millett J had expressed earlier in *El Ajou* v *Dollar Land Holdings* [1993] 3 All ER 717. In similar vein, but writing extra-judicially, Lord Nicholls has suggested that 'restitutionary liability, applicable regardless of fault, but subject to a defence of change of position, would be a better-tailored response to the underlying mischief of misapplied property than personal liability which is exclusively fault-based': Nicholls, in *Restitution—Past, Present and Future* (Cornish, ed.), Hart Publishing, 1998, at p. 231. The adoption of such an approach would mean that innocent volunteers (like some of the recipient charities in *Re Diplock* [1948] Ch 465, CA) who cannot establish the defence of change of position, would become personally liable. Lord Nicholls expressed similar views in his speech in *Criterion Properties plc* v *Stratford UK Properties LLC* [2004] 1 WLR 1846, HL. Both Lord Nicholls and Lord Scott (with whose speech the other members of the House of Lords agreed) criticised the Court of Appeal in *Akindele* for having treated the case before them as one of 'knowing receipt', when it should have been treated as one of 'want of authority'. All these comments were, however, obiter, as *Criterion* was not a case of knowing receipt.

In the absence of a clarification of the principles by the Supreme Court in a case directly concerned with knowing receipt, the basis for the imposition for liability for knowing receipt remains uncertain and unsatisfactory. There seems to be a growing recognition amongst commentators that this is an area of law that needs to be integrated into general principles of restitution, but whether such development can be effected by the courts alone or requires legislative intervention remains to be seen.

Question 8

Wynken and Nod are the two partners in a firm of solicitors, Blynken & Co. Wynken acts for the Fishnet Trust. On the instructions of the sole trustee of the Trust, Sleepy, Wynken paid out £30,000 to Chloë, believing her to be a beneficiary under the Trust and properly entitled to be paid this sum. Had Wynken looked at the trust deed in the firm's strong-room, however, he would have realised that she was neither a beneficiary under the Trust nor a person entitled to any payment. Chloë, who was Sleepy's daughter, did not realise that the sum was paid to her in breach of trust, and she spent it all on a luxury round-the-world cruise.

(a) Consider the liability to the beneficiaries of the Fishnet Trust of (i) Wynken; (ii) Nod; and (iii) Chloë.

AND

(b) Explain whether your answers to (i) and (ii) might differ if it were found that Sleepy's appointment as trustee had not been properly effected.

 Commentary

An answer to this question requires an application to specific circumstances of the principles outlined in the Suggested answer to question 7. The equitable requirements for imposing personal liability on an accessory to a breach of trust or a breach of fiduciary duty were laid down in *Royal Brunei Airlines Sdn Bhd v Tan* [1995] 2 AC 378, and were clarified by the House of Lords in *Twinsectra Ltd v Yardley* [2002] 2 AC 164. Neither case, however, involved the personal liability of a person who received property under a breach of trust. The precise requirements of recipient liability are regrettably uncertain; moreover, since liability will depend upon a detailed analysis of the facts, the candidate cannot be expected to reach any definite conclusion in a problem question. What you can be expected to do, however, is to demonstrate a knowledge of the principles involved, and to suggest how they might be applied to the facts of the problem. This is a difficult area, and the same observations might be made as regards question 7—it is not a topic for the faint-hearted!

Answer plan

(a) **(i)** Liability of W depends upon his dishonesty
- *Royal Brunei Airlines* and *Twinsectra*

(ii) vicariously liable for W's acts if W acting in ordinary course of business
- *Dubai Aluminium*; **Partnership Act 1890, s. 10**

(iii) No proprietary action to recover the money from C (since spent)
- Does C incur recipient liability?
  - may depend on her constructive knowledge, on unconscionability, or on restitutionary principles

(b) • If W realised that S was not properly appointed:
- W is acting as a trustee *de son tort*
- N would not be liable
- (not part of a solicitor's business to act as the trustee of an express trust)

• If W believed the trustee was properly appointed:
- W's liability turns on dishonest assistance as in (a)(i)
- N's liability as a partner is as in (a)(ii)

Suggested answer

(a)(i) Wynken would be personally liable to the beneficiaries of the Fishnet Trust if he has dishonestly assisted in a breach of trust in accordance with the principles for accessory liability laid down in *Royal Brunei Airlines Sdn Bhd* v *Tan* [1995] 2 AC 378, as clarified by the House of Lords in *Twinsectra Ltd* v *Yardley* [2002] 2 AC 164. Although Sleepy might have been acting dishonestly in seeking to obtain a payment for his daughter, Wynken's liability does not require dishonesty on the part of the trustee: *Brunei*, at p. 392. It must, however, be shown that Wynken was dishonest. In the *Twinsectra* case, Lord Hutton, with whose speech the majority of their Lordships agreed, held that the test for dishonesty in this context was a combined objective and subjective test. This test is that the defendant's conduct must be shown to be dishonest by the ordinary standards of reasonable and honest people, and that the defendant must himself have realised that his conduct was dishonest by those standards. Whether Wynken is dishonest is therefore a matter of evidence; but merely failing to refer to the trust instrument before making the payment, whilst perhaps amounting to negligence, does not itself indicate dishonesty.

(ii) Even if Wynken is personally liable for dishonest assistance, his partner, Nod, is not necessarily also liable. If Nod knew what Wynken was doing and stood by, doing nothing to prevent Wynken from assisting in the breach of trust, the beneficiaries might seek to make Nod also liable for dishonest assistance. It could be argued, however, that merely standing by while Wynken acts does not itself amount to 'assistance'.

The beneficiaries might seek to recover from Nod on the ground that he is liable in equity for his partner's acts. In *Mara v Browne* [1896] 1 Ch 199, at p. 208, Lord Herschell had stated obiter that 'it is not within the scope of the implied authority of a partner ... [in a solicitor's] business that he should so act as to make himself a constructive trustee, and thereby subject his partners to the same liability.' In *Re Bell's Indenture* [1980] 1 WLR 1217, this dictum was apparently interpreted to mean that, when a partner in a firm of solicitors incurred liability for dishonestly assisting in a breach of trust, his co-partner could not as a matter of law be liable, since such an act was necessarily outside the scope of his implied authority. In *Dubai Aluminium Co. Ltd v Salaam* [2003] 1 All ER 97, however, their Lordships disapproved of this interpretation and overruled *Re Bell's Indenture*. Lord Millett suggested that Lord Herschell's dictum referred only to trustees *de son tort*, these being persons who, without being appointed, nevertheless take it upon themselves to act as trustees. Lord Millett said that the expression 'constructive trustee' was best abandoned in the context of liability for dishonest assistance, and that it was more appropriate to refer to the defendant as being merely 'accountable in equity'.

Under the Partnership Act 1890, s. 10, the firm is liable where a person suffers loss 'by any wrongful act or omission of any partner in the ordinary course of the business of the firm'. In the *Dubai Aluminium* case, the House of Lords held that the phrase 'wrongful act or omission' was not confined to common law torts but included a fault-based equitable wrong such as liability for dishonest assistance in a breach of trust. On this interpretation, Nod's liability as a partner depends on the ordinary principles of partnership law. It is therefore a matter of evidence whether, in paying out money on the instructions of Sleepy in breach of trust, Wynken was acting in the ordinary course of the firm's business. As the act in question was performed by Wynken in his capacity as a solicitor, it would be difficult to argue that it was not also performed in the ordinary course of the firm's business. Assuming this to be the case, if Wynken is liable for dishonest assistance, Nod is vicariously liable.

(iii) As Chloë did not give consideration for the £30,000 paid to her, the beneficiaries could have traced it into her hands (or into its product in her hands) if she still retained it. As Chloë has spent the money, however, the beneficiaries cannot bring any proprietary action to recover it from her. The beneficiaries will be able to bring a personal action against her to recover the equivalent value, however, if they can establish the ingredients for recipient liability. The initial requirement is met, as Chloë received the money beneficially and as a result of a breach of trust. Unfortunately, the courts have expressed different views about what else is required for recipient liability.

In *Brunei*, Lord Nicholls said that recipient liability is restitution-based, and his Lordship expressed a similar view in dicta in *Criterion Properties plc* v *Stratford UK*

Properties LLC [2004] 1 WLR 1846, HL. If, therefore, the general principles of restitution were to apply to this type of liability, Chloë would be strictly liable as a beneficial recipient; but, as she has already spent the money, if she is an innocent volunteer she would have the defence of change of position. This analysis met with the approval of Lord Millett in the *Twinsectra* case, but his Lordship recognised that English law had not yet developed in that way. Where property is wrongly distributed under a will, those entitled under it may bring a personal action against the recipients, even if the latter are innocent volunteers: *Re Diplock* [1948] Ch 465, affirmed *Ministry of Health* v *Simpson* [1951] AC 251. The action *in personam* resembles what might now be termed a restitutionary claim based on the fact of receipt, and available even against an innocent volunteer. It appears, however, that the *Re Diplock* action *in personam* is limited to claims against recipients of assets wrongly distributed during the course of administration of an estate: ibid., at pp. 265–6 (Lord Simonds). If this limitation still applies today, such action cannot be brought against Chloë, who receives property wrongly distributed under an *inter vivos* trust. The beneficiaries would therefore have to content themselves with a claim based on accessory liability.

Most authorities hold that liability depends on the recipient's knowledge, but even these are in disagreement about what amounts to knowledge. Some are prepared to accept any of the five categories of knowledge set out in *Baden Delvaux* as sufficient: *Cowan de Groot Properties* v *Eagle Trust* [1992] 4 All ER 700; *Belmont Finance Corp.* v *Williams Furniture (No. 2)* [1980] 1 All ER 393, CA; and dicta of Lord Millett in *Twinsectra*. Others require knowledge within the first three categories only: *Re Montagu's Settlement* [1987] Ch 264.

In *Eagle Trust* v *SBS Securities* [1993] 1 WLR 484, it was held that liability under any of the five heads sufficed where the receipt occurred (as in *Re Montagu*) in a non-commercial transaction. If *Eagle Trust* is applied, then as Chloë was not a commercial recipient, her liability would effectively depend on whether she had constructive notice of the breach of trust. More precisely, her liability would turn on whether she had knowledge within category (iv) of *Baden Delvaux* (knowledge of circumstances that would indicate the facts to an honest and reasonable person), or category (v) (knowledge of circumstances that would put an honest and reasonable person on inquiry).

Other views have, however, been expressed judicially. In *Dubai Aluminium Co. Ltd* v *Salaam* [2000] 3 WLR 910, the Court of Appeal considered the substantive ingredient for knowing receipt to be dishonesty, not knowledge. In *BCCI (Overseas) Ltd* v *Akindele* [2000] 3 WLR 1423, Nourse LJ said that the test was rather whether the recipient's state of knowledge was such as to make it unconscionable for him to retain the benefit of the receipt.

If the correct test is dishonesty or knowledge within the first three heads of *Baden Delvaux* only (all of which seem to involve some consciousness of wrongdoing), Chloë's lack of awareness of her receipt's being in breach of trust would save her from incurring recipient liability. If, however, the correct test is knowledge within any of the five heads of *Baden Delvaux*, or merely unconscionability, then the question provides insufficient facts for any determination of her liability to be made.

(b) If Sleepy's appointment as trustee had not been properly effected, Wynken could not have been acting as an agent. In *Blythe* v *Fladgate* [1891] 1 Ch 327, Smith, a partner in a firm of solicitors continued to deal with trust funds after the death of the sole trustee. He was held liable as an intermeddler (a trustee *de son tort*), and his co-partners were also held liable on this basis. If in the problem Wynken realised that he was effectively acting as principal, he may be liable as a trustee *de son tort*, in effect as a *de facto* trustee (which latter expression Lord Millett in the *Dubai Aluminium* case thought preferable today). If Wynken were liable as a *de facto* trustee, it would appear that Nod would not be liable, since Lord Millett thought that it was still not within the ordinary scope of a solicitor's practice to act as a trustee of an express trust. These would be the precise circumstances in which Lord Herschell's dictum in *Mara* v *Browne* would apply.

If, however, Wynken believed that the trustee had been properly appointed, so that he did not realise that he was himself acting as a principal, it would be difficult to characterise him as a *de facto* trustee, since he would not be purporting to act as a trustee. In these circumstances, his liability would depend upon his having dishonestly assisted Sleepy in the breach of trust as considered in (i), and the liability of Nod would be the same as previously considered in (ii).

Further reading

Cohabitation: The Financial Consequences of Relationship Breakdown—A Consultation Paper (Law Commission Consultation Paper No. 179, Part 2, 2006).

Cohabitation: The Financial Consequences of Relationship Breakdown (Law Com No. 307, 2007).

Corporate fraud, investigation and asset recovery update, Herbert Smith solicitors' newsletter, July 2007, pp. 3–5.

Rotherham, C., *Proprietary Remedies in Context*, Hart Publishing, 2002.

Sharing Homes: A Discussion Paper (Law Com No. 278, 2002).

10

Estoppel

Introduction

If you have already studied the Law of Contract, you will have come across promissory estoppel. Proprietary estoppel, although similar, is a development of equity which is much wider than promissory estoppel and can create new substantive rights. Proprietary estoppel remains a contested area with two House of Lords' decisions, *Yeoman's Row Management* v *Cobbe* [2008] UKHL 55 and *Thorner* v *Major* [2009] UKHL 18 following on from the innovative application of estoppel to limit a person's testamentary freedom by the Court of Appeal in *Gillett* v *Holt* [2001] Ch 210. All of these cases have generated an extensive discussion about the criteria and application of proprietary estoppel in academic circles.

The Law Commission Report, which led to the passing of the **Law of Property (Miscellaneous Provisions) Act 1989**, abolished the equitable doctrine of part performance. It was envisaged that the doctrine of estoppel would take its place, and there have now been two or three cases where this doctrine has been applied to prevent a contract or deed from being declared void for failure to comply with statutory formalities. However, each case needs to be carefully examined on its facts as the House of Lords made clear in *Yeoman's Row Management*.

Estoppel cases are necessarily very varied in their results, but there is a helpful judgment of Robert Walker LJ in *Jennings* v *Rice* [2003] 1 P & CR 8 (referred to in the questions) suggesting guidelines for the courts as to how they should satisfy an estoppel.

Because estoppel can give rise to a proprietary interest, it is of considerable importance in land law where it may be necessary to determine whether a third party will be bound or not by an estoppel interest. This chapter has not considered this aspect of the subject as this is usually dealt with in Land Law. Question 4 of Chapter 16 also includes an estoppel interest.

There is a lot of case law, a book and a number of academic articles written on the subject: see the Further reading section at the end of this chapter.

Question 1

... once the elements of proprietary estoppel are established an equity arises. The value of that equity will depend upon all the circumstances including the expectation and the detriment. The task of the court is to do justice. The most essential requirement is that there must be proportionality between the expectation and the detriment. (Aldous LJ in *Jennings* v *Rice* [2003] 1 P & CR 8.)

Explain how the courts have sought to do justice in satisfying an estoppel.

 Commentary

The Court of Appeal has attempted in ***Jennings* v *Rice*** to define the limits of a remedy to be awarded in estoppel cases. The cases are of course enormously varied, and the task is not easy. In his judgment, Robert Walker LJ (as he then was) refers to two articles on the subject which contain 'a full and illuminating discussion of this area'. They are 'Estoppel and the protection of expectations' by Elizabeth Cooke (1997) 17 LS 258 and 'The remedial discretion in proprietary estoppel' by Simon Gardner (1999) 115 LQR 438, and these articles would be good reading for coursework on this subject. Elizabeth Cooke puts forward an interesting proposition that the remedy for estoppel is nearly always satisfaction of the claimant's expectations, and Simon Gardner considers four different hypotheses upon which the remedy could be based.

For further reading on this subject, see the section at the end of this chapter.

 Answer plan

- The nature of estoppel and its essential requirements
- Width of the remedies which have been given to satisfy an estoppel
- Estoppels where there is no ideally tailored proprietary remedy, and where money payments have been awarded instead of a proprietary remedy
- Identification of cases where the circumstances are very close to a contract between the parties, and other cases where the statements, expectations and detriment may all be vague and differing
- The judgment of Robert Walker LJ (as he then was) in ***Jennings* v *Rice***, where he considers proportionality in relation to expectation and detriment
- Impact of House of Lords' decision in ***Thorner* v *Major*** [2009] UKHL 18

Suggested answer

Estoppel is a doctrine of equity which has been applied to a great variety of informal dealings in order to do justice. Although at one time it was limited to situations where the five *probanda* of Fry J laid down in *Willmott v Barber* (1880) 15 ChD 96 applied, it was held to have a much wider application by Oliver J in *Taylors Fashions Ltd* v *Liverpool Victoria Trustees Co. Ltd* [1982] QB 133. The essential requirements for an estoppel to arise since then have been that a statement is made by one person as to their intention on which another person acts to their detriment in such a way that it would be unjust to allow the person who has made the statement to renege upon it.

The doctrine is extremely wide and has been applied to a variety of situations. The interests granted to satisfy an estoppel are usually (although not always) proprietary. They have included a right in the nature of an easement (*Crabb v Arun DC* [1976] Ch 179, where Scarman LJ sought, as a remedy for an estoppel, 'the minimum equity to do justice', *E. R. Ives Investment Ltd v High* [1967] 2 QB 379), a licence (*Inwards* v *Baker* [1965] 2 QB 29, *Matharu v Matharu* (1994) 68 P & CR 93), the full fee simple (*Pascoe v Turner* [1979] 1 WLR 431), a long lease (*Griffiths v Williams* (1978) 248 EG 947) and where it was applied prospectively to limit a person's testamentary freedom (*Gillett v Holt* [2001] Ch 210). However, in *Powell v Benny* [2008] P & CR D31, a sum of money was awarded. Estoppel was given proprietary recognition in the Land Registration Act 2002, s. 116.

Proprietary estoppel, unlike promissory estoppel, may be used to found an action and is not confined to setting up a defence. It is not, like promissory estoppel, limited by the terms of a contract, and the courts have jealously guarded their very wide discretion in applying it, taking into account any unconscionability and the circumstances of the parties. The statement giving rise to the estoppel may be vague and uncertain as to what was actually intended and the detriment may be conduct over a number of years; these factors mean that the courts often have difficulty in finding a just solution. In some cases it has been impossible to award an interest which exactly achieves what was required to reflect the estoppel, and the courts have awarded an interest which most nearly approximates to it. Thus, in *Ungurian v Lesnoff* [1990] Ch 206 a life tenancy under the Settled Land Act 1925 was awarded to a cohabitee, although it gave her the very wide powers of disposition under the Act, and in *Griffiths* v *Williams* a lease at a nominal rent for life. In other cases, the courts have exercised their discretion to err on the side of generosity because of the possibly difficult behaviour of one of the parties (as in *Pascoe v Turner*, where, on the expenditure of less than £700 on a house, a cohabitee was awarded the full fee simple), or have refused to make any award where the circumstances of the parties had changed so that this would have caused hardship to the party who had made the statement (*Sledmore v Dalby* (1996) 72 P & CR 196, where it was held that ten years' rent-free occupation of a house which the plaintiff had improved had satisfied the estoppel).

In some cases, the courts have taken the view that a monetary payment is the best way of satisfying the estoppel. In *Wayling v Jones* (1995) 69 P & CR 170 the property which the plaintiff had been promised would be left to him on death had already been sold, so that the only possibility of compensating him was by a money payment from the estate. In *Baker v Baker* [1993] 2 FLR 247 the relationship between the father, who had made a substantial contribution to the purchase of his son's house, and his son and his wife had broken down, so that the only practicable way of satisfying the estoppel was by a money payment. In *Dodsworth v Dodsworth* (1973) 228 EG 1115 where the promisees had spent £700 improving a house in which they were told they could live for as long as they liked, they were allowed to remain there until the expenditure had been reimbursed. In *Campbell v Griffin* [2001] EWCA Civ 990, where a similar promise was made, the court considered it preferable to make a money award rather than to encumber the property with a life tenant, and based this on a rough estimate of what the claimant's services would have cost the deceased promisor if she had had to pay for them. A money award was also deemed appropriate in *Jennings v Rice* [2003] 1 P & CR 8 where the value of the equity resulting from the estoppel was found to be less than half the value of the house which the plaintiff claimed to have been promised.

Given the wide discretion which the courts have applied in the cases, it is hardly surprising that Weeks J remarked in *Taylor v Dickens* [1998] 1 FLR 806 at first instance that in estoppel cases one might as well 'issue every civil judge with a portable palm tree', and that equity was in danger again of becoming as long as the Chancellor's foot. Whilst a discretion is desirable to do justice in a particular case, it creates problems for lawyers who have to advise their client on the merits, or otherwise, of their claim. For this reason, the judgment of Robert Walker LJ in *Jennings v Rice* is to be welcomed as an attempt to lay down some guidelines for the courts. Walker LJ said that the courts cannot exercise a totally unfettered discretion, which might anyway vary from one judge to another. He considered that any strict rules for the application of a discretion would be inappropriate, but that nevertheless, 'The need to search for the right principles cannot be avoided'. He conceded that the search would be difficult because of the unlimited variety of factual situations which could give rise to an estoppel.

Robert Walker LJ observed that in these contractual cases where the promise and the detriment are fairly clearly defined and the arrangement between the parties does not fall far short of a contract, there is not much difficulty as the estoppel can be satisfied by the implementation of the agreement. An extreme example of such a case would be *Yaxley v Gotts* [2000] Ch 162, where there was an agreement but it was void as it failed to comply with the Law of Property (Miscellaneous Provisions) Act 1989, s. 2.

Where, however, the promisee's expectations far exceed what he might have expected as a result of the detriment he has suffered, then the court should limit the expectations to make them more proportionate to the detriment. The equity from an estoppel arises from the expectations and detriment and the unconscionable behaviour of the promisor, but the expectations and the detriment must be proportionate in the remedy granted.

On the other hand, distinct from cases where the interest is immediate, in other cases the assurance may relate to a future property right (*Thorner* v *Major* [2009] UKHL 18; *Gillett* v *Holt* [2001] Ch 210). These cases present much more difficulty in satisfying the estoppel particularly where the expectation is to receive property on the death of the promisor. In *Thorner* v *Major*, the House of Lords acknowledged that an assurance as to an inheritance might well involve a change in the extent of the property between the date of the assurance and the death and that would then be relevant to the relief that the claimant was awarded. However, provided that there was still an identifiable property at the death then the court would be willing to grant the relief. In *Thorner*, the claimant was granted the beneficial ownership in the whole of the farm and the farming business although the extent of the farm had changed since the first assurances were given. But the court was prepared to make an award since the approach is to look back at the time at which the promise should have been carried out and ask whether it would be unconscionable not to give effect to it. As Lord Hoffmann expressed it cryptically in *Thorner*, 'The owl of Minerva spreads its wings at dusk'; in other words, the assessment of the equity is retrospective. The majority in *Thorner* based their view of the claimant's entitlement on the doctrine of proprietary estoppel whereas Lord Scott considered that the nature of the expectation made a claim based on estoppel difficult preferring the constructive trust as the better mechanism for realising the claimant's expectation. His view, first set out in the decision in *Yeoman's Row Management* v *Cobbe* where any equitable relief was denied, was that cases where the expectation which had been disappointed was for a future property right were more appropriately dealt with using the constructive trust. However, in *Thorner*, albeit the basis for his decision was different from the majority, his view as to the way in which the equity should be satisfied (i.e., the transfer of the farm and the business to the claimant) was the same.

Gillett v *Holt* [2001] Ch 210 is an earlier case concerning a future property right where the expectation was to receive property on death and the effect of the equity was to limit the testamentary freedom of the defendant. The Court of Appeal deemed that the promisor was estopped from denying the promise during his lifetime and undertook an inquiry into the extent of the estate—a complicated holding consisting of several separate properties—making an award which was consistent with the reasonable expectation the claimant had been led to hold. The satisfaction of the equity there was to make an evaluation of what it was reasonable for the claimant to receive in the light of the promise which had been made and his detrimental reliance.

So, it is clear that although there are some judicial guidelines as to the manner of satisfying the equity, nevertheless there remains much flexibility in the scope available to the courts in providing a particular remedy in any individual case. The scope of an estoppel appears to be as unlimited as the factual circumstances which may arise.

Question 2

Luke is the owner of a large agricultural barn which he is using for his pottery business. Two years ago, Luke was approached by Eddy, an old friend from their school days, who had inherited a large amount of money from his father which had been made mainly from buying former agricultural buildings and developing them into high-quality housing. Eddy proposed that they should convert the studios into two large houses. As Luke had no money to invest in this venture they agreed that Eddy would bear all the costs involved in acquiring planning permission; he would then buy the studios from Luke for £450,000 and undertake the development, and when the work was completed he would recoup his costs out of the sale of the housing and they would share the profits equally.

At some considerable expense, the planning permission was successfully obtained last year. However, Luke has now received an offer from AristoBuild plc to sell the studios to them, with the benefit of the planning permission, for £650,000. He is now refusing to go ahead with the original agreement with Eddy.

Advise Eddy.

Commentary

The focus of the question is proprietary estoppel and the cases on this topic are plentiful. Indeed, it is likely that such a problem as this has been triggered by a recent decision, so topicality is all-important. These cases can have small distinctions of fact which create a different emphasis in each, so a wide and up-to-date knowledge of the cases and the principles behind them is important.

As this is an area of much judicial activity, there are some useful articles to read which are listed in the Further reading section at the end of this chapter. These are essential reading, particularly if coursework is set in this area.

Answer plan

- Introduction to the context of the question and the doctrine of proprietary estoppel
- The modern application of the doctrine to include the three elements: representation, reliance and detriment
- The classic approach of the five strict *probanda*
- Discussion of the circumstances in which the reliance took place and the extent to which it is reasonable for the claimant to have relied on the representation
- Analysis and application of *Thorner* v *Major* [2009] UKHL 18 and *Yeoman's Row Management* v *Cobbe* [2008] UKHL 55 to the problem

Suggested answer

If the agreement between Luke and Eddy is in respect of an interest in land, the absence of any formalities as required by s. 2(1) of the Law of Property (Miscellaneous Provisions) Act 1989 means that no action can be brought for specific performance of a contract. The question then remains as to what rights and remedies might be available to Eddy given the fact that he has expended money in obtaining planning permission for the conversion of Luke's studios. There are various possibilities to be considered; in particular, proprietary estoppel and the remedial constructive trust. If these fail then Eddy may have to rely on personal claims for damages at common law such as unjust enrichment or quantum meruit.

The doctrine of proprietary estoppel rests on the unconscionability of the conduct of the respondent. The difficulty in applying the doctrine to the problem is that according to statute such an agreement as exists between Luke and Eddy is void and to allow equity to undermine statute on the basis of the unconscionable conduct of the person relying on the contract without the application of due principle is not judicially acceptable. The courts have considered such problems over a period of two centuries and recent judicial analysis is still developing.

The essentials to be established are threefold: representation, reliance and detriment. There must be a clear and unequivocal representation whether by words or conduct made by the legal owner on which the claimant reasonably relies (and therefore changes his position) and on which the claimant acts to his detriment or is unconscionably disadvantaged. In earlier decisions, five criteria were considered necessary to establish the grounds for the application of the doctrine (per Fry J, in *Willmott* v *Barber* (1880) 15 ChD 96; on appeal (1881) 17 ChD 772). These were that:

(i) there must have been a mistake made by the claimant as to his legal rights;

(ii) the claimant must have expended money or done some act on the faith of his mistaken belief;

(iii) the legal owner must know of the existence of his own right which is inconsistent with the right claimed by the claimant;

(iv) the legal owner must know of the claimant's mistaken belief; and

(v) the legal owner must have encouraged the claimant in the expenditure or other acts which he has performed.

It is now thought that proof of all criteria will only be required in cases where the landowner has passively stood by and acquiesced in a mistaken belief held unilaterally by the claimant (*Taylors Fashions Ltd* v *Liverpool Victoria Trustees Co. Ltd* [1982] QB 133; *Orgee* v *Orgee* [1997] EGCS 152; *Yeoman's Row Management Ltd* v *Cobbe* [2008] UKHL 55). That does not appear to be the case in the problem where both Luke and Eddy have agreed to the proposed arrangement. Cases relying on the doctrine of proprietary estoppel can rest either on a common expectation, an imperfect gift or a unilateral mistake (*Yeoman's Row* v *Cobbe* at 47 citing Gray & Gray, *Land Law*,

4th edn at 10.189). The problem posed in the question is one where there is an expectation held in common by both parties that the agreement will be carried through; that is, that Eddy will undertake the acquisition of the planning permission and will then buy the unconverted studios from Luke for £450,000.

One issue which arises therefore is the extent to which the parties, and the claimant in particular, believed that the agreement was binding, or, conversely knew that it was not. In *Ramsden v Dyson* (1866) LR 1 HL 129, Lord Kingsdown relied on the fact that the claimant mistakenly believed that the agreement was binding whereas in *Attorney-General of Hong Kong v Humphreys Estate (Queen's Gardens) Ltd* [1987] AC 114, there was no question but that the claimant (the Government of Hong Kong) knew that the agreement was binding in honour only. In *Plimmer v Mayor, Councillors and Citizens of the City of Wellington* (1884) 9 App Cas 699, when a businessman engaged in an arrangement to provide landing places with the provincial government, it was held wholly inequitable that the government should be allowed to renege on this agreement. In *Taylors Fashions Ltd v Liverpool Victoria Trustees Co. Ltd* (1979) [1982] QB 133, Oliver J delivered an important analysis of proprietary estoppel when he stated that 'it would be unconscionable for a party to be permitted to deny that which, knowingly, or unknowingly, he has allowed or encouraged another to assume to his detriment ... ' (at pp. 151–2).

These cases indicate a different approach between contexts which are commercial and those which are domestic. Cases such as *Inwards v Baker* [1965] 2 QB 29; *Pascoe v Turner* [1979] 1 WLR 431; *Windeler v Whitehall* [1990] 2 FLR 505; *Gillett v Holt* [2001] Ch 210; *Grundy v Ottey* [2003] WTLR 1253; *Jennings v Rice* [2003] 1 P & CR 8; *Lissimore v Downing* [2002] 2 FLR 308, where there is a domestic or family background to the circumstances, tend to show a greater readiness on the part of the courts to apply the doctrine. Where a claimant has a mistaken belief, on which they rely to their detriment, that they have a proprietary interest, the courts are more ready to accord them the right under the doctrine than in those cases of a commercial context where the parties are deemed to have been aware of the lack of their formal rights. In *Yeoman's Row v Cobbe*, the House of Lords held that the claimant, a man of business, knew that the agreement which was entered into as a business arrangement was binding in honour only. There was a common agreement on which the claimant had relied but it was held that he had every understanding as a businessman that the agreement was not legally binding. His claim for enforcement of the agreement based on a claim of proprietary estoppel was therefore not found. He was only able to claim damages for the expenditure he had committed to the abortive project. In *Thorner v Major* [2009] UKHL 18, a case of a familial context, the House of Lords came to an opposite conclusion. Their Lordships held that a representation had been made by the deceased that his cousin would inherit the farm and that it had been reasonable for the claimant to rely on it and conduct himself in a way that was detrimental if the promise was not fulfilled.

Difficulties have been raised about the applicability of proprietary estoppel to cases where the estoppel is conditional. For instance, in cases where the promise will only be implemented on death through inheritance as in *Gillett v Holt* then there is an argument that the promise which is conditional on death is uncertain. The property which is left at death may be different from the property which is in existence when the representation is originally made. Lord Scott in *Thorner* v *Major* at 20, argues that the remedial constructive trust is a better route to find a remedy in such cases than estoppel, 'For my part I would prefer to keep proprietary estoppel and constructive trust as distinct and separate remedies, to confine proprietary estoppel to cases where the representation, whether express or implied, on which the claimant has acted is unconditional and to address the cases where the representations are of future benefits, and subject to qualification on account of unforeseen future events, via the principles of remedial constructive trusts.' Lord Hoffmann at 8, however, in the same case, found no difficulty in applying estoppel to such cases arguing that certainty is available when the promise is realised and is achieved by ascertaining the form of the relief which equity can grant, 'The owl of Minerva spreads its wings only with the falling of the dusk.' The agreement between Eddy and Luke is for a future agreement to convey land to take place. Had the planning permission not been obtained then the question apparently remains open: would the whole agreement have fallen? Was it conditional on obtaining planning permission? It would seem unlikely in the circumstances that Eddy would have wanted to go ahead with the agreement had the potential for redevelopment of the property not been attained. In such a case, Lord Scott in *Thorner* v *Major* expresses the view that the better remedy would be the remedial constructive trust. A constructive trust based on the decision in *Pallant* v *Morgan* [1952] Ch 43 would not be effective because the land was not purchased following an agreement relating to the joint venture (*Banner Homes Group Plc* v *Luff Developments* [2000] EWCA Civ 18, [2000] EWCA Civ 3016).

Lord Scott in *Yeoman's Row* v *Cobbe* (at 15) also indicated that a flaw in the claimant's argument in that case was the fact that he was not claiming an interest in land as appeared to have been required by Oliver J in *Taylors Fashions* and Lord Kingsdown in *Ramsden* v *Dyson*. Lord Walker at 61 in *Thorner* v *Major*, indicates that the necessary requirement for proprietary estoppel to apply is for the assurance to relate to an indentified piece of land owned by the defendant (and see also *Crabb* v *Arun District Council* [1976] Ch 179). This is the case in the current problem—Luke is the owner of the barn. However, the point made by Lord Scott in *Yeoman's Row* v *Cobbe* is that the agreement was speculative. Once planning permission had been obtained then the agreement was that they would enter into negotiations to agree the precise terms of the contract. An 'expectation dependent upon the conclusion of a successful negotiation is not an expectation of an interest having [sufficient] certainty' (Lord Scott at 18). In this context, the interest to be granted lacked certainty and both parties knew that the agreement was not legally binding. So, could Luke and Eddy's agreement be distinguishable from that in *Yeoman's Row* v *Cobbe*? There seem to be two possible grounds of distinction: the agreement is clear (the land will be transferred for £450,000 and the net profits split 50:50); and the parties are arguably not operating on a commercial basis (they are old friends and Eddy may not be running a business but simply emulating his father's mode of business). The first point is problematic in the sense that the agreement is presumably conditional on obtaining planning permission. That favours an outcome as in *Yeoman's Row* v *Cobbe*, i.e., estoppel is not available because there is no certainty as to the interest to be obtained. However, the judgment in *Thorner* v *Major* clearly suggests that estoppel is retrospective—it bites not at the time of the assurance but at the point when the expectation is not realised. Once Eddy has obtained planning permission—as he has—then arguably the estoppel should be realised since there is a clear and unequivocal assurance as to the terms of the agreement. The second point relating to the argument, that the agreement was on a familial rather than a commercial basis where both parties might be considered to have clearly understood the lack of enforceability in their transactions, would rely on further evidence surrounding the knowledge and understanding and capacity of the two parties. In both *Yeoman's Row* v *Cobbe* and *Thorner* much was made of the evidence surrounding the understanding of the parties in each case. It is likely that that would be relevant again in this problem to determine the context in which Luke and Eddy were operating. Finally, even if proprietary estoppel was not available there remains the possibility of an argument that Luke holds his land on a constructive trust for himself and Eddy to take account of his unconscionable conduct. In any event, the element of unconscionability—not specifically dwelt upon in *Thorner* v *Major* although clearly acknowledged (albeit unsuccessful in *Yeoman's Row* v *Cobbe*)—is plainly in evidence here.

Failing all else, Eddy would have a personal remedy for compensatory damages on a quantum meruit basis at common law for the expenditure he committed in the acquisition of the planning permission.

Further reading

Battersby, G., 'Informal transactions in land, estoppel and registration' (1995) 58 MLR 637.

Browne-Wilkinson, N., 'Constructive trusts and unjust enrichment' (1996) 10 TLI 98.

Cooke, E., 'Estoppel and the protection of expectations' (1997) 17 LS 258.

Dixon, M., 'Proprietary estoppel: a return to principle?' [2009] Conv 260.

Etherton, T., 'Constructive trusts and proprietary estoppel: the search for clarity and principle' [2009] Conv 104.

Gardner, S., 'The remedial discretion in proprietary estoppel' (1999) 115 LQR 438.

Nield, S., 'Constructive trusts and estoppel' (2003) 23 LS 311.

Piska, N., 'Hopes, expectations and revocable promises in proprietary estoppel' (2009) 72 MLR 998.

Rose, C., 'Crystals and mud in property law' (1987–88) 40 Stanford L Rev 577.

Thompson, M. P., 'Proprietary estoppel, third parties and constructive trusts: a taste of the future?' [2002] Conv 584.

11

Administration of trusts

Introduction

Administration of trusts involves a study of a number of discrete, but related, topics. You may well find that different topics within administration of trusts form separate halves of a single question. Trustee investment, for instance, might form part (a) of a question in which part (b) is variation of trusts. You are therefore advised to revise all aspects of administration of trusts which appear on your course.

The area of review of trustees' decisions is one that has generated a fair body of case law in recent years. Question 1 examines these problems with particular regard to the extent of beneficiaries' or objects' rights to see documents relating to the trust, this being a particularly topical issue in view of the decision of the Privy Council in *Schmidt* v *Rosewood Trust* [2003] 2 WLR 1442.

The biggest changes affecting this area of the law were brought in by the **Trustee Act 2000**. Amongst many other changes, the Act introduced a single statutory duty of care for trustees, which duty applies to a wide range of trustees' functions; and it made important modifications to the law relating to remuneration of trustees, and to investment and delegation. There is little judicial guidance to the interpretation of the Act. There are four questions in this chapter that demand a knowledge of the law contained in the Act: question 1, which partly involves trustee remuneration; question 2, which deals with delegation and the validity of trustee exclusion clauses; question 3, which covers investment; and question 4, which tackles the rule in *Howe* v *Earl of Dartmouth* (1802) 7 Ves 137 (whose scope is now more restricted owing to the widening of the concept of authorised investments under the **Trustee Act 2000**).

Although the **Trustee Act 2000** has given statutory effect to the 'portfolio theory' of investment, it does not go so far as to enable trustees, under the general law, to pursue an investment policy based on the best overall return. This means that, in a trust where investments are held for A for life remainder to B, the trustees must still balance the need for income and capital growth, as they must pay whatever income is produced to A, and hold the benefit of any increased value in the capital for B. Even though the trustees may consider that it would produce the best overall profit for the trust, they cannot pursue a policy, for instance, of going mainly for capital growth and then in due course apportioning (i.e., dividing) the return between A and B (by treating some of the capital growth as income). The reverse also applies. These restrictions mean that the overall return might be lower than it would be if trustees were not fettered by the need to distinguish between a profit of an income and a capital nature. This may be set to change at some time in the future, as the introduction of a 'best overall return' policy would need to be linked with a power or duty to apportion. Apportionment was the subject of a Law Commission report: *Capital and Income in Trusts: Classification and Apportionment* (Law Com Report No. 315, 2009).

The one limited instance in which equity does provide for apportionment is where trustees are under a duty to convert assets and to invest them in authorised investments. This may arise where the duty to convert is imposed under the rule in *Howe v Earl of Dartmouth*. The scope of the duty to convert under this rule, and the accompanying duty to apportion, is dealt with in part (a) of question 4.

Question 4 deals also with trustees' powers of advancement. If your course covers advancement, it will probably also deal with trustees' powers of maintenance, and this is the subject of question 5. Maintenance would not be a difficult topic, were it not for the awe-inspiring complexity of the rules governing whether gifts carry the intermediate income.

The final question in this chapter, question 6, covers variation of trusts. This is an important topic, but relatively few cases on variation are published in the reports these days as most applications for a variation are heard in private. Like maintenance, variation of trusts is not an essentially difficult topic, but it too has one rather complicated aspect—this time, the meaning of para. (b) of s. 1(1) of the Variation of Trusts Act 1958. Your lecturer may delight in the complexities of this paragraph, and linger over the case law that has attempted to interpret it. On the other hand, he or she may prefer to scurry by para. (b) with no more than a passing reference to it. Your lecturer's approach should give you some indication of the depth in which you might need to know that paragraph in the examination.

Question 1

(a) Ann, Bob and Cindy are the trustees of a private trust set up under the will of a testator who died earlier this year; the beneficiaries are members of the testator's family. The assets of the trust comprise shares in the testator's family business, Fruitrite Ltd, which engages in market-gardening. Ann is a solicitor, Bob is an accountant and Cindy was a friend of the testator and has considerable experience of market-gardening.

The trust instrument contains no provision for remuneration of the trustees. Advise the trustees whether they are entitled to claim remuneration for acting as trustees.

(b) Trevor is the sole trustee of an exhaustive discretionary trust of income, the objects of which are the nephews and nieces of Sally. Sally has two nephews, Benjy and Damian, and one niece, Caroline. Six months ago Trevor lent Benjy the sum of £20,000 out of his

(Trevor's) own money. Caroline and Damian have now learned that Trevor has decided to pay the entire income of the trust for the present year, some £15,000, to Benjy. Caroline and Damian claim that Trevor exercised his discretion under the trust in Benjy's favour only in order that Benjy would be in sufficient funds to repay that loan. Caroline and Damian wish to have the proposed exercise of the discretion prevented, and further wish to compel Trevor to distribute the income for the present year among all three objects equally.

Advise Caroline and Damian.

Commentary

Part **(a)** of the question involves an area affected by the **Trustee Act 2000**, with which the examiners will expect you to be familiar. The answer deals mostly with the exceptions to the basic rule, but the student should always remember to state what the basic principle is before coming to the exceptions. Part **(b)** concerns review of trustees' decisions. Unless the examination paper indicates otherwise, you might reasonably assume that, where a question is in separate parts, such as this one, each part carries equal marks. The candidate should therefore try to allocate roughly an equal amount of time to tackling each part.

Answer plan

(a) • General rule: trusteeship gratuitous unless charging clause
  • Right to remuneration of trustees acting in professional capacity (A & B) (**TA 2000, s. 29**)
  • Remuneration of other trustee (C): only if beneficiaries' consent or court's approval

(b) • Improper exercise of trustee's discretion?
  • Trustee not have to give reasons for decisions
  • Inspection by beneficiaries of trust documents
  • Court's exercising trustee's discretion?

Suggested answer

(a) The general rule is that a trustee is not entitled to claim remuneration for carrying out his office: *Robinson v Pett* (1734) 2 P Wms 249. This general rule admits of a number of exceptions. A trustee is entitled to charge if the trust instrument so provides, but as the trust instrument in the problem does not contain a charging clause, this exception need not be considered further.

An important exception to the general rule was introduced in the **Trustee Act 2000**. If the requirements of that Act are met, a trustee of a private trust who acts in a professional capacity may be entitled to receive reasonable remuneration out of the trust funds for any services that he provides to the trust. The requirements are that the trustee is not a sole trustee, that each other trustee has agreed in writing that he may be remunerated (**Trustee Act 2000, s. 29(2)**)) and that no provision for remuneration is made by the trust instrument (**s. 29(5)(a)**)). A trustee acts in a professional capacity if he acts in the course of a profession or business which includes the provision of services in connection with the management or administration of trusts generally (or any particular aspect of such management or administration) or a particular kind of trust (**s. 28(5)**). A trustee is entitled to remuneration under the statutory provision even if the services in question could be provided by a lay trustee (**s. 29(4)**).

In the problem, there appear to be two trustees who might be able to take advantage of such statutory provision of remuneration. These are Ann and Bob, each of whom is likely to be able to satisfy the requirement that they act in a professional capacity. If each of them is to be entitled to remuneration, each will need the agreement in writing of the other two trustees. If such agreement is obtained, Ann and Bob will be able to charge for all work that they perform as trustees, not merely work undertaken in their professional capacities.

Cindy, however, will be unable to take advantage of the statutory provision for remuneration. Although it might be advantageous to the trust to have as one of its trustees a person, such as Cindy, who has expertise in the business in which the trust's shares are invested, she does not act in a professional capacity for the purposes of the **Trustee Act 2000**. If, therefore, Cindy wishes to claim remuneration for acting as a trustee, she will need to come under one of the other exceptions to the general rule.

Any beneficiary who consents in advance to Cindy's receiving remuneration will be estopped from bringing any claim against her to make her account for any remuneration she does receive; but Cindy could still be made to account for remuneration at the behest of those beneficiaries who did not so agree. Cindy could therefore safely receive remuneration only if she has the consent of all the beneficiaries, and only if such beneficiaries are all *sui iuris* and together form a closed class. The problem does not itself indicate whether the beneficiaries meet these requirements, but even if they do, they might not all agree.

The final avenue open to Cindy would be to seek the consent of the court to approving prospective remuneration. That the court has jurisdiction to award future remuneration was confirmed in *Re Duke of Norfolk's Settlement Trusts* [1982] Ch 61. The criterion for such award is the overall benefit of the trust; but it is clear that the power will be exercised only in exceptional circumstances, where the trustee's skill and experience are of particular value to the trust. In the *Norfolk* case, the Court of Appeal did make an award of future remuneration beyond that permitted in the trust instrument, but that was in circumstances where it became apparent that the work that would need to be undertaken as trustee considerably exceeded that which might have been apparent at the time the trustee accepted office. Unless Cindy could make out a comparable case, it is unlikely that the court would make an award of future remuneration in her favour.

(b) If Trevor has exercised the discretion vested in him in order to ensure that he is repaid the debt Benjy owes him, this is an improper exercise of the discretion. It is improper because the power of selection must be exercised in good faith and for its proper purpose: the trustee must consider the objects' interests, not his own. If Caroline and Damian can prove that the exercise was so motivated, they can apply to the court to have the improper appointment set aside, and Trevor will be personally liable to them for any loss resulting from the breach of trust: *Molyneux v Fletcher* [1898] 1 QB 648.

The problem for Caroline and Damian, however, is essentially one of proof. A trustee is not obliged to give reasons for the exercise of his discretions: *Re Beloved Wilkes' Charity* (1851) 3 Mac & G 440 and *Re Londonderry's Settlement* [1965] Ch 918, CA. If, however, a trustee does give reasons, and these are improper, the objects can have the exercise set aside: *Klug v Klug* [1918] 2 Ch 67.

In *O'Rourke v Darbyshire* [1920] AC 581, at pp. 619–20, Lord Wrenbury expressed the view that a beneficial interest under a trust carried with it a proprietary right to see trust documents. On this analysis, it would be important to determine whether objects of a discretionary trust, such as Caroline and Damian, have proprietary rights under the trust, and also whether the documents at issue can be characterised as trust documents: *Re Londonderry's Settlement* [1965] 1 Ch 918, at p. 938.

More recently, however, Lord Walker, delivering the advice of the Privy Council in *Schmidt v Rosewood Trust Ltd* [2003] 2 AC 709, said that the right to seek disclosure of trust documents was not based on any proprietary right, but was rather an aspect of the court's inherent jurisdiction to supervise, and if necessary to intervene in, the administration of trusts. Although not strictly binding in English law, the views expressed by the Privy Council in this case are highly persuasive. Applying the principles there laid down, it would seem that, although an individual object of a discretionary trust (such as Caroline or Damian) does not have any proprietary right under the trust, such object may seek the protection of equity.

Whether any protection will be awarded to Caroline and Damian, and the nature of any such protection, is at the court's discretion, and will vary with the circumstances. In the *Schmidt* case, Lord Walker said that, in determining whether an object may see trust documents, the court may have to balance the interests of the different beneficiaries or objects, the trustees and third parties. In performing this balancing exercise, the court will accord greater weight to the claims of an object with a real (as opposed to a mere theoretical) possibility of benefit. The fact that Caroline and Damian are members of a very small class of discretionary objects is therefore favourable to their claim.

Lord Walker said that the balancing of the various interests must also take into account any issues of personal or commercial confidentiality. In *Re Londonderry*, the object of a fiduciary power complained of the small amount of capital allotted to her by the trustees. She asked to see copies of the minutes of trustees' meetings and other correspondence in the hope that these would reveal the basis for the trustees' allocation. The Court of Appeal held that the trustees were not bound to disclose the documents: it considered that the disclosure of such confidential information could cause trouble in the family out of all proportion to any resulting benefit. It also said that, if the trustees knew that they could be required to make such disclosure, it might interfere with the proper exercise of their discretion.

As the discretionary trust in the question involves a very small group of family members, there is a real possibility of family strife were Trevor to be compelled to disclose the documents giving the reasons for his decision to pay the entire income to Benjy. This factor might lead the court either to decline to order Trevor to reveal such documents to Caroline and Damian, or to compel them to reveal only such parts of them as do not indicate the reasons for his decision.

The Court of Appeal in *Re Londonderry* commented that the position would be different if an object were to make a case of *mala fides*. The problem for Caroline and Damian, however, is that evidence of *mala fides* might be difficult to obtain without recourse to such documents. Unless Trevor has made statements disclosing bad faith, the objects might find it difficult to prove that the exercise was improper.

In *O'Rourke* v *Darbyshire*, Lord Parmoor did not consider it important to determine whether the right of a beneficiary to inspect trust documents was based on a primary proprietary right, or whether it was a right under the law of disclosure to be enforced in the course of litigation: ibid., at pp. 619–20. In the light of these and other comments in *Re Londonderry*, it was suggested that where objects have no initial right to ask to see the documents in question, they might circumvent this problem by bringing an action alleging an improper exercise of the trustees' discretions, and then obtaining disclosure of documents in the proceedings: Megarry (1965) 81 LQR 196. In *Scott* v *National Trust* [1998] 1 WLR 226, Robert Walker J opined that trustees might be compelled through disclosure to reveal the substance of their reasons for their decision if such decision were directly attacked by legal proceedings. On the other hand the courts are unwilling to award disclosure in a claim that is merely a 'fishing expedition', i.e., where the substance of the claim depends entirely on what might be revealed by the disclosure itself. In *Re Murphy's Settlements* [1999] 1 WLR 282, Neuberger J said that the absence of any suggestion that the trustees have acted wrongfully is a factor affecting whether the court will compel them to reveal information; and this seems to be consistent with the view of the Privy Council in the *Schmidt* case.

The fact that Trevor exercised his discretion in favour of an object to whom he had lent some of his own money only a short while before, might raise a suspicion that Trevor has not exercised his power for its proper purpose, and this might just weigh the scales in favour of disclosure in an action for breach of trust brought by Caroline and Damian.

Even if Caroline and Damian succeed in having the exercise set aside, they cannot themselves compel Trevor positively to exercise his discretion as they direct. All three objects together, assuming they are all *sui iuris* and form a closed class, could compel the distribution of the income to them under an extension of the rule in *Saunders* v *Vautier* (1841) 4 Beav 115. Caroline and Damian, however, are only two of the three objects of the discretionary trust of income.

It is unclear, however, whether the court would itself be able (or willing) to exercise the trustee's dispositive discretion under a discretionary trust. In *Klug* v *Klug* itself, the court did order the advancement to be made; but it may be that it was merely giving effect to the wishes of the remaining trustee whose decision was not tainted by improper considerations. In *McPhail* v *Doulton* [1971] AC 424, the House of Lords stated that the court would, if called upon to do so, execute a discretionary trust in the manner best calculated to give effect to the settlor's intentions; and, ultimately, where a proper basis for distribution appears, this could be by itself directing the trustees so to distribute. In so holding, it revived the authority of eighteenth-century cases where the court had itself executed a discretionary trust: *Warburton* v *Warburton* (1702) 4 Bro PC 1 and *Richardson* v *Chapman* (1760) 7 Bro PC 318. This jurisdiction will be exercised only in the last resort: cf. *Mettoy Pension Trustees* v *Evans* [1990] 1 WLR 1587, where the court exercised the same jurisdiction to execute a fiduciary power. In practice, therefore, where a trustee persistently fails properly to exercise his discretion to appoint amongst the objects, the latter might be better advised to seek such trustee's removal and replacement: *Re Gestetner Settlement* [1953] Ch 672 admits of such possibility.

Question 2

Six months ago, Topaz, a trustee, wished to sell some jewellery which belonged to the trust. He asked Jade, a jeweller whom he knew to have been fined for smuggling stones into the country a few years earlier, to carry out a valuation. Jade valued the jewellery at £100,000. In reliance upon this, Topaz instructed Jade to sell the jewellery for that amount to Sapphire, which he did. A month later, Sapphire sold the jewellery at an auction for five times that amount.

Three months after the sale, Jade had still not accounted to Topaz for the proceeds. Topaz then began to press Jade for payment, but was met with evasive replies. Last week, Topaz learned that Jade lost the entire £100,000 proceeds whilst gambling, and is now insolvent.

(a) Advise the beneficiaries of the trust as to their rights against Topaz.

(b) How would your advice differ if the trust had contained a clause excluding the trustee from all liability other than for 'wilful default'?

Commentary

The need to answer only what is asked and no more is vividly illustrated in part **(a)** of this question. You should deal with the rights against Topaz only. It earns no marks whatever to consider any rights the beneficiaries may have against any other parties mentioned. Differently worded, it could easily have become a question on tracing and third party receivers or dealers—but it is not. If you know your stuff, your answer should be a little gem.

The powers of a trustee to delegate have been considerably extended by the **Trustee Act 2000**; the examiners will expect you to be fully acquainted with the law. It should be noted that the appointment of an 'agent' under the statutory provision is not restricted to the appointment of an agent in the contractual sense, i.e., for entering into agreements with third parties. Thus, although a person appointed to value property is not a contractual agent, the **Trustee Act 1925, s. 22(3)**, expressly permits trustees to have the trust property valued 'by duly qualified agents'. It seems likely that the term 'agent' is used in a similarly wide sense in the **Trustee Act 2000**. A trustee is, for example, under a duty to keep proper accounts (***Pearse v Green*** (1819) 1 Jac & W 135, 140). Such a duty comprises a 'delegable function' (**s. 39(1)**) of a trustee of a private trust, so it seems that an accountant might be appointed to maintain the trust accounts as an agent under **s. 11**.

Part **(b)** concerns the validity of trustee exclusion clauses. These are quite common in trust instruments nowadays, and it seems generally to be accepted that the **Unfair Contract Terms Act 1977** does not apply to trustee exclusion clauses: Goodhart, 'Trust Law for the Twenty-First Century' (1996) 10(2) TLI 38. Since the Court of Appeal in ***Armitage* v *Nurse* [1998] Ch 241** upheld the validity of a very wide exclusion clause, however, such clauses have been a matter of concern, being the subject of a Consultation Paper, *Trustee Exemption Clauses*, produced by the Trust Law Committee in 1998.

During the passage of the **Trustee Act 2000** through the House of Lords, some of their Lord-ships expressed concern that professional persons acting for a settlor in drawing up a trust instrument are effectively free to insert an exclusion clause protecting them from liability, whilst at the same time charging for their professional services to the trust. The Lord Chancel-lor agreed that the matter needed to be looked into and referred it to the Law Commission, which subsequently published a Report, *Trustee Exemption Clauses* (Law Com No. 301, 2006). The Report indicates that the Law Commission has retreated from the view expressed in its earlier Consultation Paper (CP No. 171, 2002) which had favoured legislation; instead the Law Commission now only recommends the introduction of rules of practice. For an analysis of the validity of trustee exclusion clauses at present, see Luxton, 'Trustee Exclusion Clauses: Lost in the Heather?', in *Modern Studies in Property Law: Volume 1: Property 2000* (Elizabeth Cooke, ed.), Hart Publishing, 2001, chapter 3, at pp. 59–75.

Answer plan

(a) • Appointment of agent (**Trustee Act 2000, s. 11**)

  – in compliance with statutory duty of care?

  – did T actively consider valuation?

  – asset management function

 • Supervision of agent (**Trustee Act 2000, ss. 21–22**)

(b) • Meaning of 'wilful default' in earlier Trustee Acts

 • Express exclusion clause

  – cannot exclude liability for dishonesty

  – dishonesty in context of solicitor-trustee

Suggested answer

(a) The sum of at least £100,000 has been lost to the trust as a result of Jade's gambling. It may be that a further £400,000 has been lost through a sale to Sapphire at a considerable undervalue. The beneficiaries have a personal right of action against Topaz to require him to make good this loss if they can establish that Topaz has committed a breach of trust.

In the absence of any provision in the trust instrument, trustees may authorise any person to exercise any delegable function as their agent; and the appointment of an agent to value and to sell trust assets is a delegable function (Trustee Act 2000, s. 11(1), (2)). More specifically, trustees may have trust property valued by duly qualified agents (Trustee Act 1925, s. 22(3)). Topaz may nevertheless be liable to the beneficiaries on various grounds.

First, it could be argued that the appointment of Jade as an agent was wrongful in itself. In appointing a person to act as agent, a trustee is under the statutory duty of care set out in the Trustee Act 2000, s. 1(1) and Sch. 1, para. 3(1)(a). In appointing an agent, Topaz must therefore exercise such care and skill as is reasonable in the circumstances, having regard in particular to any special knowledge or experience he holds himself out as having, or, if he acts as a trustee in the course of a business or profession, to any special knowledge or experience that it is reasonable to expect such a person to have. A trustee will not be liable for any act or default of the agent unless he has failed to comply with that duty of care (Trustee Act 2000, s. 23(1)). In its Report which led to the Trustee Act 2000, the Law Commission took the view that the statutory duty of care codified the liability of a trustee in equity: *Trustees' Powers and Duties* (Law Com No. 260, 1999), para. 3.24. Assuming that this is correct, the principles laid down in the case law before the Trustee Act 2000 continue to apply. The cases establish that a trustee is to be judged by the test of the prudent man of business acting in his own affairs: *Speight v Gaunt* (1883) 9 App Cas 1. A prudent man of business would employ an agent only in his proper field (*Fry v Tapson* (1884) 28 ChD 268); and in appointing a jeweller to value and sell jewellery, Topaz has probably satisfied this requirement. A prudent man of business, however, would probably not appoint as his agent to value and sell jewellery belonging to the trust a person whom he knows to have been convicted of a crime involving dishonesty. It is therefore likely that the choice of Jade as agent was itself a breach of trust, so that Topaz is personally liable for the loss to the trust.

Secondly, whilst the Trustee Act 2000 permits a trustee (subject to specified exceptions) to delegate discretions as well as duties, on the facts of the problem Topaz initially asked Jade merely to value the jewellery. The decision to instruct Jade to sell would therefore have needed to be made on the basis of that valuation. If Topaz simply accepted Jade's valuation without himself considering it, this would itself be a breach of trust.

Thirdly, a trustee may not appoint an agent to exercise any 'asset management function' as his agent, except by an agreement which is in, or is evidenced in, writing and on terms that the agent will comply with a policy statement which the trustee has prepared (Trustee Act 2000, s. 15(1), (2)). An asset management function includes the acquisition of property which is to be subject to the trust (s. 15(5)(b)). If Jade was appointed to deal with the sale of the jewellery on the basis that the proceeds of sale would be paid to him, his appointment involved the exercise of an asset management function. Topaz will therefore be liable if his appointment of Jade did not meet the requirements of s. 15.

Fourthly, when a trustee has appointed an agent, he must keep under review the arrangements under which the agent acts, and must consider if there is a need to exercise any power of intervention (which includes giving the agent directions, and revoking the appointment) (Trustee Act 2000, ss. 21, 22). The trustee is therefore effectively under a duty to supervise the agent after appointment, in respect of which he is again subject to the statutory duty of care (s. 2 and Sch. 1, para. 3(1)(e)). It might therefore be argued that Topaz was in breach of his duty as trustee to protect the trust assets, in that he left a large sum of money (the sale proceeds) in Jade's hands for an undue length of time. Three months is surely longer than a prudent man of business would allow. It is likely that Topaz's inaction amounts to a breach of trust.

(b) An exclusion of liability for wilful default first appeared in trust instruments in the eighteenth century; but the exclusion of liability was put on a statutory footing in various Trustee Acts of the nineteenth century, where the phrase was construed objectively, i.e., so as not to derogate from the principle laid down in *Speight* v *Gaunt* (1883) 9 App Cas 1 that a trustee must act as a prudent man of business would act in his own affairs: *Re Brier* (1884) 26 ChD 238, CA. The same phrase was used in the Trustee Act 1925, s. 30(1) (now repealed), which Maugham J in *Re Vickery* [1931] 1 Ch 572, however, interpreted literally, i.e., as requiring consciousness of wrongdoing. Maugham J reached this conclusion by relying upon *Re Equitable City Fire Insurance Co. Ltd* [1925] 1 Ch 407, a case which concerned the liability of auditors, not trustees. Maugham J's view conflicted with earlier cases such as *Re Brier*, and effectively made the section a fool's charter. Nevertheless, in *Armitage* v *Nurse* [1998] Ch 241, Millett LJ expressed support for Maugham J's interpretation.

The Trustee Act 1925, s. 30(1) was repealed by the Trustee Act 2000, so that a trustee no longer has the benefit of the statutory exclusion of liability. A trustee may, however, have the benefit of an exclusion of liability clause contained in the trust instrument. The Trustee Act 2000 does not invalidate trustee exclusion clauses; indeed, it effectively provides that the statutory duty of care may be restricted or excluded by the trust instrument (Sch. 1, para. 7). An exclusion clause in the trust instrument may be very wide in scope: the Court of Appeal held in *Armitage* v *Nurse* that such a clause may exclude the liability of a trustee for acts and defaults in carrying out his functions as trustee except those which involve dishonesty. This principle applies even if the trustee is a solicitor and himself prepared the trust instrument: *Bogg* v *Raper* (1998) *The Times*, 22 April, CA. The principle in *Armitage* v *Nurse* was slightly qualified in *Walker* v *Stones* [2000] 4 All ER 412, CA, where it was said that, at least where the trustee is also a solicitor, the test for honesty is not purely subjective. Thus a solicitor-trustee who deliberately acts in breach of trust may be dishonest for this purpose, regardless of his subjective belief, if no reasonable solicitor-trustee could have thought that what he did was for the benefit of the beneficiaries (at p. 443, per Sir Christopher Slade).

The exclusion clause in the trust instrument in the problem will therefore be effective to protect Topaz from liability for breach of trust according to its terms for all acts except those involving 'wilful default' or dishonesty. The question does not state whether Topaz was a solicitor-trustee, but it does not seem that he deliberately acted in breach of trust. In any event, it would not appear from the facts given that he was dishonest, and it may well be that he was not conscious of any wrongdoing. In these circumstances, it seems likely that he will be able to rely on the clause to exclude his liability.

Question 3

By his will, Edward, who died earlier this year, gave £500,000 to his trustees, Sam and Giles, in trust for Edward's daughter, Daphne, for life, remainder to Edward's nephew, Norris. The will gave the trustees an express power to invest in shares quoted on the London Stock Exchange, 'except in shares of Maropet plc'. Sam is a solicitor; Giles is a farmer and an old friend of Edward. Sam and Giles would like to invest part of the trust fund in Old Masters. Norris is a keen environmentalist, and he has written to the trustees asking that they do not make investments in companies which engage in the emission of greenhouse gases.

In the light of these circumstances, advise Sam and Giles:

(a) of their powers of investment;

AND

(b) as to their duties in selecting investments.

 Commentary

The law relating to trustee investment was considerably altered and simplified by the **Trustee Act 2000**. This question covers what qualifies as an investment, and the equitable and statutory duties of trustees relating to the selection and review of investments.

 Answer plan

(a) • General power of investment

• Restriction

• Capital appreciation only?

(b) • Statutory duty of care

  • Standard investment criteria

  • Duty to act even-handedly between beneficiaries

  • Ethical investment

Suggested answer

(a) Subject to any provisions in the trust instrument, a trustee may make any kind of investment that he could make if he were absolutely entitled to the trust assets (**Trustee Act 2000, s. 3(1)**). This power is called 'the general power of investment' (**s. 3(2)**). The general power of investment does not itself give trustees a power to make investments in land (other than in loans secured on land) (**s. 3(3)**); trustees are, however, given a separate power to acquire as an investment freehold or leasehold land in the United Kingdom (**s. 8(1)(a)**).

The general power of investment is additional to any express powers of investment, but is subject to any restriction or exclusion that the trust instrument may contain (**s. 6(1)**). Had the investment clause in the question provided that the trustees were to be empowered to invest *only* in shares quoted on the London Stock Exchange, the general power of investment would have been effectively excluded. The positive inclusion of a power to invest in shares quoted on the Stock Exchange is not, however, to be treated as an exclusion of the general power of investment. Sam and Giles therefore have the general power of investment, subject only to the restriction on investing in shares in Maropet plc. That this is the intended effect of the statute is apparent from an explanatory note which the Law Commission attached to the clause of its Draft Bill which later became **s. 6** of the **Trustee Act 2000**: Law Commission, *Trustees' Powers and Duties* (Law Com No. 260, 1999).

The older view of an investment is that it is the purchase of property from which interest or income is expected to accrue: *Re Wragg* [1919] 2 Ch 58. More recently, however, it has been accepted that an investment includes any laying out of money with a view to obtaining a return, which suggests that even the purchase of an asset which can produce a return only on sale is included: *Re Lilly's Will Trusts* [1948] 2 All ER 906. The modern view is that investment may include a capital, as well as an income, return: *Cowan* v *Scargill* [1985] Ch 270; *Harries* v *Church Commissioners for England* [1992] 1 WLR 1241, at p. 1246. On this basis, the purchase of Old Masters, which do not themselves produce an income, could today be regarded as an investment. The risk for the trustees, however, is that if such paintings were sold soon after purchase, it might be argued that they were acquired not for investment but for purposes of trading, with the result that the profits of the sale could be liable to income tax.

(b) The **Trustee Act 2000** subjects trustees to a statutory duty of care, which applies when a trustee is exercising the general power of investment or any other power of investment, however conferred, or when carrying out his statutory duties in relation to the exercise of a power of investment or to the review of investments (under ss. 4 and 5) (Trustee Act 2000, ss. 1 and 2 and Sch. 1, para. 1).

The duty of care requires a trustee to exercise such care and skill as is reasonable in the circumstances, having regard in particular to any special knowledge or experience that he has or holds himself out as having, and (if he acts as a trustee in the course of a business or profession) to any special knowledge or experience that it is reasonable to expect of such a person (**Trustee Act 2000, s. 1(1)**). It would appear that this puts into statutory form a distinction which had been previously drawn in the case law, under which a professional trustee (namely a trust corporation) is treated as subject to a higher standard of care than an unpaid (lay) trustee: *Re Waterman's Will Trusts* [1952] 2 All ER 1054; *Bartlett* v *Barclays Bank Trust Co. Ltd (No. 1)* [1980] Ch 515, at p. 534. It would appear from the question that Giles is a lay trustee; he will therefore be judged by the standard of care established in the case law, namely that of the prudent man of business investing for the benefit of persons for whom he feels morally bound to provide: *Re Whiteley* (1886) 33 ChD 347, at p. 355 (Lindley LJ). In investing, therefore, Giles may not take more than a prudent degree of risk: *Learoyd* v *Whiteley* (1887) 12 App Cas 727, at p. 733; *Bartlett* v *Barclays Bank Trust Co. Ltd (No. 1)* [1980] Ch 515, at p. 531. Although he is not a professional trustee, Sam is a professional person, so that it would seem that he will be required to exercise a higher degree of skill in relation to the legal work which he performs for the trust.

In exercising any power of investment, whether under the **Trustee Act 2000** or otherwise, a trustee must have regard to the standard investment criteria, and must from time to time review the investments of the trust and consider whether, having regard to such criteria, they should be varied (**Trustee Act 2000, s. 4(1), (2)**). The standard investment criteria require the trustee to have regard to the suitability of the investment to the trust and to the need for diversification so far as is appropriate to the circumstances of the trust (s. 4(3)). The statutory duty to select suitable investments is twofold: if, for instance, trustees are considering investing in shares in X plc, they must consider both whether investment in shares is suitable for the trust, and whether shares in X plc are a suitable investment within that class. Diversification is important in order to spread the risk of investment. Sam and Giles might therefore be in breach of trust were they to invest the entire trust fund, for instance, in the shares of one company. The trustees are not, however, guarantors of the success of their investment policy, and so are not liable merely because the investments do not, in the course of time, turn out to have been the most profitable that could have been made: *Nestle* v *National Westminster Bank plc* [1993] 1 WLR 1260, CA.

Both duties effectively require the trustees to have regard to the particular trust; and the trustees must act even-handedly between the beneficiaries. In the problem, therefore, the investments should be selected so as to provide, so far as possible, both a reasonable income for Daphne for her life, and reasonable capital growth for the remainderman, Norris. The trustees would therefore probably be in breach of trust were they to invest the entire trust fund in Old Masters, since, apart from breaching the duty to diversify, they would be investing in a way that would produce no income for Daphne.

In selecting investments, and having regard to the above, the trustees' duty is to secure the maximum financial return for the trust: *Harries v Church Commissioners for England* [1992] 1 WLR 1241, at p. 1246. The consequence is that, in a private trust (such as that in the question), the trustees may not have a policy of ethical investment which would be likely significantly to reduce financial returns. The only exception to this in the case of a private trust is where all the beneficiaries are *sui iuris*, form a closed class and unanimously agree to such a policy: *Cowan v Scargill* [1985] Ch 270. Therefore, even assuming Norris is at least 18 years of age, the trustees would probably be in breach of trust in pursuing the ethical policy he proposes unless Daphne expressly agrees to it.

Question 4

Alex died last year. By his will he left his residuary estate to his trustees in trust for his sister, Samantha, for life, remainder to her son, Edwin. The residuary estate comprises the following assets:

(i)   Rocky, a two-year-old racehorse with many wins to her credit;

(ii) an interest in remainder under a trust which will fall into possession on the death of Lionel, who has a life interest thereunder; and

(iii) a lease of land in Yorkshire which has 40 years unexpired.

Advise the trustees:

(a)   of their duties to the beneficiaries in relation to these assets;

AND

(b)   whether, and to what extent, the trustees may make advancements to Edwin under the Trustee Act 1925, s. 32.

 Commentary

Questions involving the rules in **Howe v Earl of Dartmouth** and **Re Earl Chesterfield's Trusts** should appeal to students with an interest in technical details, but wise candidates will not allow the technicalities of the rules to obscure an appreciation of the principles underlying them. It is important to note how the impact of the rules was affected by the **Trustee Act 2000**, as virtually all investments are now authorised (the exception being land outside the United Kingdom: **s. 8(1)**).

The fact that the two parts of the question deal with different areas illustrates the risk that you run if you pick and choose individual topics for revision.

Answer plan

(a) • Rule in *Howe v Earl of Dartmouth*

   • Apportionment under *Re Earl of Chesterfield's Trusts*

(b) • Advancement under **Trustee Act 1925, s. 32**

   • Restrictions on advancement

   • Meaning of 'advancement or benefit'

   • Methods of making an advancement

Suggested answer

(a) It must be considered whether any of the assets comprising residue fall within the rule in *Howe v Earl of Dartmouth* (1802) 7 Ves 137, which is designed to promote equality among beneficiaries. The rule applies (subject to a contrary intention) where residuary personalty is settled by will upon persons in succession; it obliges the trustees to convert into authorised investments such parts as are of a wasting, hazardous, future or reversionary nature, or which consist of unauthorised securities.

The rule is therefore applicable to Rocky, the racehorse, which for a short time might produce a great deal of income, but whose capital value might eventually be no more than horsemeat. The interest in remainder is also subject to the rule: but for the duty to convert, this property would be of no immediate benefit to the life tenant, Samantha.

Under the **Trustee Act 2000, s. 8(1)**, trustees have power to acquire (*inter alia*) leasehold land in the United Kingdom for investment, for occupation by a beneficiary or for any other reason. They would therefore have power to acquire even a short lease. The rule in *Howe v Earl of Dartmouth* cannot therefore apply to the lease of land in Yorkshire. Samantha, the life tenant, will therefore be entitled to all the rent or other income that it produces.

In respect of the racehorse and the interest in remainder, however, the trustees are under a duty not merely to convert, but also to apportion until conversion takes place.

In the absence of a power to postpone sale, Rocky must be valued one year after Alex's death. Whatever income Rocky produces, Samantha is entitled to interest at the rate (subject to the discretion of the court) of 4 per cent per annum on this sum from the date of Alex's death until the conversion is effected. Any shortfall in the actual income in any year must be made good, first out of any surplus in future years and then (if necessary) out of capital when the asset is sold.

Although an interest in remainder is saleable, the uncertainties surrounding the date it will fall into possession, and the amount of inheritance tax that it may have to bear, considerably discount its market value. Generally, therefore, it is better for trustees to retain such interest until it falls into possession. Apportionment is effected under the rule in *Re Earl of Chesterfield's Trusts* (1883) 24 ChD 643. This requires a reversionary interest to be valued at the date of its sale or (if later) its falling into possession. A proportion of this sum ranks as capital, the balance as income. Let us suppose that the valuation produces a figure of £10,000. The proportion treated as capital is that part of £10,000 which, if invested at 4 per cent interest with yearly rests, would (after deducting income tax at the basic rate) produce the sum of £10,000. Edwin receives that part; the balance goes to Samantha.

(b) The power of advancement under the **Trustee Act 1925, s. 32**, is a power to advance capital money, which therefore excludes money arising by way of income. The statutory power is not applicable to capital monies arising under the **Settled Land Act 1925**, but that is not relevant in the problem because the trust of the leasehold land in Yorkshire arose only on Alex's death, which was after 1996, since which date no new settlements under the **Settled Land Act 1925** can be created. The power is therefore exercisable in respect of all the items of property comprising Alex's residuary estate. Monies raised on the sale (pursuant to the rule in *Howe v Earl of Dartmouth*) of Rocky and the interest in remainder could be advanced to Edwin under **s. 32**, as could any securities (e.g., shares) in which the trustees might invest the proceeds of such sales. Bearing in mind the discounted market value of an interest in remainder, the trustees might be better advised to sell one or more of the other assets. Although the power is to apply only money, in practice the courts have permitted trustees to transfer trust assets, such as land or shares, directly to a beneficiary by way of advancement under the statutory power, rather than requiring the trustees to sell the assets in question to provide the beneficiary with the funds to purchase them for himself: *Re Collard's Will Trusts* [1961] Ch 293.

The power under **s. 32** is to advance up to one-half of a beneficiary's vested or presumptive share of capital. Since Edwin has a vested interest in the entire capital, the power could extend to a maximum of one-half the value of the residuary estate. The written consent of any person with a prior interest (i.e., Samantha) is necessary.

The statutory power is exercisable only for the beneficiary's 'advancement or benefit'. 'Advancement' means establishing the beneficiary in life; 'benefit' is broadly interpreted. Together they mean any use of the money which improves the beneficiary's material situation: *Pilkington v IRC* [1964] AC 612, HL. Usually a benefit is a financial benefit (e.g., from tax saving); but it can include even a purely moral benefit. In *Re Clore's Settlement Trusts* [1966] 1 WLR 955, an advancement by way of a gift to charity was held to be for the benefit of a wealthy beneficiary: but the court emphasised that the moral compunction must be that of the beneficiary, not that of the trustees. In *X v A* [2005] EWHC 2706 (Ch), Hart J held that it was not open to the trustees to make advancements of sums which the beneficiary intended to give to charity. Although the beneficiary considered herself under a moral obligation, the advancement could not be for her material benefit since (unlike the circumstances in *Clore*) the amount proposed to be advanced exceeded the value of her own free resources. An advancement may take the form of a sub-trust, and beneficiaries of such sub-trust might even include other persons—such as any children Edwin may have in the future: *Pilkington v IRC*. It remains unclear whether an advancement under which the beneficiary is merely a discretionary object suffices. The trustees may make the advancement directly to Edwin, or to Edwin's parent or guardian for Edwin's benefit; but if the advancement is for a specified purpose, the trustees should not pay the money directly to Edwin unless they consider that they can trust him to carry out the prescribed purpose: *Re Pauling's Settlement Trusts* [1964] Ch 303, CA.

Question 5

Mole, who died recently, made the following dispositions in his will:

(a) £10,000 to his son Bill, provided he attained the age of 18;

(b) his shares in Midnight Oil Ltd to his daughter Delia, provided she attained the age of 25; and

(c) his freehold house, 'Dunroamin', to his other daughter Elizabeth, defeasible upon her marrying under the age of 21.

It was further provided that neither of the dispositions to the daughters should take effect until the death of Mole's widow.

Mole's wife has survived him. Bill is now aged 14, Delia is 16 and Elizabeth is 19.

Advise Mole's executors and trustees whether they may (or must) use income to assist Mole's children; and, if so, to what extent.

Commentary

This is a tricky question: the law is extraordinarily complex, and the things asked are very precise. Some examination papers carry at least one treacherous question like this for those who have worked hard and really enjoy the subject. A cool-headed and well-prepared student can earn high marks; a persistent waffler, however, will be skating on very thin ice. If you do decide to attempt this sort of question, it is better to leave it until later in the examination, when you already have at least a couple of good answers under your belt. This is definitely not a question for 'writing yourself in'.

Answer plan

(a) • Contingent pecuniary legacy
  • Does it carry intermediate income?
  • **Trustee Act 1925, s. 31**

(b) • Contingent and future specific bequest
  • Does it carry intermediate income (**LPA 1925, s. 75**)?
  • *Re McGeorge*
  • **Trustee Act 1925, s. 31(1)**

(c) • Future specific devise

• Does it carry intermediate income (**LPA 1925, s. 175**)?

• *Re McGeorge*

• **Trustee Act 1925, s. 31(1)(ii)**

Suggested answer

It is convenient to deal with each child in turn.

(a) Bill. The Trustee Act 1925, s. 31, provides for the circumstances in which trustees may (or must) pay the trust income to beneficiaries who are not entitled to it under the terms of the trust instrument. In the case of a contingent interest, the section applies only if the limitation carries the intermediate income or interest for the maintenance of the legatee (s. 31(3)).

Since the gift to Bill comprises a sum of money, it is a pecuniary legacy. It is also contingent since it vests only if Bill attains 18. Generally, a contingent pecuniary legacy does not carry the intermediate income: *Re Raine* [1929] 1 Ch 716. However, such a gift does carry interest if (*inter alia*) it was made to a minor by his father. Two requirements must, however, be met. First, there must be no other fund provided for his maintenance: *Re George* (1877) 5 ChD 837. Secondly, the contingency must not be the attaining of an age greater than the age of majority (presently 18): *Re Abrahams* [1911] 1 Ch 108. This latter requirement is clearly satisfied. Assuming that the former is also met, and that there is no expression of a contrary intention in the will, the gift will carry interest and so fall within the Trustee Act 1925, s. 31. This exceptional case is indeed expressly recognised by s. 31(3), which states that the section applies to a contingent legacy made (*inter alia*) by a parent of the legatee if, under the general law, the legacy carries interest for the maintenance of the legatee, and it specifies a rate of interest of 5 per cent (s. 31(3)). Whether such legacy does carry such interest is determined by reference to the cases, including those mentioned above.

Assuming the gift carries such interest, the Trustee Act 1925 imposes a trust to accumulate this income during Bill's minority, but gives the trustees a power to pay to Bill's (surviving) parent or guardian, or otherwise apply for or towards his maintenance, education or benefit, the whole or such part of the income as may be reasonable, whether or not there is any other fund applicable to the same purpose. The trustees must have regard (*inter alia*) to the age of the minor, his requirements and generally to the circumstances of the case (Trustee Act 1925, s. 31(1)). Accumulations may be applied for the benefit of the minor as if they were income of the current year (Trustee Act 1925, s. 31(2) proviso).

When Bill attains 18, his gift vests and he is entitled to the capital and accumulations. If Bill dies under 18, the gift does not vest and (in the absence of a gift over) it will go on a resulting trust to Mole's estate. Any sums previously paid to or for Bill's benefit under s. 31, however, need not be repaid.

(b) Delia. This gift is a contingent and future specific bequest of personality. Under the Law of Property Act 1925, s. 175, such a bequest carries the intermediate income from the death of the testator, except so far as such income is otherwise expressly disposed of. There being no such express disposal here, Delia will receive the intermediate income eventually if she attains 25.

This does not, however, mean that the income is in the meantime subject to s. 31; for that section gives way to a contrary intention in the will (Trustee Act 1925, s. 69(2)). The deferring of the gift suggests that the testator did not intend Delia to have the intermediate income until the widow's death. In *Re McGeorge* [1963] Ch 544, the testator specifically devised land to his daughter but stated that the devise was not to take effect until the death of his widow. Cross J held that by so deferring the enjoyment of the property the testator had shown an intention that the intermediate income should not be subject to s. 31, but should be accumulated for 21 years (the relevant period of accumulation) or until the earlier death of the widow. If Mole's disposition indicates a similar intention, the same result will ensue.

If, however, the court does not find a contrary intention from the postponement of the bequest, the application of the income is governed by the Trustee Act 1925, s. 31(1). Thus there is an accumulation trust during Delia's minority, and the trustees have power to apply income for her maintenance or benefit. The position is the same as that in respect of Bill during his minority. When Delia attains 18, the trustees must pay her the income that arises thereafter: this is indicated by s. 31(1)(ii), which gives a beneficiary who at 18 'has not a vested interest in such income' the right to such income. Since her interest is contingent, however, any accumulations made during her minority are not paid to her at 18, but remain part of the capital of the fund subject to her interest vesting at the age of 25.

(c) Elizabeth. This gift is a future specific devise of property which carries the intermediate income unless it is otherwise expressly disposed of (Law of Property Act 1925, s. 175). As in the case of Delia, however, the postponement of the gift may evidence an intention that it should not carry such income until the widow's death. In support of his decision in *Re McGeorge*, Cross J pointed out that, if such a disposition were to be treated as carrying the intermediate income, an adult devisee with a vested interest would be able to call for an immediate conveyance in disregard of the instruction that the gift be deferred.

There was another ground for the decision in *Re McGeorge*. The daughter in that case (like Elizabeth in the problem) was over 18 and had an interest which, although future and defeasible, was vested. Cross J held that she was not entitled to the income under the Trustee Act 1925, since s. 31(1)(ii) confers the right to income at majority only on a beneficiary who does not then have a vested interest in such income.

On either of these bases, therefore, the result is that the income must be accumulated until the widow's death, or (if earlier) until Elizabeth's interest ceases to be defeasible on her attaining 21 without having already married.

Question 6

(a) Consider the classes of persons on whose behalf the court is empowered to approve an arrangement under the **Variation of Trusts Act 1958**.

AND

(b) In 2000, Mark, a wealthy businessman, settled a large sum of money in trust for such of his two sons, Luke and John, as should attain the age of 30, if both in equal shares, with remainders over in default to their respective issue (if any).

Mark had for several years expressed a desire to retire to the Channel Islands, and last year he went to live on Jersey. His sons, Luke and John, however, who are presently aged 16 and 18 respectively, are at school in Yorkshire and hope to read law at a university in England. Both are presently unmarried and without children. Mark's solicitor has advised him that, on grounds both of administrative convenience and tax-saving, the trust should be transferred to Jersey.

Advise the trustees whether such transfer can be sanctioned by the court under the **Variation of Trusts Act 1958**; and, if so, of the likelihood that the court's consent will be obtained.

Commentary

The suggested answer to part **(b)** illustrates the importance of not giving a definite answer to problems likely to turn upon a multiplicity of facts which are not stated. Do not be afraid, in such cases, to indicate what further information you may require. Indeed, sometimes the question will expressly ask you to do this.

Answer plan

(a) • VTA 1958, s. 1(1), paras (a)–(d)
  • Cases on of scope of **para. (b)**
  • Need for 'benefit' in **paras (a)–(c)**
(b) • Consent on behalf or minors or unborns
  • 'Benefit' for persons within **paras (a) and (c)**
  • Case law on different sorts of 'benefit'

Suggested answer

(a) The Variation of Trusts Act 1958, s. 1, empowers the High Court to approve an arrangement varying or revoking the trusts on behalf of four classes of persons, these being listed in paras (a) to (d) of s. 1(1).

Paragraph (a) comprises minors and other persons who by reason of incapacity are incapable of assenting; the interest of such person can be either vested or contingent. Paragraph (c) applies to persons unborn. Paragraph (d) refers to persons who have an interest under the discretionary trust which will arise under protective trusts where the interest of the principal beneficiary has not yet failed or determined.

The definition of persons falling within para. (b) is, however, the most complex. It includes any person (whether ascertained or not) who may become entitled to an interest under the trusts as being at a future date or on the happening of a future event a person of any specified description or a member of a specified class. The proviso however excludes any person who would be of that description or a member of that class if the said date had fallen or the said event had happened at the date of application to the court.

Case law has indicated the scope of para. (b). In *Re Suffert's Settlement* [1961] Ch 1, the settlor's daughter had a life interest under the trust together with a general testamentary power of appointment. In default of appointment, the property was to be held for those persons who would be her statutory next of kin if she died intestate and unmarried. The daughter, who was unmarried and aged 61, applied to the court for approval to be given to an arrangement dividing the fund between herself and her statutory next of kin. Buckley J held that he was not empowered to give consent on behalf of the daughter's two cousins because they fell within the proviso. If the daughter had died at the date of application to the court, the two cousins would be her statutory next of kin: they 'would be' persons of that description. Other potential next of kin, however, are not within the proviso, and the court is empowered to give its consent on their behalf. *Re Moncrieff's Settlement Trusts* [1962] 1 WLR 1344 is to similar effect.

In *Knocker v Youle* [1986] 1 WLR 934, it was held that para. (b) does not enable the court to give its consent on behalf of persons who have contingent (albeit very remote) interests. This is because the paragraph refers only to persons 'who may become entitled', not to those who already are. *Re Suffert's* and *Re Moncrieff 's Settlement Trusts*, were distinguishable because prospective next of kin of a living person have no interest in that person's estate, they have merely an expectation (a spes). Riddall, however, has argued that *Knocker v Youle* is wrong, and that the word 'interest' in the first part of para. (b) refers to a vested interest: Riddall [1987] Conv 144. This would mean that para. (b) would include persons who have merely a contingent interest, provided such contingency is more than one step removed.

It might also be pointed out that s. 1 does not enable the court to give its consent on behalf of persons merely on the ground that they are untraceable. In such cases, however, a *Benjamin* order might be appropriate: *Re Benjamin* [1902] 1 Ch 723.

Lastly, it is provided that, except in the case of para. (d), the court shall not approve an arrangement unless it is satisfied that it is for the benefit of the persons on whose behalf approval is given.

(b) An arrangement varying or revoking the terms of a trust under the Variation of Trusts Act 1958 has been held to include the sanctioning of the 'export' of a trust to a foreign jurisdiction. The court has power to consent on behalf of beneficiaries who fall within paras (a) to (d) of s. 1(1). As a minor having a contingent interest under the trusts, Luke falls within para. (a). Moreover, any issue of either son fall within para. (c), since these are persons unborn. Consent cannot be given on behalf of John, however, since he no longer falls within any of the paragraphs: he has already attained majority, and has an interest under the trust, albeit contingent. Under the statute, therefore, John's own consent to the export of the trust is required.

The court is not obliged to sanction an application to the court under the Variation of Trusts Act 1958: the court may give its approval 'if it thinks fit'. Furthermore, the court may not approve an arrangement on behalf of persons within paras (a) to (c) unless it would be for the benefit of those persons. In *Re Seale's Marriage Settlement* [1961] Ch 574, the court approved, on behalf of the children, the export of a marriage settlement to Canada, which was the country to which the family had emigrated many years earlier and in which they were permanently settled. The benefit to the children was one of administrative convenience.

By contrast, in *Re Weston* [1969] 1 Ch 223 the Court of Appeal refused to give its consent, on behalf of minor beneficiaries, to the export of a trust to Jersey. Unlike their counterparts in the aforementioned case, the family here had only just moved to Jersey and there was no evidence that they intended to stay there any length of time. The judges involved, however, gave different reasons for their refusal. Stamp J at first instance castigated the arrangement as a blatant piece of tax avoidance: yet tax avoidance is lawful, and most applications under the Act have tax-saving as a main object. In the Court of Appeal, Lord Denning MR, in Shakespearian vein, considered that the minors' welfare might be imperiled were they to be uprooted from England. This outweighed any benefit from tax-saving. Harman LJ, by contrast, decided on the ground that Jersey law could not administer trusts; but this opinion was evidently made *per incuriam*: *Re Windeatt's Will Trusts* [1969] 1 WLR 692. Moreover, in the later case of *Re Chamberlain* (1976, unreported) the court approved an export of a trust to Guernsey where the main beneficiaries were resident in France and Indonesia.

It therefore appears that the export of a trust upon the grounds proposed in the problem will be permitted unless the welfare of unborn or minor beneficiaries is endangered. There is probably little likelihood of endangerment as regards the unborn beneficiaries; but more evidence is needed to assess the impact upon Luke's welfare. Such evidence would include whether it is intended that Luke should cease to be educated in England, or whether he is to remain in the country while the rest of his family move to Jersey.

Further reading

Griffiths, G., 'Antipodean Revelations? The Beneficiary's Right to Information after "*Rosewood*"' [2005] Conv 93.

Hayton, D., 'The Irreducible Core Content of Trusteeship', in *Trends in Contemporary Trust Law* (A. J. Oakley, ed.), Oxford University Press, 1996, chapter 3.

Luxton, P., 'An unascertainable problem in variation of trusts' (1986) 136 NLJ 1057.

Luxton, P., 'Variation of trusts: settlors' intentions and the consent principle in *Saunders* v. *Vautier*' (1997) 60 MLR 719.

Nobles, R., 'Charities and ethical investments' [1992] Conv 115.

Riddall, J., 'Does it or doesn't it? Contingent interests and the Variation of Trusts Act 1958' [1987] Conv 144.

12

Pension-fund trusts

Introduction

For trusts lawyers, both professional and academic, pension funds are an area of increasing importance and interest, not to mention their high profile in the political and economic arenas. Most pension-fund trusts are created by an employer (which it is here convenient to call 'the company') with separate trustees who hold the fund upon trust to pay pensions to retired employees in accordance with each employee's contractual entitlement. Under some schemes (non-contributory schemes) the whole fund is provided by the company alone; but many schemes are contributory in that the employees also make contributions of a specified amount.

Most of these funds take the form of a trust, and there are two principal reasons for this. First, the trust enables the assets of the pension fund to be distinguished from those of the employer company. This offers some safeguards against an unscrupulous employer and makes it more difficult (though, as the Robert Maxwell saga revealed, not impossible) for the employer to treat the pension fund as its own property. Secondly, very important tax exemptions are available to pension funds, but only to those which exist in the form of an irrevocable trust. The Maxwell scandal led to a review of the law relating to pension funds, and to the introduction of special rules to regulate them in the **Pensions Act 1995**. This Act set up a regulatory authority with supervisory powers over trustees of pension funds, it introduced minimum funding requirements and restrictions on an employer's receipt of surplus while a scheme is ongoing and it requires one-third of the trustees to be member-nominated trustees. The **Pensions Act 2004** further strengthened the legislative protection by replacing the minimum funding rules with a more flexible scheme, by setting up the Pensions Protection Fund and by creating the office of the Pensions Regulator. It also permits the proportion of member-trustees to be increased, by regulation, to one-half: **Pensions Act 2004, s. 243**.

Pension funds increasingly feature in courses on equity and trusts. In the context of trusts law, it is possible to identify three important areas: the extent to which the law of trusts is developing special rules for pension funds; the beneficial ownership of a surplus; and the control of the exercise of powers under a pension fund. Each of these areas is covered by one of the three questions and answers in this chapter.

Useful discussions of pension funds generally are to be found in the following books: Parker and Mellows, *The Modern Law of Trusts* (A. J. Oakley, ed.) 9th edn, Sweet & Maxwell, 2008; Hayton and Mitchell, *Hayton and Marshall: Cases and Commentary on the Law of Trusts and Equitable Remedies*, 13th edn, Sweet & Maxwell, 2010; Martin, *Hanbury and Martin: Modern Equity*, 18th edn, Sweet & Maxwell, 2009.

Question 1

To what extent is the law of trusts developing a distinct set of principles for pension-fund trusts?

Commentary

The question raises interesting issues and admits of no definite answer. As with many essay-style questions, it is for the candidates to create their own structures for their answers. The suggested answer examines three ways in which pension-fund trusts tend to differ from the traditional family trust (the number of beneficiaries, the large size of their investments and their contractual nature). It then considers the question in relation to each of them in turn.

Answer plan

- Large number of beneficiaries
  - potential problem: uncertainty of objects
  - judicial response: *McPhail* v *Doulton*
- Large size of many pension funds: cf. large charitable trusts
  - potential problem: unduly restrictive investment clause
  - judicial response: *Mason* v *Farbrother*
- Essential contractual nature
  - potential problem: adequate control of powers
  - judicial response: *Mettoy* case; *Imperial Group Pension Trust*; *Wilson* v *Law Debenture Trust*

Suggested answer

Although pension funds normally adopt the trust form, they differ in a number of ways from family trusts. One important difference is in the sheer number of beneficiaries: a family trust is likely to have a small range of beneficiaries, whereas under a pension fund the beneficiaries may be reckoned in the hundreds of thousands. The House of Lords in *McPhail* v *Doulton* [1971] AC 424 recognised the need for trust law (which was largely developed in the context of family trusts) to adapt to take account of the modern large-scale trusts for the benefit of employees. This it did by discarding the 'complete list' test for discretionary trusts. It appears that the House of Lords intended its decision to be of general application, and not to be restricted to pension-fund trusts.

It is therefore evident that the growth in pension-fund trusts has had an impact upon the general law of trusts. What is more difficult to ascertain is the extent to which the law of trusts is developing, or ought to develop. rules of special application to these pension-fund trusts. In addition to the large number of beneficiaries, there are other elements which distinguish such trusts from family trusts. Thus some pension-fund trusts contain many millions of pounds—far larger than the majority of family trusts. In the context of trustees' investment policy, Megarry V-C in *Cowan* v *Scargill* [1985] Ch 270 saw no reason to hold that different principles should be applied to pension-fund trusts from those which apply to other trusts. In contrast to this, in *Mason* v *Farbrother* [1983] 2 All ER 1078, the judge considered that the very size of the pension fund involved (£127 million) meant that it had 'something of a public element in it'. He treated this as a special circumstance justifying the court's sanctioning an extension of the trustees' investment powers under the Trustee Act 1925, s. 57, beyond that permitted under the general law at that time. (The courts showed a similar willingness to permit a widening of the investment powers of trustees of very large charitable trusts: see *Trustees of the British Museum* v *A-G* [1984] 1 WLR 418 and *Steel* v *Wellcome Custodian Trustees Ltd* [1988] 1 WLR 167.) The Pensions Act 1995, s. 34(1), gave trustees of an occupational pension scheme the same powers of investment as if they were entitled to the assets absolutely; and similarly wide powers were conferred on trustees of other trusts by the Trustee Act 2000, s. 3(1). Future applications to the court are therefore more likely to comprise attempts to have restrictions on investment imposed by the trust instrument removed. It remains to be seen if the courts will adopt a different approach for pension-fund trusts in these circumstances.

Most important of all, perhaps, is the fact that the beneficiaries of pension-fund trusts (unlike the majority of beneficiaries under family trusts) are not volunteers but provide consideration for their benefits. This was first acknowledged judicially in *Kerr* v *British Leyland (Staff) Trustees Ltd* [2001] WTLR 1071 and has been accepted in subsequent cases, notably *Mettoy Pension Trustees* v *Evans* [1990] 1 WLR 1587 and *Davis* v *Richards & Wallington Industries Ltd* [1990] 1 WLR 1511. The consideration may take the form of direct contributions to the fund; but even if the fund is non-contributory, the employees can be treated as furnishing consideration by working for the employer in the expectation that they will eventually receive a pension from the fund. Indeed, pensions are sometimes considered to be a form of deferred remuneration. Since the employees in a pension fund provide commercial consideration for their benefits, a pension-fund trust is therefore an example of a commercial (or at least a quasi-commercial) trust, in contradistinction to the traditional family trust, which is essentially a creature of the settlor's bounty. It appears, however, that the underlying contractual basis of a pension fund does not itself preclude the employees from being entitled to any surplus by way of resulting trust: *Davis v Richards & Wallington Industries Ltd*.

It was the contractual nature of the employees' rights that impressed Warner J in the *Mettoy* case that the power to appoint the surplus, although vested in the company rather than the trustees, was a fiduciary power rather than a personal power. Furthermore, as the company was in liquidation and there was nobody who could exercise that power (a position since modified by the **Pensions Act 1995, s. 25**), it was appropriate for the court to exercise it in the most appropriate manner. There is no comparable instance of the court's executing a fiduciary power in the context of a family trust. At first sight, *Klug v Klug* [1918] 2 Ch 67, may appear to run counter to this view. In that case, which involved a family trust, one of two trustees (the Public Trustee) wished to exercise the power of advancement in favour of the beneficiary in remainder, but the other trustee objected on grounds which indicated that she had taken improper considerations into account. The court ordered the advancement to be made. It is arguable, however, that the court was not exercising the discretion itself, but was merely giving effect to the wishes of the untainted trustee. The remedy in the *Mettoy* case may therefore, in practice, be available only in the peculiar circumstances of a pension-fund trust.

There is now implicit judicial recognition that established principles of trust law are inadequate to control the exercise of all powers under a pension fund. Thus it is evident that not all powers exercisable under a trust can be fiduciary powers, so that equity is powerless to intervene. New duties in relation to the exercise of powers under a pension-fund trust are therefore being imported from the law of contract. Thus, the employee's right to have the pension fund properly managed, and the correlative duties imposed on those with powers in relation to the fund, are being treated as derived from the employee's contract of employment: see particularly *Imperial Group Pension Trust Ltd* v *Imperial Tobacco Ltd* [1991] 1 WLR 589. Since it is equity which traditionally fills the gaps left in the common law, this might be considered a reversal of roles! It appears, however, that the courts are unwilling to permit the commercial nature of a pension-fund trust to justify a departure from the general rule of trust law, that a beneficiary is not entitled to see documents which reveal the reasons for the exercise of the trustees' discretion: see *Wilson v Law Debenture Trust Corp.* [1995] 2 All ER 337.

Question 2

In the absence of an express indication in the trust deed establishing a pension fund or the exercise of any power to deal with surplus funds, it is difficult to ascertain who is beneficially entitled to any surplus that arises. This is largely the fault of trust law itself.

Discuss.

Commentary

The question deals with an important aspect of pension-fund trusts: the ownership, subject to any appointment, of any surplus. 'Surplus' means the amount by which the value of the trust's assets exceed its actuarial liabilities. The liabilities are the payments which the fund needs to make to satisfy the contractual entitlements of its pensioner-beneficiaries, these being retired employees currently receiving a pension, and present employees when they eventually retire. So long as the pension-fund trust continues, the surplus is merely actuarial. There is no actual surplus until the trust is wound up, which may occur if the company which created it is taken over or is dissolved on insolvency.

Surpluses began to be amassed in the 1980s, largely owing to higher than expected interest rates and redundancies, which reduced the anticipated demands on the funds. To combat this, the **Finance Act 1986** imposed a ceiling on the permitted size of surpluses, so that schemes which operated with excessive surpluses lost the tax advantages. If the company which set up and (at least partly) funded the scheme was beneficially entitled to a large surplus, it could become a target of a 'corporate raid', i.e., an attempted takeover by another company seeking to get its hands on the surplus funds. For primarily these reasons, the issue of the application of surplus funds came to prominence in the 1990s, and, in view of the recession and insolvencies of that period and beyond, seems likely to remain important.

Answer plan

- Introduction
  - significance of determining beneficial ownership
- Theories
  - overfunding by employer
  - resulting trust
- Conclusion
  - more meaningful to consider how surplus is applied

Suggested answer

The need to identify the beneficial ownership in a pension-fund surplus can arise in two sets of circumstances: where the pension fund is continuing, and where it is wound up (which may occur when the company which established it is dissolved or taken over). The trust instrument may specify how, in either event, any surplus is to be applied. Most instruments, however, in order to retain flexibility, do not. Instead, most confer a variety of powers (either on the trustees or the company) to enable them to deal with the surplus. Since, however, the exercise of a power is necessarily discretionary, it is important to ascertain who is entitled to the surplus should there be no exercise of the power, i.e., to ascertain who has a beneficial interest subject to defeasance.

Identifying such beneficial ownership can be difficult, and the Pensions Act 1995 does not provide a solution. Superficially, it might appear that the law of trusts is to blame, since most pension funds (in order both to create funds distinct from the employer's own assets and to take advantage of various tax exemptions) are created as trusts; and, on the recent occasions when the courts have applied principles of trust law, there has been no consistency of result. A deeper analysis, however, suggests that the uncertainties are not wholly a result of trust law, but arise also from the nature of pension funds themselves.

In *Re Courage Group Pension Schemes* [1987] 1 WLR 495, Millett J noted that, under most pension schemes, the employees cannot be asked to increase their contributions, even if the fund is in deficit, and it will be the company which must make good any shortfall. Any surplus is therefore to be treated as the result of overfunding by the company alone, and so would appear to belong (so far as not appointed) to the company beneficially.

A different view, however, was taken in *Mettoy Pension Trustees Ltd* v *Evans* [1990] 1 WLR 1587. There, Warner J thought that, if the company were effectively at liberty to apply the surplus in any way it wished, it was difficult to appreciate why the trust instrument should expressly give it a power to do something it was in any event entitled to do: namely, to apply the surplus to the benefit of the employee-objects. Warner J's judgment seems, therefore, to proceed on the basis that, subject to the exercise of any power of appointment, the surplus belonged beneficially to the employees.

Only a few weeks after judgment was delivered in *Mettoy*, the court was again asked to rule on the application of a surplus in *Davis* v *Richards & Wallington Industries Ltd* [1990] 1 WLR 1511. It is therefore not surprising that *Mettoy* was not cited in the later case, where Scott J adopted a different approach. Here, the pension scheme had been wound up with a surplus of £3 million. Contributions to it were derived from three sources: the company, the employees and other companies' pension schemes which had joined and whose assets had been transferred (the transferred funds). The scheme had in fact been amended to enable the surplus to be applied to the employees; but the court was asked to decide (*inter alia*) how, in the absence of the valid exercise of such power, the surplus should be held.

Scott J decided that, in the absence of any indication in the trust instrument, there was a presumption that the surplus was held on a resulting trust for those who had contributed to it. He did not think that the fact that the contributions from all sources had a contractual origin under the pension scheme was itself sufficient to exclude any claim under a resulting trust. Under this particular scheme, the company had been required to contribute whatever sums were necessary to enable the trustees to maintain the benefits. The benefits should therefore be treated as having been funded first by the employees' contributions and by the transferred funds, and only secondly by the company's contributions. It was therefore logical to treat the surplus as being provided first by the company's contributions. In effect, the company had made an overpayment, and thereby acquired an equitable right to its repayment; and the device whereby such repayment was effected was the resulting trust. The practical result of this approach (which was similar to that adopted in *Re Courage*) was that the company was entitled to the entire surplus.

Scott J also rejected any claim under a resulting trust by the employees or the trustees of the transferred funds. He gave two reasons. First, the value of the benefits would be different for each employee, depending upon when he joined and how old he was when he left. A resulting trust was unworkable as between the employees, and the court would not impute to the employees an intention that would lead to such a result. Secondly, the scheme was established to take advantage of various tax exemptions, and the relevant legislation placed a ceiling on the amounts that could be returned to employees. A resulting trust for the employees would have breached these requirements, and equity would not therefore impute an intention to the employees that any part of the surplus derived from their contributions should be returned to them under a resulting trust. A resulting trust of the transferred funds was rejected on similar grounds. Scott J therefore held that any part of the surplus derived from either of these two sources was to devolve as *bona vacantia*.

In *Air Jamaica Ltd* v *Charlton* [1999] 1 WLR 1399, at p. 1412, however, Lord Millett, giving the advice of the Privy Council, expressed the view that Scott J's reasoning in the *Davis* case was erroneous. Lord Millett said that evidence that the employees did not intend to retain a beneficial interest could not prevent them having an interest under a resulting trust.

There is, therefore, a conflict of authority as to where, subject to the exercise of any power of appointment, the beneficial interest in any surplus in fact lies. Where the pension fund is wound up, the allocation of a surplus will usually be determined by the exercise of a power, and it has been held that the mere fact that a surplus on winding up might be attributable to overpayments by the employer is not a sufficient reason for the trustees to refuse to exercise the power so as to allow the surplus to go to the employer: *Thrells Ltd (1974) Pension Scheme* v *Peter Lomas* [1992] PLR 1.

Where the pension fund is still continuing, any surplus is merely actuarial: the extent of the surplus depends upon which of a variety of methods of calculation the actuary employs, and there can be no certainty that the surplus will continue or that it will not, in a future year, turn into a loss. It may therefore be inappropriate to seek to identify the ownership of a surplus in a continuing fund. There is much to be said for Knox J's observation in *Re London Regional Transport Pension Fund Trust Co. Ltd* (1993) *The Times*, 20 May that 'the question of whether a continuing fund is in surplus or in deficit cannot be answered with any precision, ... and the concept of ownership of a surplus is even more uncertain than that of ownership of the fund as a whole.'

In practice, the issue before the court tends not to be the abstract question of who owns a surplus, but the rather more concrete problem of construction of the trust instrument consistently with the **Pensions Act 1995** and other statutory provisions. The issue then resolves itself into determining whether the trust instrument authorises, or can be amended to authorise, the application of the surplus in the way proposed. As was said by the Court of Appeal in *National Grid Co.* v *Mayes* [1999] PLR 37, 'The solution lies within the terms of the scheme itself, and not within a world populated by competing philosophies as to the true nature and ownership of actuarial surplus.'

Question 3

Consider the extent to which the court can control the exercise of a power to appoint a surplus under a pension-fund trust.

Commentary

Most pension-fund trusts confer a variety of powers upon the trustees or the company (or the trustees with the consent of the company) to enable them to deal with any surplus. Examples of commonly found powers are: a power to amend the trust deed or the rules made under it in order to increase pensions or other benefits to the employees and pensioners beyond their contractual entitlements; a power to enable the company (and, more rarely, the employees) to take a 'contributions holiday' (i.e., to reduce or suspend its contributions to the fund in the event of there being an excessive surplus); and a power to make a payment out of the pension fund to the company. The power of the court to control the exercise of the power derives originally from equity, which means that the manner of the exercise of the power can be controlled only if it is a fiduciary power. Recent case law, however, has revealed the existence of duties derived from the law of contract. The suggested answer deals with duties of both types.

Answer plan

- Fiduciary power (power conferred on trustees)
  - relevant duties
- Trustees need not disclose reasons for decisions
- No-conflicts rule
  - effect of **Pensions Acts 1995** and **2004**
- Contractual duties
  - good faith

Suggested answer

If the power to appoint a surplus is vested in the trustees of the pension fund, it is inevitably a fiduciary power. In equity, the trustees of such a power must actively consider its exercise, must exercise it for its proper purpose, must consider fairly the respective claims of the objects of the power and must exclude any improper considerations.

The appointment of a surplus may be effected by the exercise of a power of amendment contained in the scheme itself. In *Edge v Pensions Ombudsman* [2000] Ch 602, the trustees had dealt with an actuarial surplus by exercising a power of amendment so as to reduce the contributions of employees and employers, to give additional service credit for members in service. Benefits for existing pensioners were not, however, increased, and some of these pensioners argued that, in exercising their discretion, the trustees had not acted impartially as between the different classes of beneficiaries. The Court of Appeal rejected this argument. The power to amend was a discretionary power, so that the decision of the trustees to prefer one class of beneficiaries to another could not be criticised. There being no evidence that the trustees had not exercised the power for its proper purpose, or that they had failed to give proper consideration to relevant matters or had not excluded from consideration irrelevant matters, there was nothing to indicate a breach of trust.

Even if the trustees of a pension fund have acted in breach of trust, as where they have taken improper considerations into account, it may be difficult for the beneficiaries to obtain evidence of such breach of trust. The problem is that it has been held that, like the beneficiaries under a family trust, the employee-beneficiaries cannot, in the absence of evidence of bad faith, compel the trustees to disclose the reasons for their decisions: *Wilson* v *Law Debenture Corp.* [1995] 2 All ER 337. In the view of Rattee J, the fact that the employees were not volunteers did not justify a departure from the general principles established in *Re Londonderry's Settlement* [1965] Ch 918. Sir Robert Walker, writing extra-judicially, has expressed cautious criticism of the decision in *Wilson*, both because the rationale for the *Londonderry* principles may not apply to commercial trusts such as pension funds, and also because it runs counter to the trend in administrative law towards a general duty to give reasons for decisions: Walker, chapter 5 in *Trends in Contemporary Trust Law* (A. J. Oakley, ed.), Oxford University Press, 1996, at p. 131.

Trustees are under a duty to prevent putting themselves in a position where their duties as trustees conflicts with their personal interests. The no-conflicts rule would have the potential to prevent trustees of pension funds who are also members of the fund from benefiting from decisions they make as trustees, e.g., through a decision to increase pensions. The **Pensions Act 1995, s. 39**, however, has restricted the application of the rule, so that trustees are not subject to the rule merely because they exercise their powers as trustees in a manner that benefits, or might benefit, them as members of the scheme.

Generally, a power conferred, not on the trustees, but on a third party, would be construed as a non-fiduciary (i.e., a personal) power, with the result that the manner of its exercise (or non-exercise) would not be subject to equity's scrutiny. Were this construction to be applied to pension funds, then, where (as happened in the past) a power to apply surplus assets was conferred on the company employer that was not itself a trustee of the fund, equity would not be able to prevent the employer from exercising (or from refraining from exercising) the power solely in order to benefit itself. In *Mettoy Pension Trustees* v *Evans* [1990] 1 WLR 1587, in rather special circumstances, Warner J treated the power vested in the employer (which was not itself a trustee) as a fiduciary power. His Lordship was influenced by the fact that the beneficiaries under a pension fund are not volunteers, but provide consideration for their pensions, and they might be thought to have earned a right to have the company properly consider the exercise of the power in their favour. He also took into account the desirability of preventing a company's pension-fund surplus from being raided by another company in a takeover bid.

The specific problem considered (but circumvented) by the decision in *Mettoy* was addressed by the Pensions Act 1995 (as amended by the Pensions Act 2004): where the employer is insolvent (as it was in *Mettoy*), any fiduciary powers vested in it are exercisable only by an independent trustee: ibid., s. 25. The same Act also dealt with the more general problem (highlighted by *Mettoy*) of the employer being in a position of conflict in relation to the exercise of a power. Thus, where there is an ongoing scheme, a power conferred on any person (including the employer) to make payments to the employer is exercisable only by the trustees: ibid., s. 37(2), and only in compliance with proposals approved by the Revenue and designed to protect the members: ibid., s. 37(4). A power vested in the employer to take a contributions holiday, however, is not a power to make payments to the employer, and so is not subject to these statutory safeguards.

The donee of a power under a pension scheme (whether himself a trustee of the fund or a third party) may owe duties to the employee-beneficiaries of the fund in relation to the exercise of that power which derive, not from equity (and so are not dependent upon the power's being construed as fiduciary), but rather from the common law: namely, the implied duties which arise by virtue of the contract of employment. These other duties (such as to act in good faith, and to exercise the power for its proper purpose and not for a collateral purpose) are similar to the particular duties which are imposed by equity on the donee of a fiduciary power. Provided these duties are fulfilled, there is no conflict in the exercise of the power resulting in a benefit to the donee of the power.

Thus in *Imperial Group Pension Trust Ltd* v *Imperial Tobacco Ltd* [1991] 1 WLR 589, Browne-Wilkinson V-C held that, as the employee-beneficiaries were not volunteers, the company's power to withhold consent to an amendment to a pension scheme had to be exercised in good faith. The company was not entitled to use its power to induce members to transfer to a new scheme. The duty of good faith implied into the contract of employment itself was therefore to be implied into the contract underlying the pension-fund trust. Similarly, in *British Coal Corporation* v *British Coal Superannuation Scheme Trustees Ltd* [1995] 1 All ER 912, Vinelott J stated that a company with a power to amend its pension scheme must exercise the power so as to fulfil the legitimate expectations of the members and pensioners; but, provided it does so, it may exercise the power so as to reduce or suspend its own contributions.

The emergence of these duties is not, however, without problems: since the duties are necessarily expressed in general terms, there may be practical difficulties for the company to know whether it is doing what is necessary to comply with them, particularly where the fund is still continuing so that the surplus is purely actuarial.

Further reading

Hayton, D., 'Pension Trusts and Traditional Trusts: Drastically Different Species of Trusts' [2005] Conv 229.

Moffatt, G., 'Pension Funds: a Fragmentation of Trust Law?' (1993) 56 MLR 471.

Nobles, R., 'Don't Trust the Trustee' (1990) 53 MLR 377.

Nobles, R., 'The Exercise of Trustees' Discretion under a Pension Scheme' [1992] Journal of Business Law 261.

Pittaway, 'Pension funds—is a separate branch of trust law evolving?' (1990) 4 Trust Law & Practice 156.

Scott of Foscote, Lord 'The fetters in trustees' discretions' (2002) 16 TLI 214.

Walker, Sir Robert, 'Some Trust Principles in the Pensions Context', in *Trends in Contemporary Trust Law* (A. J. Oakley, ed.), Oxford University Press, 1996, chapter 5.

13

Breach of trust

Introduction

This chapter includes real and personal remedies against trustees and other persons into whose hands property has passed in breach of trust. Questions are usually predictable. This topic often occurs chronologically at the end of a course and may, therefore, be reasonably fresh in the student's mind—always a bonus.

A question concerning the process of tracing is often popular and an important first step is to read *Re Diplock* [1948] Ch 465, where the Court of Appeal dealt thoroughly with the fundamental principles relating to equitable tracing. You should also read *Boscawen v Bajwa* [1996] 1 WLR 328, where the Court of Appeal indicated that aspects of the reasoning in *Re Diplock* are in need of reappraisal in the light of the significant developments in the law of restitution which have taken place in the last 50 years.

Here comes a difficulty. You need to know the extent to which tracing is permitted at law before you can embark on an examination of equitable tracing. So, you have spent the best part of the academic year studying equity and now you are expected to exhibit a familiarity with the common law. That, after all, smacks of real life which is not always conveniently departmentalised. It may be that your course covers the law of obligations and you have dealt with the common law and equity side by side. On the other hand, your lecturer may be an equity lawyer who feels unhappy with common law concepts. You should, therefore, know from the content of your course what is expected of you.

To what extent could you be expected to deal with the personal common law action of conversion or the action for money had and received in a course on equity? The answer is, probably, not at all. It is likely that you will only need to be able to deal with the tracing process at law rather than concern yourself with the precise nature of the claim. You should also bear in mind that, although the House of Lords' decision in *Lipkin Gorman v Karpnale Ltd* [1991] 2 AC 548 concerned only tracing at common law, their Lordships' observations on the defence of change of position are very broad, and are likely to be held applicable to tracing in equity also: *Boscawen v Bajwa* (though see Lord Millett's dicta in *Foskett v McKeown* [2001] 1 AC 102).

For additional reading (and you will find numerous articles referred to in the textbooks), look at Goff and Jones, *The Law of Restitution*, 7th edn, Sweet & Maxwell, 2006.

Question 1

The only restriction on the ability of equity to follow assets is the requirement that there must be some fiduciary relationship which permits the assistance of equity to be invoked. (Per Millett J, *Agip (Africa) Ltd* v *Jackson* [1990] Ch 265.)

Discuss, in the light of this quotation, the requirement that there must be some fiduciary relationship before tracing in equity is permitted.

Commentary

The central issue in this question is the requirement of a fiduciary relationship, so the answer requires a thorough discussion of the case law on this point. The crucial thing for the candidate is to ensure that the answer does not deteriorate into one of the 'write all you know' type. Related ideas can therefore be explored, but only to the extent that they throw light on the central issue.

The suggested answer explores the question in the following manner. First, it puts the requirement into context by briefly setting out what all the requirements are to trace in equity. Secondly, it examines the background and emergence of the requirement since the **Judicature Acts**, and mentions cases in which such requirement has been accepted or criticised. Thirdly, it compares the need for a fiduciary relationship with the need for an equitable (or perhaps a legal) proprietary right, looking in particular at the issue of theft from a legal beneficial owner. Fourthly, it looks at the ways in which the courts have treated the requirement flexibly: in not insisting that it necessarily exist between claimant and defendant, and in treating such relationship as arising in the case of mistaken payments.

Answer plan

- Brief statement of requirements for assets to be followed in equity
- Requirement of need for both an equitable proprietary right and a fiduciary relationship—discussion of cases where doubt as to this point (*Westdeutsche Landesbank* case compared with *Bristol and West Building Society* v *Mothew*; *Foskett* v *McKeown*)
- Extent of requirement for equitable proprietary right
- Discussion of types of fiduciary relationship and the courts' flexible approach

Suggested answer

There are certain requirements which must be satisfied before a claimant may follow assets in equity. These are: there must be an equity to trace; the property must be traceable; and the result must not be inequitable. The issue in the question is whether the first of these requirements, the equity to trace, imports the need for a fiduciary relationship.

Before the Judicature Acts 1873–75, the courts of common law and the Court of Chancery applied their own distinctive rules relating to tracing. Just as tracing at common law was available only to a person who had a proprietary right at law, so tracing in equity was available only to a person who had a proprietary right in equity. Following those Acts, it might have been thought that equitable tracing would be available to a beneficial legal owner where common law tracing proved inadequate. This indeed appears to have been recognised in *Banque Belge Pour L'Etranger* v *Hambrouck* [1921] 1 KB 321, CA. In *Re Diplock* [1948] Ch 465, however, the Court of Appeal expressed the view that, in order to be able to trace in equity, it was not sufficient for the claimant merely to have an equitable proprietary right, there also had to be a fiduciary relationship. In *Westdeutsche Landesbank Girozentrale* v *Islington LBC* [1996] AC 669, the House of Lords seemed to accept the correctness of this proposition. Other cases, however, reveal some judicial reluctance to accept such a requirement. Doubts were expressed by Millett LJ in *Bristol and West Building Society* v *Mothew* [1998] Ch 1, at p. 23; and in *Foskett* v *McKeown* [2001] 1 AC 102, Lord Millett (then in the House of Lords) stated that he could see no logic in the requirement. These observations may indicate that the Supreme Court might at some future time wish to reconsider *Re Diplock*. The requirement for a fiduciary relationship in order to trace in equity remains, however, for the present at least.

Where the claimant has an equitable proprietary right, there will be a fiduciary relationship. The classic example of this is, of course, the trust, whether express, implied or constructive. A trust is not, however, a prerequisite: a person who entrusts property to a fiduciary, for instance, will retain an equitable proprietary interest sufficient to enable her to trace. Thus, in *Re Hallett's Estate* (1880) 13 ChD 696, one Mrs Cotterill paid money to her solicitor to invest on her behalf; instead he paid part of this into his personal bank account. It was held that, in these circumstances, Mrs Cotterill was entitled to trace her money in equity. The same principles apply to all fiduciary relationships, such as those between a company and its directors, between a principal and agent, and between partners in a business *inter se*.

It is clear, however, that a fiduciary relationship is not itself sufficient to enable the claimant to trace. Tracing is, after all, the process of identifying the claimant's property or its product in a third party's hands, so there can be no right to trace if the claimant has no proprietary right to the assets in question. In the *Westdeutsche Landesbank* case, the House of Lords held that the bank retained no proprietary interest in money which it had paid to the defendant local authority under an interest rate swap arrangement which was *ultra vires* the local authority. The claimant would therefore have had no right to trace such money in equity. On the other hand, it may be that the requisite proprietary right need not be equitable. In *Aluminium Industrie Vaassen BV v Romalpa Aluminium Ltd* [1976] 1 WLR 676, it was held that, where a fiduciary relationship existed, even a legal owner (with no distinct equitable proprietary right) could trace in equity.

Because no fiduciary relationship exists in respect of property vested in a beneficial legal owner, it might appear that tracing is not available to such owner if the property is stolen from him by a thief. If the property stolen is money and is mixed by the thief in his own bank account, the victim, whilst possessing a personal remedy against the thief, cannot claim any legal proprietary remedy against the money in the account. In such circumstances, however, the House of Lords accepted that, once the victim's legal title to the money passes (upon mixing in the account), a constructive trust is imposed upon the thief, and it is this trust which gives rise to a fiduciary relationship enabling the victim to trace in equity into the mixed fund: see *Lipkin Gorman* v *Karpnale Ltd* [1991] 2 AC 548 (Lord Templeman); and the *Westdeutsche Landesbank* case (Lord Browne-Wilkinson).

The case law provides other illustrations of the courts' willingness to interpret the requirement for a fiduciary relationship flexibly. It does not, for example, matter that such relationship does not exist between the claimant and the person against whom the tracing claim is brought. In *Re Diplock* itself, money was wrongfully distributed by the executors of a will to a number of charities. It was held that the next of kin, who should have been entitled to such money, were entitled to trace into the hands of the money's innocent recipients. The right of the next of kin to trace arose from their equitable right against the executors to have the estate properly distributed. In that case, therefore, the fiduciary relationship was between the next of kin and the executors.

Another example of the court's flexible approach is in relation to payments made under a mistake. A fiduciary relationship, giving rise to a right to trace in equity, can also arise where the defendant receives the claimant's property as a result of a mistake. In *Chase Manhattan Bank NA v Israel-British Bank (London) Ltd* [1981] Ch 105, the plaintiffs, as a result of a bookkeeping error, wrongly made a double payment of $2 million into the account of the defendant bank. At that time, the common law action of money had and received did not apply to money paid as a result of a mistake of law, which that was (but this is no longer so: see *Kleinwort Benson Ltd* v *Lincoln City Council* [1999] 2 AC 349, HL). The plaintiffs therefore needed to be able to trace in equity. It was held that the mistaken second payment gave rise to a fiduciary relationship, which gave the plaintiffs a right to trace. The House of Lords in the *Westdeutsche Landesbank* case has since doubted that the fiduciary relationship arose at the time of the mistaken second payment; rather, their Lordships considered that it arose only when the defendant's conscience was affected, i.e., when it became aware of the mistake two days later. The decision in *Chase Manhattan* nevertheless remains good law in so far as it illustrates that the fiduciary relationship needed to trace does not need to be a pre-existing one.

Question 2

Brown is a solicitor and a trustee of the Rainbow Trust. His co-trustee, Grey, is not a solicitor, but is a member of the Rainbow family. Grey is content to leave the entire management of the trust to Brown. Under the terms of the trust, Leone has a life interest, and the capital is held for Azure and Grey in equal shares.

In 1990, Brown invested half of the trust fund in the family company, Rainbow Ltd, which he understood to be an authorised investment within the terms of the trust deed. In fact, the trust deed expressly prohibited the trustees from investing more than one-fifth of the trust fund in Rainbow Ltd. When Rainbow Ltd went into insolvent liquidation in 2009, the trust's total investment in that company was lost. All the other investments which Brown made have been very successful, however, and during the period he has been administering the trust a healthy capital growth has been achieved.

Between 1993 and 2000, Brown made advances of capital sums out of the trust to Leone, which comprised breaches of trust. Brown did not realise that these payments were in breach of trust, as he did not check the terms of the trust deed, which he kept in his office safe.

Advise Azure.

Commentary

This question covers breach of trust by trustees where they fail to comply with the terms of the trust. Distinctions between professional and non-professional trustees need to be considered, and between active and non-active trustees.

The question is not difficult but requires a knowledge of the statutory provisions imposing liability and providing defences. Discussion of the case law dealing with the possibility of setting off a profit made by successful investments against losses sustained by an improper investment is required, however, to achieve a good mark.

There is only one devious point hidden in the question and that relates to the limitation period. The clue to look out for is the careful use of dates. If they are not relevant, the examiner would probably have simply set the events in the previous year.

Answer plan

- Establishing the breaches of trust in the problem and the nature of the liability of the trustees

- Effect of breach which results in enhancement of profits for beneficiaries (rule in *Dimes* v *Scott*)

- Reversal of rule where gain and loss made in single transaction (*Fletcher* v *Green*)

- Effect of limitation in the **Limitation Act 1980, s. 21(3)** on problem

- Relief for trustee acting honestly and reasonably and who ought fairly to be excused (**Trustee Act 1925, s. 61**)

- Distinction between status of professional trustee (Brown) and lay trustee (Grey)

- Unjust enrichment of Leone; tracing and the defence of change of position

- Partial indemnities

Suggested answer

The basic principle is that trustees who commit a breach of trust which results in a loss to the trust estate are personally liable to the beneficiaries to make good the loss. Brown's excessive investment in Rainbow Ltd and the wrongful advances of capital were both in breach of the terms of the trust deed. Brown is therefore prima facie liable to make good such losses to the trust fund. The liability of trustees is personal, not vicarious: *Townley* v *Sherborne* (1643) J Bridg 35. Grey is not therefore vicariously liable for Brown's breaches of trust. Grey may be personally liable for his own breach, however, in failing to participate in the management of the trust and merely leaving matters in the hands of his co-trustee: *Bahin* v *Hughes* (1886) 31 ChD 390. Equity does not, after all, countenance a sleeping trustee.

The investment in Rainbow Ltd is a breach of trust to the extent that the amount invested exceeded the one-fifth limit imposed by the trust instrument. The measure of the trustees' liability is the loss caused to the trust. In this instance, the onus would be on Azure to establish that there is a loss which would not have occurred but for the breach: *Target Holdings Ltd* v *Redferns* [1996] 1 AC 421, HL, at p. 440. Unless there are circumstances which indicate that the trustees were in breach of trust in investing in Rainbow Ltd at all, it would seem that the trustees' liability would be limited to the loss of the excess over one-fifth only.

Brown has, however, invested the remaining assets profitably. Normally, a gain made in one transaction may not be set off against a loss suffered in another. This is the rule established in *Dimes* v *Scott* (1828) 4 Russ 195, where the trustees retained an unauthorised investment for longer than the prescribed period. When the investment was eventually sold, the trustees were able to invest extensively in Consols, as the price had dropped. This resulted in a greater gain for the remaindermen. The trustees were nevertheless held liable for the loss caused by the retention of the unauthorised investment without being allowed to set off the gain.

If the gain and the loss were made in a single transaction, though, then the rule is reversed. In *Fletcher* v *Green* (1864) 33 Beav 426, the proceeds of sale of an unauthorised investment were invested in Consols, the value of which then rose. It was held that the trustees were entitled to take advantage of such rise. The difficulty, as these cases illustrate, is often in determining whether the gains and losses occur in the same or in separate transactions. In *Bartlett* v *Barclays Bank Trust Co. Ltd (No. 1)* [1980] Ch 515, the trustees had engaged in a sequence of speculative investments. One of these, the Guildford project, was successful; but another, the Old Bailey project, was a disaster. The bank pleaded that it should be permitted to set off the profit from one against the loss on the other. Brightman J allowed them to do so, expressing the view that it would be unjust to deprive the bank of the element of salvage in assessing the cost of the shipwreck. In the question, Brown and Grey would be able to set off the gains only if they could show that the activities which produced such gains were so connected to the losses as to form part of one transaction. On the facts as stated, there is no evidence of such connection, and so the trustees are unlikely to succeed.

A claim brought by a beneficiary against a trustee for breach of trust must be brought within six years from the date on which the right of action arose (Limitation Act 1980, s. 21(3)). There is a proviso to the sub-section that time does not start to run against a remainderman until his interest falls into possession. As the advances made by Brown were in breach of trust, they would not cause Azure's interest to fall into possession for the purposes of the Limitation Act: *Re Pauling's Settlement Trusts* [1964] Ch 303, CA. Azure's interest falls into possession only on the death of Leone, and as the question suggests that Leone is still alive, it would appear that time has not yet even started to run against Azure. He will not, however, be permitted to bring any claim against the trustees if it is shown that he participated in, or consented to, the breach, or if it can be shown that he later acquiesced in the breach: *Re Pauling's Settlement Trusts*.

A trustee who would otherwise be liable for breach of trust may be relieved if he can show that he acted honestly and reasonably and ought fairly to be excused (Trustee Act 1925, s. 61). It is unlikely that the court would grant relief under this section to a person who is professionally involved with the management of trusts, such as Brown. It is the trustee who has the onus of showing that he acted honestly and reasonably: *Re Stuart* [1897] 2 Ch 583. There are no general principles in applying the statute; every case turns on its own circumstances: *Re Turner* [1897] 1 Ch 536. Nevertheless, it might be surmised that if Grey left everything to Brown and never asked for explanations, he would probably not be considered to have acted reasonably, and he might not even count as honest for this purpose: *Re Second East Dulwich Building Society* (1899) 79 LT 726. A trustee may also be able to escape liability by relying on an express exclusion clause in the trust instrument; the question does not indicate, however, whether the Rainbow Trust contained any such clause.

The fact that Brown is a solicitor and Grey apparently a layman may be a relevant factor in determining the liability of Brown and Grey *inter se*: if it can be shown that Brown exercised a controlling influence over Grey, the latter might be entitled to an indemnity from the former (*Re Partington* (1887) 57 LT 654). It seems unlikely, however, that an indemnity could be claimed by a non-participating trustee. Apart from this, it might be possible for Grey to claim a contribution from Brown under the Civil Liability (Contribution) Act 1978, although there is no reported case law as yet to indicate what the attitude of the courts might be where such a claim is brought by a passive trustee. Rights of indemnity or contribution between the trustees do not, however, affect the personal liability of each to Azure; so that if each of the trustees is personally liable, Azure could recover the full amount of the loss from either of them, leaving it to that trustee to make a claim against his co-trustee.

Leone received the advances in breach of trust. Leone has therefore been unjustly enriched, and she will be liable to repay to the trust the sums advanced to her if they can be traced into her hands, unless she can rely on the defence of change of position. The trustees' personal liability will be reduced to the extent of any sums so recovered from her. If, however, Leone can establish such a defence (so that she can show that she is an innocent volunteer who has, for example, spent the money so that it cannot be traced), *Re Diplock* [1948] **Ch 465** suggests that she will not be personally liable to repay the advances, since she did not receive the money from the personal representatives of an estate in the course of administration. The modern principle of unjust enrichment nevertheless suggests that she should remain personally liable, since she has still had the benefit of the sums she received (as where she spent them on a holiday). If Leone is held personally liable to repay, her liability is reduced to the extent that such sums can be personally recovered from the trustees (*Re Diplock*, at p. 503). If, on the other hand, Leone instigated or requested the breach, the trustees are entitled to impound her beneficial interest by way of indemnity: *Chillingworth* v *Chambers* [1896] **1 Ch 685**; **Trustee Act 1925, s. 62**. The trustees will also be entitled to withhold payments of income from Leone in order to repair the breach: cf. *Re Balfour's Settlement Trusts* [1938] **Ch 928**.

If it were to be shown that Grey had participated in the breach of trust, he will be required to indemnify Brown to the extent of his beneficial interest under the trust, which would effectively give Brown a partial indemnity: *Chillingworth* v *Chambers*.

Question 3

George was appointed the sole executor of Harriet's will. Harriet died last year leaving her entire estate, worth £130,000 after payment of debts, to her cousin Albert in Australia. George died recently. Albert has only just learned of this and has discovered that George, believing that as executor he was entitled to the estate beneficially and knowing that he was terminally ill, has made the following dispositions of the estate:

(a) £40,000 of the estate was contributed to the purchase of a house by George's daughter, Peggy. The house was purchased for £60,000 and Peggy contributed the remaining £20,000. The house is now worth £80,000.

(b) George settled £40,000 on trust for his son Felix as part of a marriage settlement on the occasion of his marriage to Matilda.

(c) George used £20,000 to buy a valuable antique Grecian urn which he gave to his service club.

(d) George used £20,000 to finance his gambling habits and this has all been lost at the Spend Casino.

(e) George gave the remaining £10,000 to his housekeeper May. May paid this into her current account, in which there was a balance of £5,000, but has since drawn out £10,000.

Advise Albert whether he has any claim against the recipients of Harriet's estate.

Commentary

This problem raises a number of different permutations of the tracing remedy. Most problems raised in this field relate to the issue of tracing in equity. The limitations of the remedy of tracing at common law need to be known.

The issue of the up-and-coming defence of change of position is also raised and merits some discussion of the important House of Lords' decision in **Lipkin Gorman v Karpnale Ltd [1991] 2 AC 548**, although this case is concerned with tracing at common law.

Answer plan

(a) • Position of Peggy as innocent volunteer; equitable proprietary interest of Albert; mixing of funds; inequitable results and the loss of the tracing remedy; equitable claims *in personam*

(b) • Marriage consideration and status of Felix with an equitable interest; Felix not 'equity's darling'; claim *in personam*

(c) • Status of club as volunteer; equitable tracing into volunteer's hands; identifiable proceeds of trust money

(d) • Position where trust money dissipated; tracing into hands of the casino which is a volunteer; defence of change of position; claim *in personam*

(e) • Mixing of trust money with that of innocent volunteer; rule in **Clayton's Case**; position where money used to buy investment

Suggested answer

The right to trace is available at common law if the claimant retains the legal title to the property. Here, tracing at law is not available because George, the legal owner, has disposed of the property and the legal title has passed. It is necessary, therefore, to consider the availability of the remedy in equity.

(a) Peggy is presumably an innocent volunteer. The trust funds have been mixed with her money. The mixed funds have been used to purchase a house. The value of the house has now risen.

Albert is the true beneficiary, and therefore has an equitable proprietary interest. £40,000 of the trust property is in the hands of an innocent volunteer and has been used for the acquisition of property. An equitable proprietary remedy may be available which will enable Albert to trace the property.

In equity, where the trust property has been transferred in breach of trust to an innocent volunteer who has mixed it with her own, the trust and the volunteer share *pari passu* in the property purchased with the mixed fund: *Sinclair* v *Brougham* [1914] AC 398, HL, *Re Diplock* [1948] Ch 465, CA. They will share the profits and the capital in the proportions in which they contributed.

The right to trace may be lost where it would produce an inequitable result. In *Re Diplock* it was held that where trust money was spent on altering or improving land then it would be inequitable to force the innocent volunteer to sell the land to satisfy a charge on it. Peggy has used the money to buy land. It might be argued, therefore, that her circumstances have changed as a result of the receipt of the trust money, thus rendering it inequitable for the remedy to be enforced against her. This would, however, mean that Peggy would be unjustly enriched. In the light of *Boscawen* v *Bajwa* [1996] 1 WLR 328, the most appropriate solution would be for the court to defer Albert's right to enforce the equitable charge until Peggy has had a reasonable opportunity to raise and pay the amount due, e.g., by mortgaging the house.

If the proprietary claim fails, then an equitable claim *in personam* can be brought for the principal sum of £40,000 without interest. However, Peggy will only be liable to the extent that the money cannot be recovered directly from George's own estate. The claim in these circumstances is limited to claims arising out of the administration of estates and is subject to the primary liability of the executor: *Re Diplock*.

(b) £40,000 was settled on trust under a marriage settlement for Felix. He is within the marriage consideration and, therefore, not a volunteer. Where trust property has been transferred to a bona fide purchaser of a legal estate for value and without notice of the equitable interest, the property is taken free from the claims of the beneficiaries. However, Felix has acquired merely an equitable as opposed to a legal interest and does not receive the protection of 'equity's darling'.

Alternatively, and especially if the tracing remedy does not satisfy Albert's loss, he may recover the loss (or the balance) in a claim *in personam*. In this case, Albert should look to the personal remedy against George's estate in the first instance, but may recover the balance from Felix in a claim *in personam*.

(c) The service club is a volunteer as it has given no consideration for the urn. Presumably it is also innocent. Equitable tracing is, however, available against an innocent volunteer if the property can be traced into the volunteer's hands. The trust money has been exchanged for the urn with no mixing of other funds. The club have the identifiable proceeds of the trust money. Albert can therefore trace in equity into the urn and obtain an order to restore the urn, being property acquired with the £20,000.

(d) £20,000 of trust property was dissipated by George on gambling at the Spend Casino.

The right to trace is lost where the property has ceased to be identifiable. Where the money has been dissipated, therefore, it can no longer be identified and cannot be traced. However, the money has passed into the hands of the Spend Casino, which is a volunteer, as no valuable consideration is given: *Lipkin Gorman* v *Karpnale Ltd* [1991] 2 AC 548. However, a casino stands the risk of losing or winning when it permits someone to place bets. The defence of change of position was considered in *Lipkin Gorman* v *Karpnale Ltd*, a case which was concerned with legal tracing only. In *Lipkin Gorman* v *Karpnale Ltd*, it was held by the House of Lords that a casino was entitled to set off any winnings made by the gambler on the basis that it had changed its position by paying such winnings to him. Change of position was not a complete defence and the club was held liable in an action for money had and received for the net amount he had lost gambling at the club. It was stated, *per curiam*, by the House of Lords, that it is right to recognise the defence of change of position in good faith in restitution claims, based on the unjust enrichment of the defendant. The House of Lords, however, left the development of this doctrine to future cases. So, although it is likely that future courts will develop this doctrine, there is presently no direct authority for this defence to be raised by the Spend Casino in a claim to trace in equity.

The Spend Casino will also be subject to a claim *in personam* under *Re Diplock*, as confirmed on appeal in *Ministry of Health* v *Simpson* [1951] AC 251, HL. This will be for the amount which Albert has been unable to claim from George's estate and will be limited to the principal sum without interest.

(e) £10,000 of trust money has been mixed in May's current account with £5,000 of her own money. Where trust money is mixed with that of an innocent volunteer, tracing in equity is available. However, May has withdrawn £10,000. As the account is a current account, the rule in *Clayton's Case* (1816) 1 Mer 572, first in, first out applies. The rule in *Clayton's Case* is a rule of convenience and applies unless it is impracticable or would result in injustice (*Barlow Clowes International Ltd (in liquidation)* v *Vaughan* [1992] 4 All ER 22). If the prima facie rule is to apply here, then, as May had £5,000 of her own money in the account, she is presumed to draw that out first, followed by £5,000 of trust money. The remaining money is, therefore, trust money.

If the £10,000 withdrawn has been used to buy an investment, Albert will be able to claim a charge on the investment and rank *pari passu* with May. If, however, the £5,000 trust money cannot be traced (if, for example, it has been dissipated), Albert will be left to pursue a claim *in personam* as discussed previously.

Question 4

On 1 January 2010, Tonto, who was trustee of the Una Charitable Trust, in breach of trust paid into his bank account £10,000 of the charity's money. There was already £6,000 of his own money in his account. One week later he bought shares to the value of £5,000 and withdrew this amount from his account. The next day, he drew out £3,500 which he used to buy a boat. On 1 March 2010, he paid into the account in breach of trust £5,000 belonging to the Duo Trust Fund, of which he was also trustee. The next day he drew out £5,000 which he used to pay debts which he had incurred in his business. The following day he withdrew a further £5,000 which he gave to his daughter, Dora, which she used as a deposit on a house she was buying.

The boat has now been destroyed in a hurricane. The shares are now worth £6,000.

Tonto has just been declared bankrupt.

Advise the beneficiaries of the two trusts.

Commentary

This question deals with the mixing of monies in a bank account. Once money or other property has been mixed, it is not possible to trace at common law. The question therefore requires an application of the rules for tracing in equity. The answer takes account of the significant decision of the Court of Appeal in *Boscawen v Bajwa* [1996] 1 WLR 328.

It is important to be aware that different rules apply to the mixing of trust monies with a trustee's own money, and the mixing of the monies of two trusts that are both treated as innocent volunteers.

Where there is a series of transactions involving payments into and out of a bank account, as here, it is essential to work the transactions through in draft form first, calculating the amounts remaining in the bank account and to whom they belong after each transaction.

You should also apportion the rights to any property purchased from the mixed account according to whose money has been used for its purchase.

You should, of course, explain which rule you are applying in each transaction, so that a kind-hearted marker will be able to give you credit for legal knowledge even if you slip up on your arithmetic!

Answer plan

- First transaction: mixing of Tonto's own funds with Una's in Tonto's bank account: tracing in equity available (*Re Diplock*; *Re Hallett's Estate*). Calculation
- Principle applied to purchase of boat
- Displacement of rule in *Re Hallett's Estate* where balance dissipated (*Re Oatway*)
- Application of Hayton's approach that trustee should not be allowed to allocate profitable transactions to himself
- Calculation

Suggested answer

As Tonto is bankrupt, a personal claim against him for breach of trust is likely to be of little value to the Una Charitable Trust ('Una') or to the beneficiaries of the Duo Trust ('Duo'). Una and Duo should therefore first try to trace their funds into the property to which the funds have been applied.

The first transaction involves the mixing in Tonto's bank account of Tonto's own money and money belonging to Una. Tracing at law is not possible as the money has been applied by its legal owner, Tonto; and, in any event, money or other property cannot be traced at law once it has been mixed. Tracing is, however, possible in equity, as Tonto is a trustee and therefore in a fiduciary relationship (*Re Diplock* [1948] Ch 465), and property can be traced in equity even after it has been mixed.

The shares which Tonto buys for £5,000, paid for from the account, are prima facie deemed to have been purchased out of his own £6,000 in the account, on the basis that a trustee is deemed not to be acting in breach of trust: *Re Hallett's Estate* (1880) 13 ChD 696. If this is the case, the shares belong to Tonto, and the money remaining in the account belongs as follows:

Tonto   £1,000

Una   £10,000

If the same principle is applied on the purchase of the boat, then the boat represents £1,000 of Tonto's money and £2,500 of Una's money. The bank account then has no money of Tonto's left in it, and there is £7,500 of Una's money remaining.

The rule in *Re Hallett's Estate*, however, is displaced where the trustee, having purchased an investment, subsequently dissipates the balance in the account, which, on the application of *Re Hallett's Estate*, would mean that the beneficiary's money would have been dissipated. In such circumstances, *Re Oatway* [1903] 2 Ch 356 held that the beneficiary is entitled to treat the investment as having been purchased first out of the trust monies, so as to enable the beneficiary to trace into the investment. Hayton has cogently argued that the rule in *Re Oatway* exemplifies the underlying principle that a trustee should not be permitted to allocate profitable transactions to himself, as this would allow him to benefit from his own wrongdoing: Underhill and Hayton, *Law Relating to Trusts and Trustees* (David J. Hayton, ed.), 18th edn, LexisNexis, 2010. The fact that some money of Una remains in the bank account should not, therefore, affect Una's right to trace into the shares, which, in view of the boat's destruction, it would obviously be better advised to do.

The remedy granted in *Re Oatway* itself was an equitable charge over the investment to the value of the trust monies used in its purchase. That case did not deal with the position in the event of the investment's increasing in value. It would, however, appear to follow from dicta in *Re Tilley's Will Trusts* [1967] Ch 1179 (where trust money had been mixed with the trustee's own), that Una should be able to benefit from the entire increase in value, i.e., to claim that the shares are held for it upon a constructive trust.

Assuming that Hayton's view is applied, the money remaining in the bank account immediately after the shares have been purchased belongs as follows:

Una   £5,000

Tonto   £6,000

The rule in *Re Hallett's Estate* is then applied to the purchase of the boat, which is therefore bought entirely from Tonto's own money. After the purchase of the boat, the money remaining in the bank account is as follows:

Una   £5,000

Tonto   £2,500

The rest of this answer proceeds on the basis that Hayton's approach to the application of *Re Oatway* represents the law.

Tonto's payment into the account of £5,000 belonging to Duo means that there is then £12,500 in that account. When Tonto subsequently withdraws the first £5,000 from the account, the withdrawal first comprises £2,500 of Tonto's own money (*Re Hallett's Estate*). As between innocent volunteers, the appropriation of withdrawals from an active bank account is governed by the rule in *Clayton's Case* (1816) 1 Mer 572, whereby withdrawals are treated as made in the same order as payments in, i.e., first in, first out. As Una and Duo are both innocent volunteers, the balance of £2,500 withdrawn is treated as Una's money. The second withdrawal of £5,000 therefore comprises the remaining £2,500 of Una's money, and £2,500 of Duo's. This leaves £2,500 in the bank account which can be traced by Duo.

Assuming that the creditors are bona fide purchasers without notice, Una cannot trace its £2,500 applied in the discharge of Tonto's debts into their hands. Una can, however, claim to be subrogated to the creditors' claims against Tonto: *Boscawen* v *Bajwa* [1996] 1 WLR 328, CA. If the creditors' claims were secured, e.g., by a mortgage over Tonto's assets, Una would be able to claim an equitable charge over those assets to the extent of £2,500. If, however, the creditors' claims were unsecured, there is no advantage to Una, as a personal claim would not give it priority over Tonto's creditors in Tonto's bankruptcy.

Assuming that Dora is an innocent volunteer, Una and Duo can prima facie trace the monies which she has received into the house she has bought. In *Re Diplock*, however, the Court of Appeal held that, where an innocent volunteer had applied trust monies in building an extension to its existing premises, tracing would not be permitted as this would produce an inequitable result, i.e., the plaintiff could compel a sale of the entire premises. That principle, however, seems to be giving way to a broader principle that tracing will be permitted unless the defendant can establish the defence of change of position. In *Lipkin Gorman* v *Karpnale Ltd* [1991] 2 AC 548, the House of Lords held that such a defence was available to a tracing claim; *Lipkin Gorman* itself concerned tracing at common law, but it has been suggested by Millett J that such a defence is also available in equitable tracing: *Boscawen* v *Bajwa* (supra). More recently, however, in

Foskett v *McKeown* [2001] 1 AC 102, Lord Millett (as he now is) suggested that the defence of change of position is available only where the basis of the claim is unjust enrichment. Where the claimant uses the tracing process to vindicate a property right, by contrast, the only defence is that of the bona fide purchaser for value.

The most appropriate remedy might be for the court to grant Una and Duo an equitable charge over the house, but to defer their right to enforce it for a reasonable time in order to enable Dora to raise (e.g., by mortgaging the house) the amount necessary to satisfy the equitable charge. If the house has increased (or fallen) in value, Dora, Una and Duo, all being innocent volunteers, share the increase (or the loss, as the case may be) rateably: *Sinclair* v *Brougham* [1914] AC 398, HL; *Re Diplock* (supra).

If Dora is indeed an innocent volunteer, no personal claim will lie against her: *Ministry of Health* v *Simpson* [1951] AC 251. If, however, she receives the £5,000 with constructive notice that it is trust money, she will be personally liable as a constructive trustee to account for it under the principle of knowing receipt: *Agip (Africa) Ltd* v *Jackson* [1990] Ch 265 (Millett J).

Further reading

Chambers, R., 'Liability', in *Breach of Trust* (P. Birks and A. Pretto, eds), Hart Publishing, 2002, chapter 1.

Lowry, J. and Edmunds, R., 'Excuses', in *Breach of Trust* (P. Birks and A. Pretto, eds), Hart Publishing, 2002, chapter 9.

Payne, J., 'Consent', in *Breach of Trust* (P. Birks and A. Pretto, eds), Hart Publishing, 2002, chapter 10.

Smith, L., *The Law of Tracing*, Clarendon Press, 1997.

14

Equitable doctrines

Introduction

The maxims of equity are the general principles upon which the Chancery Court developed this system of law and reflect the desire to be fair and even-handed between litigants. The maxims underlie the equitable doctrines and remedies. Their origins are to be found in the history of property law but they are sometimes applied to more modern situations and not always very happily. The application of conversion to trusts for sale of land led to some surprising results and the **Trusts of Land and Appointment of Trustees Act (TLATA) 1996** converted all trusts for sale of land existing on 1 January 1997 (when the Act came into force) into trusts of land to which the doctrine does not apply. (There is one very limited exception to this which is referred to in question 2(a)(iii) in this chapter.) Although it is still possible to create a trust for sale of land, there is little point in it, as the power to postpone sale overrides any provision to the contrary (**s. 4(1)**), and **s. 3** abolishes the application of the doctrine of conversion to a trust for sale of land.

Questions on the doctrines of equity may well be general essay questions which will draw on your overall knowledge of the subject. It would be unwise to attempt these types of questions perhaps, unless you feel you have read generally and widely enough on the background of equity. Problem questions involving the more modern applications of the doctrines are a possibility if your lectures have covered these areas.

In deciding how much attention to give to these more general areas of equity, you should look at past examination papers and consider the emphasis given to equity itself by your lecturer. Although all courses on trusts will include some background of equity, some lecturers will not regard it as worthy of examination questions, whilst other lecturers may set questions on it. You will only know which type of course your lecturer favours by looking at the past examination questions and listening to your lecturer!

Question 1

Equity looks on that as done which ought to be done.

Discuss critically the applications of this maxim in the equitable doctrine of conversion.

Commentary

The equitable doctrine of conversion is an anachronism which can produce unfortunate results in its present day applications. It probably has more significance in land law than in trusts, although it is still capable of affecting interests on succession. The material for this type of question is more likely to be found in a book on equity rather than a book on trusts, and some reference may well be made to it in books on land law, e.g., Maudsley and Burn's, *Land Law: Cases and Materials*, 9th edn, Oxford University Press, 2009.

It is essentially only something which would be examined on a course which covers equity as well as trusts.

Answer plan

- Wherever there is an obligation to convert property to another form, e.g., to sell land and thereby convert it to money, equity regards the obligation as carried out

- Where there is a contract for the sale of land, equity therefore regards the purchaser as having already acquired the beneficial interest in the land; the vendor has the bare legal title and an interest in the proceeds of sale (personalty)

- This was extended in the rule in **Lawes v Bennett** to options to purchase and applied in **Re Sweeting** to a conditional contract

- Trustees of residuary personalty left in succession must also convert wasting or future assets into authorised investments (rule in **Howe v Dartmouth**)

Suggested answer

Although equity did not have the same rigid rules of precedent as the common law, the Court of Chancery did have certain principles which it applied in administering equity. These became known as the 'maxims' of equity, and 'equity looks on that as done which ought to be done' is one of these. Its application is evident in several areas of equity and it underlies the doctrine of conversion.

The doctrine applies wherever there is an obligation to convert property into another form. Equity will then notionally convert the property before the actual conversion takes place. This has the curious result that realty may sometimes be regarded as personalty, and vice versa, in the eyes of equity. This was significant on the passing of property on an intestacy before 1926, when realty devolved upon the heir and personalty to the next of kin, and may still be relevant after 1925 in the case of a will leaving realty to one person and personalty to another.

Jekyll MR gave the reason for the doctrine in *Lechmere v Earl of Carlisle* (1733) 3 P Wms 211 as the fact that a *cestui que trust* should not be prejudiced by a trustee's possible delay in dealing with trust property in accordance with his obligations. It has received some unfortunate extensions however, in certain areas, which have produced criticisms from the judges, and it was abolished as regards trusts for sale of land by s. 3 of the **TLATA 1996**.

The doctrine of conversion still applies, however, to a contract for the sale of land. As soon as there is an enforceable contract, equity will impose a constructive trust on the vendor. From the contract, the vendor's interest is treated as being in the proceeds of sale which, if the vendor dies before completion, are payable to the persons entitled to his personalty. The purchaser, who is regarded as having a beneficial interest in the land, should therefore insure it. The position as to insurance may of course be varied by the terms of the contract for sale, and the Standard Conditions applicable to domestic conveyances provide that insurance of the property shall remain the responsibility of the vendor until completion.

In *Re Sweeting (deceased)* [1988] 1 All ER 1016, the doctrine was applied to a conditional contract where the condition was not fulfilled until after the testator's death. An unfortunate extension of its application is the rule in *Lawes v Bennett* (1785) 1 Cox 167, which decided that the doctrine applies retrospectively when an option to purchase is exercised after the grantor's death. Moreover, if the option is granted after a specific devise of the property by will, on exercise of the option the devise is adeemed and the property, which becomes personalty retrospectively, passes to the residuary legatee: *Weeding v Weeding* (1861) 1 J & H 424.

A duty to convert property also arises under the rule in *Howe v Earl of Dartmouth* (1802) 7 Ves 137. The rule aims at achieving fairness as to investments between a life tenant and a remainderman. It requires trustees of a residuary personalty fund which is left in succession to convert any wasting assets, or future assets not yielding an income, into authorised investments, unless the will reveals a contrary intention. The income from any such part of the fund before conversion is apportioned between the life tenant and the remainderman.

A strict application of the doctrine of conversion can produce some unfortunate results, and it is hardly surprising that the courts have sought to avoid it in some circumstances.

Question 2

James, who died earlier this year, appointed Tina and Tom as executors and trustees of his will and devised all his realty to his son Sam and all his personalty to his daughter Doris. Advise the executors as to who is entitled to the following properties owned by James:

(a) (i) 'The Beeches', held by James and his wife Wynne upon trust for sale for themselves as tenants in common.

(ii) Would your answer differ if James and Wynne had held 'The Beeches' as joint tenants?

(iii) Would your answer differ if James had died before 1 January 1997?

(b) 'The Larches', which James contracted to sell to Peter shortly before he died, subject to Peter obtaining planning consent for an extension. Peter has now obtained planning consent.

(c) 'The Firs', upon which he had granted an option to purchase to Frank. Since James died, Frank has given notice to Tina and Tom of his intention to exercise the option. Would your answer differ if the will had included a specific devise of 'The Firs' to Sam?

Commentary

This question requires a knowledge of some of the circumstances in which the doctrine of conversion applies.

Like all questions in parts, it is probably unwise to attempt it unless you know the answer to at least two parts of it! If you have revised this topic, however, it is a fairly straightforward question, with almost arithmetical answers. You should achieve at least a pass if you can apply the principles, although a more detailed knowledge of the cases would be required to pass well.

Part **(a)(iii)** will have an increasingly limited relevance as its only importance now is in tracing title to unregistered land where there is such a will disposing of property subject to a trust for sale.

Answer plan

(a) (i) A trust for sale takes effect as a trust of land under **TLATA 1996** and the doctrine of conversion does not apply to it (**TLATA, s. 3**). 'The Beeches' is regarded by equity as land and passes to Sam

(ii) Wherever there is a joint tenancy, property passes by the right of survivorship to the surviving joint tenant or joint tenants and not under the will. 'The Beeches' would therefore go to Winifred

(iii) This is the only exception to **TLATA, s. 3**. The doctrine of conversion still applies to land held on a trust for sale in the will of a testator who dies before 1 January 1997 leaving 'realty' and 'personalty' specifically in the will. 'The Beeches' would therefore pass as personalty to Doris

(b) The doctrine of conversion applies to a binding contract for sale, and 'The Firs' is therefore regarded as personalty which passes to Doris

• This includes a conditional contract once the condition is fulfilled (**Re Sweeting**), and so the proceeds of sale of 'The Larches' would go to Doris

(c) As soon as an option to purchase is exercised, there is a binding contract to sell, and 'The Firs' is therefore regarded as personalty which passes to Doris

• If 'The Firs' had been specifically devised by name before the option was granted, the option would override the devise and the position would be as above

• If the specific devise was made after the option was granted, then 'The Firs' would go to Sam together with the benefit of the option

Suggested answer

(a)(i) Wherever there is co-ownership of land, this must take effect behind a trust. Before 1 January 1997, s. 34 of the Law of Property Act 1925 imposed a statutory trust for sale. Because a trust imposes a binding obligation on trustees and 'equity looks on that as done which ought to be done', the equitable doctrine of conversion operated to convert property held on a trust for sale to personalty. In the eyes of equity, there was a notional sale and the property was regarded as money.

On or after 1 January 1997 when the TLATA 1996 came into force, co-ownership takes effect behind a trust of land under the Act, and any trusts for sale existing at that date became trusts of land. It is still possible expressly to create a trust for sale (as here), but the requirement to sell can be overridden (TLATA 1996, s. 4(1)) and it will take effect as a trust of land under the Act. Section 3 of the Act abolishes the doctrine of conversion as regards any trust for sale of land (with one exception referred to in (iii) below).

James and Wynne will therefore hold the legal estate to 'The Beeches' as joint tenants at law on a trust of land under TLATA 1996, for themselves as tenants in common in equity. The right of survivorship does not apply to a tenancy in common and James's share of 'The Beeches' will therefore pass under his will to his son Sam as realty.

(ii) If James and Wynne held 'The Beeches' as joint tenants, the position as regards the legal estate is the same, and co-ownership takes effect behind a trust of land under TLATA 1996. The right of survivorship applies to a joint tenancy at law or in equity, however, so that James's equitable interest in 'The Beeches' will pass to Wynne and not under James's will at all.

(iii) Although s. 3 of the TLATA 1996 abolished the application of the doctrine of conversion to a trust for sale of land, a saving was made by the section for a will such as James's where the testator died before the Act came into force. If James had died before 1 January 1997, therefore, at his death the doctrine of conversion would have applied to the trust for sale on which 'The Beeches' was held, and his share would have passed under his will as personalty to Doris.

The position would have been the same even if there had been no express trust for sale but one had been imposed by reason of co-ownership by s. 34 of the Law of Property Act 1925.

This provision can now be relevant only in tracing title, and in practice, wills leaving personalty to one person and realty to another are rare (except perhaps in examination questions!). A testator is much more likely to specify the property he is leaving by name ('The Beeches') in his will.

(b) As soon as a valid and enforceable contract to sell property exists, equity regards the beneficial interest as having passed to the purchaser, and the vendor holds the legal title as a constructive trustee for the purchaser. Because the contract is enforceable by equity, equity regards the transaction as a notional sale. The interest of the vendor is therefore in the proceeds of sale, which are personalty.

In *Re Sweeting (deceased)* [1988] 1 All ER 1016, conversion applied to property subject to a conditional contract for sale when the condition was fulfilled after the testator's death.

The proceeds of sale of 'The Larches' will therefore go to Doris as personalty.

(c) The application of the doctrine of conversion to contracts for the sale of land was extended by the rule in *Lawes v Bennett* (1785) 1 Cox 167 to options to purchase. As soon as an option to purchase land is exercised, the property becomes personalty in the hands of the vendor because there is a binding obligation to sell it. This is still the case, even if the option is made exercisable after the death of the grantor (*Re Isaacs* [1894] 3 Ch 506). Therefore, as soon as Frank gives notice to Tina and Tom of his intention to exercise the option, it is regarded as personalty in their hands and will again go to Doris.

However, if the will makes it clear that the devisee of property is to take all the testator's interest in it, then the devise may operate to override the rule in *Lawes v Bennett*. Moreover, it is relevant whether the option was granted before or after the devise in the will. If it was granted before the devise, then there may be a presumption that the testator intended to give the whole of his interest in the property to the devisee, including any rights under the option. In *Calow v Calow* [1928] Ch 710, a devise of land or 'the proceeds of sale of the land' was held to survive a subsequent contract to sell the land completed after the testator's death. Conversely, if the option was granted after the devise, then the option is regarded as overriding the devise: *Re Carrington* [1932] 1 Ch 1.

If James's will specifically devising 'The Firs' to Sam was made before the option to purchase was granted, then the effect of Frank's notice to Tina and Tom to exercise the option is to operate the doctrine of conversion retrospectively. 'The Firs' becomes personalty in their hands and will go to Doris.

If James's will was made after the option was granted, however, then it is likely that the option will be regarded as a right attaching to the property, and 'The Firs' will pass, together with the right, to Sam as realty.

Question 3

(a) Two sisters, Amy and Bertha, were joint tenants of a house. Amy, who died recently, by her will purported to leave the house to Bertha and their brother Cyril in equal shares. There was also a bequest in the will of valuable jewellery worth at least half of the value of the house to Bertha.

Advise Bertha and Cyril.

(b) John, who died recently, made a will in which he gave a legacy of £5,000 to Bill. Bill had lent John £5,000 secured by a charge on John's house. There is a sum of £3,000 outstanding on this debt.

Advise Bill as to whether the debt will be satisfied by the legacy.

Commentary

The first part of this question is on the application of the doctrine of election, and the second part on a possible application of the doctrine of satisfaction.

Both of these doctrines have their origins in equity's desire to be fair to the children of a family in the distribution of family wealth. The doctrines were extended, however, beyond the family circumstances and the doctrine of satisfaction particularly, in its application to creditors to whom a legacy was left. There are few recent cases on the doctrines although they are still occasionally applicable today.

This is not a subject to cover unless your lecturer directs you to do so or deals with it in your lectures. The doctrines, which were included in the 15th edition of Hanbury and Martin's *Modern Equity* (Sweet & Maxwell, 1997) were left out of the 16th edition (2001) and all later editions, no doubt to allow room for more modern developments and applications of the subject.

Answer plan

(a) • Where a person receives a benefit but also suffers a loss from a transaction or a will, he may elect to reject it or to accept it; if he accepts the benefit of the transaction, he must also suffer the loss

• The doctrine would therefore apply to Bertha with regard to Amy's half share of the house and the jewellery

(b) • The doctrine of satisfaction, which had its origins in allowing for portions advanced to beneficiaries under a family settlement, was extended to debts owed by a testator

• The satisfaction of a debt by a legacy left to a creditor became subject to certain technical rules (listed in the answer) which may mean that it will not apply here

Suggested answer

(a) The doctrine of election means that a person who receives a benefit from a transaction, from which he also suffers a loss, must elect to take with the transaction or against it; that is, he may elect to take the benefit and suffer the loss, or not to accept the benefit at all. It usually applies to a will and arises where property is left to A and some of A's property is left by the same will to B. A cannot accept the gift under the will unless he compensates B from his own property. It is irrelevant that the testator has made a mistake as to the ownership of A's property which he has purported to leave to B.

Because Amy and Bertha were joint tenants of the house and the right of survivorship applies to a joint tenancy, the house automatically passes to Bertha on Amy's death. Amy is therefore leaving to Cyril property which is not hers to dispose of. In *Re Gordon's Will Trusts* [1978] Ch 145, where a mother and son owned a house as joint tenants and the mother devised it to her trustee upon trust for sale and left furniture and £1,000 to her son, Buckley LJ accepted that the doctrine of election could apply to those gifts to the son.

In that case, other property given in trust for the son was not freely alienable by him, which in fact prevented the application of the doctrine to it. If the property of the elector is not freely alienable, no case for election arises (*Re Lord Chesham* (1886) 31 ChD 466). The jewellery in this question would appear to have been given outright to Bertha, however, so it would seem that the doctrine would apply.

Bertha will therefore have to elect to take with the will, in which case she may keep the jewellery but must convey half of the house to Cyril, or against it, in which case she may keep the whole of the house but must compensate Cyril by letting him have the jewellery. She will be obliged to let him have the whole of the jewellery, however, and not just jewellery to the value of half of the house.

Hanbury and Martin's *Modern Equity*, 15th edn, Sweet & Maxwell, 1997, criticised the doctrine of election as 'too uncertain an instrument of equity', pointing out that the ultimate donee of the elector's property will always benefit, whereas the person put to their election may not benefit at all. This would seem to be the position here.

(b) The doctrine of satisfaction evolved in order to ensure, as far as possible, an equal distribution of family wealth among the children of a family. It was applied in certain circumstances to adeem a legacy left to a child who had previously received a portion (a sum of money to set him up in life).

It also applies where a legacy is left to a creditor, the underlying maxim for this being that 'equity imputes an intent to fulfil an obligation'. It must be possible to presume from the circumstances that the testator did intend to pay the debt with the legacy and, like all presumptions, it is rebuttable. Certain technical rules have developed to rebut the presumption.

First, the legacy must be as beneficial to the creditor as the debt (see *Re Van den Bergh's Will Trusts* [1948] 1 All ER 935). As Bill's loan was secured by a charge on John's house, this would not be the case.

Secondly, the doctrine applies only if the will was made after the debt was incurred. We are not told the dates of the will or the debt.

Thirdly, it will not apply if the will includes a clause (which is frequently included in wills) directing the testator's executors to pay the testator's debts and funeral and testamentary expenses. In these circumstances, both the debt and the legacy will be payable. This principle was established in *Chancey's Case* (1717) 1 P Wms 408. It is not even necessary for the clause to include reference to the payment of legacies (*Re Manners* [1949] 2 All ER 201).

For all these reasons, it is possible that the doctrine of satisfaction will not apply to the legacy in John's will, and Bill will be able to recover his debt from the estate and also take his legacy of £5,000.

15

Equitable remedies

Introduction

Equitable remedies are available in all fields of law, so do not assume that you will be confined to discussing cases involving trusts. Contract and commercial law, employment law, tort and breach of confidence are all areas which may be used to consider the application of an equitable remedy. Although you are not being examined on your knowledge in these fields, you will clearly need to have some background knowledge. Since equity and trusts is normally taught towards the end of a degree course this should not present too much of a problem. If it happens to occur earlier in your course then do not panic, your examiner will probably take this into account.

During your course of study some controversial or notorious case may arise where equitable remedies are sought. A claim may be brought based on the **Human Rights Act 1998** in respect of the right to respect for private and family life (as in, for example, *Venables and Thompson* v *News Group Newspapers* [2001] 1 All ER 908, [2001] 2 WLR 1038 and *Douglas and Zeta-Jones* v *Hello! Ltd* [2001] 2 WLR 992, [2001] 2 All ER 289); a breach of confidence claim may be brought in a case involving national security such as the *Spycatcher* case (*A-G* v *Guardian Newspapers Ltd (No. 2)* [1990] 1 AC 109), or even by a member of the Royal Family. It is likely that your examiner will frame a question round such a case. So, keep abreast of current case law, particularly if it features on the national news. If your lecturer starts referring you to newspaper reports as an example of the topicality of the subject, take the hint and read up on the material. It is very gratifying for your lecturers when they can prove to you how relevant to the modern world their subject is. If they can, they will try to reflect it in the examination.

The most likely remedies to be examined are specific performance and injunctions. They can occur as either essay or problem questions. The question might deal more narrowly with types of injunctions, such as freezing injunctions or search orders, where there have been a number of recent developments. Rescission and rectification are less commonly examined, but listen to your examiner for pointers on this one. For that reason the sample questions in the chapter concentrate on specific performance and injunctions.

As equitable remedies are discretionary you will need to bear in mind general equitable principles, for example, the maxims of equity, when answering the questions. As usual, the area is mainly case law except for the provisions of the **Senior Courts Act 1981**.

Question 1

The Draconian and essentially unfair nature of [search] orders from the point of view of respondents against whom they are made requires, in my view, that they be so drawn as to extend no further than the minimum extent necessary to achieve the purpose for which they are granted, namely the preservation of documents or articles which might otherwise be destroyed or concealed. (Per Scott J in *Columbia Picture Industries Inc.* v *Robinson* [1987] Ch 38.)

Discuss critically.

Commentary

A quotation of this sort can be followed by various commands: 'comment', or 'examine', or, as in this question, 'discuss'. Sometimes, as here, you are required to perform the test 'critically'.

Whatever the form adopted by your examiner you are required to do two things for a degree-level answer to this question. First, you must show you know what the procedure entails. So, in this question you must explain what the search order is all about. You will be expected to cite the relevant authorities.

Secondly, you must be critical. The key is to read the quotation. This may seem obvious, but there is a great temptation in the exam room to read and digest only key words. In this question the key words are 'search orders'. An answer which simply describes the search order procedure will achieve a pass, but little more. What is required is a critical analysis of the current use of the procedure.

The quotation gives the lead. You should explain in what respects the procedure is considered by the judge to be 'Draconian'. The quotation is provocative so your answer can be argumentative, even bullish. Give both sides of the argument, then come down on one side and give reasons for your decision. Provided you have argued your case well, you will not lose marks if your examiner happens to disagree with your verdict.

As with all discussion questions, beware of losing your way. Plan your arguments in advance. Prepare a checklist of the points to be made, then tick them off as you make them. A question of this sort gives you the opportunity to show off your skills in arguing a case, provided you have a sound knowledge of the law involved.

This type of question may also occur as an assessment which would require a deeper analysis of the literature. For example, more should be made of the article by Dockray and Laddie (1990) 106 LQR 601 and the judgment of Nicholls V-C in *Universal Thermosensors Ltd v Hibben* [1992] 1 WLR 840. The application to the European Court of Human Rights in *Lock International plc* v *Beswick* [1989] 1 WLR 1268, noted in the article by Dockray and Laddie, should also be considered in the light of the implementation of the **Human Rights Act 1998**. There is a decision of the Court of Appeal (*C plc* v *P* **[2007] EWCA Civ 493**) on the effect of the **Human Rights Act 1998** and the applicability of the privilege against self-incrimination (PSI) under the Convention, and a discussion of the decision in Corporate Fraud Investigation and Asset Recovery Update for July 2007 on the Herbert Smith website 'European Freezing Injunctions?' at p. 10 (‹http://www.herbertsmith.com/NR/rdonlyres/F8926D13-4D76-4431-A505-23F9106C5B82/4460/5939FraudUpdateD102.pdf›, accessed 1 August 2011).

Answer plan

- Search orders and **Civil Procedure Act 1997, s. 7**
- Problems regarding the abuse of search orders
- Purpose of search orders
- Conditions in *Anton Piller* for grant of order
- Conditions for injunctions in *American Cyanamid* case compared
- Necessity for full disclosure
- Procedure in *Universal Thermosensors* case

Suggested answer

Search orders have sometimes been described as civil search warrants, enabling the applicant to enter on the respondent's premises, search and take relevant evidence.

Since their initial use, originally in *EMI Ltd* v *Pandit* [1975] 1 WLR 302, and subsequently in *Anton Piller KG* v *Manufacturing Processes Ltd* [1976] Ch 55 from which they derived their previous name '*Anton Piller* orders', these orders have been extensively used. They now have a statutory basis in **s. 7** of the **Civil Procedure Act 1997**, and are also governed by the **Civil Procedure Rules 1998**.

Their popularity has ensured that the injustice which they were created to remedy has been ameliorated. However, applicants have not always been entirely honest when seeking this remedy; they have not always come to equity with clean hands. Concern has been expressed, both on the Bench and by academic writers, that such orders are being abused. In *Universal Thermosensors Ltd* v *Hibben*, Nicholls V-C laid out a series of guidelines for the use of these orders. He recognised that they can be both a virtue in eliciting evidence which would otherwise not have seen the light of day, and a vice in that the procedure is open to abuse. These guidelines are now laid out in *Practice Direction* [1996] 1 WLR 1552.

Search orders are sought where there is a risk that vital evidence may be lost or destroyed. Their use has been particularly appropriate in cases where the defendant is suspected of infringing the claimant's intellectual property rights or of breaching trade secrets. They have also been used in one reported case within the field of family law (*Emanuel* v *Emanuel* [1982] 1 WLR 669), to enable the wife's solicitors to enter the husband's home and inspect documents relating to his financial means.

In order to bring such a case, a claimant needs evidence which might be in the hands of the defendant. It might consist of confidential documents or material such as videotapes. In the *Anton Piller* case, the defendants were the plaintiff's selling agents. The plaintiffs believed that the defendants were selling confidential information about their electrical equipment and plans to their competitors. However, to prove this they needed access to documents kept at the defendants' premises. The Court of Appeal granted an order which permitted them to enter the defendants' premises and inspect the documents.

It is crucial that the application is made without notice. If the other side knew of the application the risk is that the evidence would be destroyed forthwith. Surprise is a key element of the procedure. Herein lies the danger. The judge, at the hearing without notice, must rely exclusively on the word of the applicant.

In the first place, the judge may be required to determine to what extent any particular scientific or technical knowledge is the subject of patent or copyright, or is merely legitimately accepted scientific research. As Hoffmann J said in *Lock International plc* v *Beswick* [1989] 1 WLR 1268, 'It may look like magic but turn out merely to embody a principle discovered by Faraday or Ampère'.

Secondly, an unscrupulous applicant might abuse the power in a commercial situation by seeking to crush a competitor by the use of oppressive tactics. In *Lock International plc* v *Beswick*, the *Anton Piller* order was carried out by five representatives of the applicant. These were solicitors or employees of the applicant. They were, however, accompanied by 11 or 12 police officers who were armed with a search warrant in respect of alleged criminal activities of the respondent.

On appeal (noted (1990) 106 LQR 173), it was said that what had happened was regrettable, and it was unfortunate that the judge had not been informed of the involvement of the police.

Three conditions for the grant of the order were laid down in *Anton Piller KG* v *Manufacturing Processes Ltd* by Ormrod LJ:

(i) There must be a very strong prima facie case.

(ii) There must be actual or potential damage of a very serious nature.

(iii) There must be clear evidence that the defendant has in his possession incriminating documents or things and a real risk that they might be destroyed before an application with notice can be heard.

Lord Denning MR added to these the condition that the order must do no real harm to the defendant. It would seem, however, that the fact that disclosure might expose the defendant to the risk of violence from his associates is not a defence (*Coca-Cola Co.* v *Gilbey* [1995] 4 All ER 711).

These conditions are more onerous than the conditions laid down in *American Cyanamid Co.* v *Ethicon Ltd* [1975] AC 396 for the issue of interim (formerly known as 'interlocutory') injunctions. This reflects the concern of the courts to protect the respondent from an abuse of process. The procedure should not be used as a means of finding out what proceedings can be brought (*Hytrac Conveyors Ltd* v *Conveyors International Ltd* [1983] 1 WLR 44). In other words, the material sought should be specific and should support the cause of action proposed by the claimant for the trial of the main claim. Fishing expeditions are not permitted. The orders are not, in fact, search warrants. They are precisely limited.

When applying for the order, the applicant must make a full disclosure to the court. There is clearly a potential weakness in a procedure which only hears one side of the case. Therefore, there is a particularly strict duty for a full and frank disclosure of all relevant facts. As Scott J pointed out in *Columbia Picture Industries Inc.* v *Robinson* [1987] Ch 38, the procedure constitutes an apparent breach of the rule of natural justice that citizens should not be deprived of their property without a fair hearing.

In carrying out the order the applicant should be accompanied by a solicitor. Documents or other evidence may be inspected and removed according to the terms of the order. They may not be used for any other purpose unless the respondent has consented or the court has so ordered. If damage is caused to the respondent then the applicant may be obliged to pay damages which could be exemplary in nature.

Two cases have sought to limit the scope of search orders: *Tate Access Floors Inc.* v *Boswell* [1991] Ch 512 and *Rank Film Distributors Ltd* v *Video Information Centre* [1982] AC 380. The former case emphasises a requirement for the claimant to make a full disclosure. In the latter case it was held that the privilege against self-incrimination could be raised by a defendant. This decision was abrogated by the **Senior Courts Act 1981, s. 72**, in cases relating to intellectual property.

Since the decision, the **Human Rights Act 1998** has adopted the European Convention on Human Rights, of which Art. 8(1) states that everyone has the right to respect for his private and family life, his home and his correspondence. Article 8(2) states that there shall be no interference by a public authority with this right except in the interests of the society to which that person belongs and makes it clear that the domestic courts are to balance the rights of the individual under the Article with protection of the society in which he lives. In *C plc* v *P* [2006] EWHC 1226 (Ch), [2007] EWCA Civ 493, CA, C obtained a search order against P and took his computer in pursuance of the order. It was subsequently discovered that P had downloaded child pornography. This was a pre-existing document to which the defence of privilege from self-incrimination (PSI) does not apply under the Convention. The Court of Appeal found (for different reasons) that the case was not an 'exceptional case' requiring departure from the **Human Rights Act 1998**, that the material had been found in the course of execution of a valid court order, and was therefore not protected by PSI. The protection afforded by the PSI rule had previously been criticised (see, e.g., Lord Templeman in *Istel (AT&T)* v *Tully*) and the court in *C plc* v *P* was in something of a dilemma as to how the offending material should be disposed of as it is an offence to be in possession of such material.

In *Universal Thermosensors Ltd* v *Hibben*, Nicholls V-C set out seven points of procedure. The defendant must have the opportunity to get legal advice, so the order should be served at a time that enables this to happen. If the defendant is a woman alone in a private house, the claimant's solicitor must be a woman, or accompanied by a woman. A detailed list of items removed should be prepared at the premises and checked by the defendant. The defendant should be restrained from communicating with others, apart from a lawyer, only for a limited period of time; a week is too long. Orders at business premises should be executed in the presence of an officer or employee. The claimant should not use the opportunity for a general search of the defendant's papers. The order should be served and supervised by an experienced solicitor independent of the claimant, who should submit a written report to the defendant and to the court at a subsequent hearing with notice.

The courts are clearly concerned to ensure that the procedure is not abused. As an equitable remedy, the search order has shown the willingness of the courts to adapt well-established remedies to new situations. The maxim that equity will not allow a wrong to be without a remedy is still valid today, yet the dangers of the procedure are acknowledged by the courts that developed it. Concern over abuse of search orders has been expressed both by the judges and the legal profession as a whole. While such orders provide a valuable remedy, the balance must be maintained between the potential parties to a claim. Although it is unlikely that this remedy will disappear, it is likely that, in future, judges will need very cogent evidence before granting search orders.

Question 2

Lex Ltd produces videos and tapes of lectures and accompanying notes for the purpose of teaching law to overseas students by distance learning. Ten staff are employed on a full-time basis. Portia, a senior member of staff, and author of a leading textbook on European law, is employed on a five-year contract to develop new materials within her field. Her contract requires her not to work for any other firm of law tutors during the period of her contract and for one year thereafter. Portia is a member of the National Union of Law Teachers (NULT).

Negotiations over conditions of service between Lex Ltd and its staff have now broken down. The following circumstances have occurred:

(a) Portia, who has three years left to run on her contract, has written a letter of resignation to Lex Ltd. She has accepted an offer of employment at the Cambridge base of the tutorial firm, Law sans Larmes, which has its headquarters in Brussels.

(b) All the materials that Portia had been working on have disappeared from the office, and Lex Ltd fears that they may now be in the possession of Law sans Larmes. The company has also discovered that its current students have received advertisement material from Law sans Larmes, and believes that Portia took a list of clients with her. It also believes that Law sans Larmes have bank accounts in Cambridge and Brussels, and that fees received are transferred on a regular basis to the Brussels account.

(c) After conducting a ballot in which the majority of members voted in support of industrial action, NULT has called a strike at Lex Ltd's premises as a result of the breakdown in negotiations. Picketing is taking place on a daily basis.

Advise Lex Ltd of any equitable remedies it may have in these circumstances.

Commentary

This problem question has a variety of points in it and mixes both specific performance and injunctions. They are, however, quite straightforward and not too difficult to spot. You should be able to score a good 2(i) if you work methodically through the various remedies, explaining their availability in each instance. For a first-class answer, some critical analysis of their usage would be necessary.

Answer plan

(a) • Contracts of service; claim for injunction to enforce express negative stipulation (cases); problem where effect to prevent employee working at all (cases); difficulties in reconciling *Warner Bros* case with later case law

(b) • Injunction to restrain abuse of confidential relationship; confidential information; maxim that equity will not act in vain; use of search orders

(c) • Interim injunction against trade union; *American Cyanamid* principles; statute law

Suggested answer

(a) Portia is in breach of her contract of employment with Lex Ltd. An employment contract, that is, a contract *of* service, cannot be enforced specifically against an employee (Trade Union and Labour Relations (Consolidation) Act 1992). This statutory provision stems from the equitable principle that such contracts should not be turned into 'contracts of slavery' (per Fry LJ in *De Francesco* v *Barnum* (1890) 45 ChD 430 at p. 438). A claim for damages would provide an adequate remedy since, although Portia is a leading author and a senior member of staff, it is likely that she could be replaced.

Lex Ltd may, however, wish to enforce the express negative stipulation in her contract restraining her from working for anyone else during the remaining period of her contract. Earlier case law indicates that a claim for an injunction to this effect would be successful. In *Lumley* v *Wagner* (1852) 1 De GM & G 604, an opera singer broke her contract which required her to sing at the plaintiff's theatre for three months. The remedy of specific performance was refused but an injunction preventing her singing at any other theatre during the contractual period was granted. This was followed in

Warner Bros Pictures Inc. v *Nelson* [1937] 1 KB 209 where the actress, Bette Davis, was prevented from working for a rival film company in breach of a no-competition clause.

However, these cases have been modified where it appears that to grant the remedy would mean that the defendant was prevented from working in any capacity (*Whitwood Chemical Co.* v *Hardman* [1891] 2 Ch 416). In *Rely-A-Bell Burglar and Fire Alarm Co. Ltd* v *Eisler* [1926] Ch 609, an injunction was refused which would have enforced compliance with a stipulation by an employee not to enter into any other employment during the term of his contract. In effect, the defendant would be required to work for the plaintiff or starve. It is considered unrealistic to expect an individual with a particular talent to work in an entirely different capacity. *Warner Bros Pictures Inc.* v *Nelson* was disapproved in *Warren* v *Mendy* [1989] 1 WLR 853, a case where an injunction preventing a boxer from seeking financial services from anyone other than his manager was refused. The principle was stated that an injunction will not be granted if its effect is to prevent a person from working for anyone other than the claimant. In *Page One Records Ltd* v *Britton* [1968] 1 WLR 157, 'The Troggs', a group of musicians, appointed the plaintiff company to act as their agent for five years, and agreed not to engage any other person to act in that capacity. An injunction enforcing the negative stipulation was refused since the practical effect would have been to oblige the group to continue to employ the plaintiff company.

The case of *Warner Bros Pictures Inc.* v *Nelson* is clearly difficult to reconcile with the later cases of *Page One Records Ltd* v *Britton* and *Warren* v *Mendy*. One significant difference is the length of the contracts: in *Warner Bros Pictures Inc.* v *Nelson* the term of the contract was for not more than 20 weeks, while in *Warren* v *Mendy* it was for two years. Issues of mutual trust and confidence are also relevant. So, where mutual confidence continues to exist between employer and employee, the court may be ready to grant an injunction (*Hill* v *Parsons & Co. Ltd* [1972] Ch 305). However, in this problem there is no mutual trust or confidence left.

The negative stipulation in Portia's contract is that she has expressly agreed not to work for any other firm of law tutors in the UK during the contractual period. If an injunction were to be granted, then, in effect, she would be obliged to resume employment with Lex Ltd, notwithstanding that a decree of specific performance would be unlikely to be available. Such a result is contrary to the principles expressed in the later cases and an injunction is, therefore, likely to be refused.

The principle would remain the same whether the injunction was sought against either Law sans Larmes or Portia.

(b) Lex Ltd may seek an injunction to prevent Portia taking its latest teaching materials. There is a right in equity to restrain an abuse of confidential information. This does not necessarily rely on an employment relationship.

Knowledge of the list of customers is critical to Lex Ltd's commercial enterprise and would also amount to confidential information. An interim injunction could have been sought to prevent this information being divulged (*Robb* v *Green* [1985] 2 QB 315). However, the information has already been acted upon, and equity will not act in vain.

In the *Spycatcher* case (*A-G* v *Guardian Newspapers Ltd (No. 2)* [1990] 1 AC 109), the final injunction was refused. The information had already been published world-wide and the injunction would have been futile. A claim for damages against Law sans Larmes might be appropriate if a profit has been made (*Seager* v *Copydex Ltd (No. 2)* [1969] 1 WLR 809).

It is unlikely that either party will be able to rely on the Human Rights Act 1998. Under that Act, freedom of expression is guaranteed subject to qualifications, under Art. 10, but the nature of the publication of the teaching materials is not likely to fall under this protection. Any potential dissemination of these materials by Portia would be to the rival company and for personal profit. The information which Portia has taken is not material which is likely to be made available to the public or where publication would be in the public interest. Likewise, reliance on Art. 8, which guarantees protection of the family and home, would not be appropriate in respect of any claim by Lex Ltd (*Douglas and Zeta-Jones* v *Hello! Ltd* [2001] 2 WLR 992, [2001] 2 All ER 289) since the nature of the material is commercial.

If Lex Ltd fears that the teaching materials have also been taken, it may seek a search order against both parties (formerly called an *Anton Piller* order after the case of *Anton Piller KG* v *Manufacturing Processes Ltd* [1976] Ch 55). This would permit the company's agents to inspect the evidence at the premises of Law sans Larmes and at Portia's home. The application is made without notice where there is a risk that the evidence might be destroyed before a claim could be brought. The application must be made, and the order served, in accordance with the procedures established in *Universal Thermosensors Ltd* v *Hibben* [1992] 1 WLR 840. In particular, as the defendant is a woman, the order must be served by, or in the presence of, a woman.

Lex Ltd must show a very strong prima facie case and actual or potential damage of a very serious nature. It already has evidence that the information is in the hands of Law sans Larmes and the damage to its business could be irreparable.

Lex Ltd is clearly concerned that if it sues Law sans Larmes for damages the latter may be unable to satisfy the claim if assets are transferred abroad. It may, therefore, consider seeking a freezing injunction under the procedure established in *Mareva Compañía Naviera SA* v *International Bulkcarriers SA* [1975] 2 Lloyd's Rep 509. This is an order which prevents the defendant from transferring assets abroad. It is usually obtained without notice and could be sought at the same time as the search order.

The principles in *American Cyanamid Co.* v *Ethicon Ltd* [1975] AC 396 must be satisfied. Further to the Senior Courts Act 1981, s. 37(3), the injunction may be granted to prevent the defendant removing the assets from the jurisdiction of the court or dissipating them in some way.

Lex Ltd must show that it has a good arguable case and will be required to give an undertaking in damages in the event that it is unsuccessful at trial. In addition, it must comply with the guidelines originally established in *Third Chandris Shipping Corp.* v *Unimarine SA* [1979] 2 All ER 972. The remedy will only be available where there is good reason to believe that assets will be moved out of the jurisdiction or otherwise disposed of so as to defeat the claim.

Some of the assets of Law sans Larmes appear to be in Brussels. Lex Ltd may consider the possibility of seeking a freezing injunction which covers not only the English bank account, but also the Brussels account. The Court of Appeal have affirmed in the cases of *Babanaft International Co. SA* v *Bassatne* [1990] Ch 13, *Republic of Haiti* v *Duvalier* [1990] 1 QB 202 and *Derby & Co. Ltd* v *Weldon* [1990] Ch 48, that there is no geographical limit to the jurisdiction of the court. However, an injunction in this form would not be available where it may adversely affect third parties and where its effect may be oppressive to the defendant.

(c) In order to obtain an interim injunction against the union to prevent picketing, Lex Ltd must first show that there is a serious question to be tried according to the principles in *American Cyanamid Co.* v *Ethicon Ltd*. Secondly, it must show that it would suffer irreparable damage if the injunction is not granted and the dispute continues. Lex Ltd may decide to seek an injunction without notice. This is permitted under the Trade Union and Labour Relations (Consolidation) Act 1992, provided that all reasonable steps have been taken for the defendant to be notified and heard.

The Trade Union and Labour Relations (Consolidation) Act 1992, as amended, provides that the court shall have regard to the possibility of the defendant establishing a defence of immunity to tortious liability under the 1992 Act. This modifies the *American Cyanamid* principles to the extent that Lex Ltd may have to show a prima facie case. This is particularly important in cases of this type where the outcome of the claim for an interim injunction pending trial may be decisive. In *NWL Ltd* v *Woods* [1979] 1 WLR 1294, where an interim injunction was sought restraining industrial action, the merits of the case were considered on an interim basis pending trial.

Question 3

To what extent have the requirements for interim (formerly known as 'interlocutory') injunctions laid down by the House of Lords in *American Cyanamid Co.* v *Ethicon Ltd* [1975] AC 396 been followed by subsequent cases?

Commentary

This essay question requires a discussion of the way in which the leading case, *American Cyanamid Co.* v *Ethicon Ltd*, changed the rules relating to interim injunctions, and the further development of those rules in subsequent cases. It is one of those colourful areas where Lord Denning MR robustly defended a certain position, and where other developments have occurred in particular fields.

As with all essay questions, the way to a high mark is to launch into a critical analysis of the case law. You would not be asked a question of this sort if the case law were straightforward.

One of the difficulties in dealing with a question of this sort in an exam is what to put in and what to leave out. You could spend all the allotted time dealing with search orders and freezing injunctions. It is preferable, however, to deal with the central issue: that is, should the defendant be required to establish a prima facie case? Then show, by example, the extent to which this point has moved from the position established in the leading case.

This also is a question which could be encountered as an assessed essay, in which case you will have much more scope to expand the examples and refer to the literature, e.g., Christine Gray, 'Interlocutory Injunctions since *Cyanamid*' [1981] CLJ 307.

Answer plan

- Position prior to *American Cyanamid*
- Changes brought about in *American Cyanamid*
- Problems with this approach
- Examples of statutory modifications in **Human Rights Act 1998** and employment law legislation which operate as exceptions
- Special factors taking cases outside *American Cyanamid*
- Search orders
- Freezing injunctions

Suggested answer

The House of Lords in *American Cyanamid Co.* v *Ethicon Ltd* [1975] AC 396 established new criteria for the granting of an interim (formerly known as an 'interlocutory') injunction.

Prior to *American Cyanamid* it had been necessary for the plaintiff to show a prima facie case before the injunction would be granted. See, for example, *J. T. Stratford & Son Ltd* v *Lindley* [1965] AC 269. In addition, it had to be shown that the balance of convenience supported the grant. So, if the plaintiff could show that damage would be suffered which could not be compensated by an award of damages at the trial, then, once a prima facie case was made out, the injunction would be granted. This meant that frequently the issues which were to be heard at the trial of the action were rehearsed at the hearing of the motion for the injunction.

In *American Cyanamid* the House of Lords disapproved of the court conducting a trial on affidavit evidence, when the essential purpose of an injunction is to preserve a party's position until trial. They decided that it was no longer necessary to establish a prima facie case at the interim proceedings. Provided that it could be shown that there was a serious question to be tried, then the remedy would be granted. Subject to this, the main test was the balance of convenience between the parties. The balance of convenience would be tested primarily by the adequacy of damages. If the balance of convenience was not clearly established then the status quo would be maintained. There is only one qualification made, which is that in individual cases special factors might have to be considered. The House of Lords did not classify these special factors.

One of the difficulties encountered with this approach is that frequently the claim never comes to trial. Litigation is expensive, and a party against whom an injunction has been made may feel sufficiently discouraged to settle or drop the case. So the decision to grant the injunction at the interim hearing may dispose of the claim and the issues may never be fully aired. Under the former position, this did not matter. If a prima facie case had to be made out, then the evidence would be presented and cross-examined.

An example of this occurs in trade disputes. The strength of the workers' case often lies in their ability to withdraw their labour. If an injunction is sought barring them from strike action then, on the *American Cyanamid* principles, the balance of convenience will invariably be in favour of the employer. This was recognised in the **Trade Union and Labour Relations (Consolidation) Act 1992**, and the court is to have regard to the likelihood of the defendant establishing the defence of immunity to tortious liability.

A further statutory modification to the principles in *American Cyanamid* is made in the **Human Rights Act 1998**. Where an interim injunction is sought to restrain publication before the trial, this may potentially affect the right to freedom of expression protected under **Art. 10 of the European Convention on Human Rights**. Thus, s. 12 of the Act provides that publication before trial should not be restrained unless the court is 'satisfied that the applicant is likely to establish that publication should not be allowed'. In any event, even if s. 12 is satisfied, the 'balance of convenience' argument may still prevail (*Douglas and Zeta-Jones v Hello! Ltd* [2001] 2 WLR 992, [2001] 2 All ER 289).

However, these statutory modifications to the *American Cyanamid* principle are exceptions. Criticism of the application of the principle has been left to the judges in later cases.

In *Fellowes & Son v Fisher* [1976] QB 122, the Court of Appeal had differing views on the application of the *American Cyanamid* principles. The majority of the court refused an injunction to prevent a breach of a restrictive covenant in an employment contract, on the ground of the balance of convenience. Lord Denning MR, however, refused the injunction on the ground that no prima facie case had been made out. He stated that *American Cyanamid* did not apply because the facts of *Fellowes & Son v Fisher* fell within one of the exceptional cases outlined by Lord Diplock where special factors could be considered.

In *Hubbard v Pitt* [1976] QB 142, Lord Denning MR again took a different approach from the rest of the Court of Appeal. An injunction was granted by the majority of the court to restrain protesters obstructing access to the premises of an estate agent.

The majority took the view that there was a serious question to be tried and the balance of convenience supported the grant. They did not require that a prima facie case should be made out. Lord Denning MR, dissenting, argued that a prima facie case was required and that the case fell outside *American Cyanamid* because 'special factors' applied. These 'special factors' related to freedom of speech and the right to demonstrate.

Thus Lord Denning MR has relied on the reference to 'special factors' to take cases outside *American Cyanamid* and rely on the former rule that a prima facie case must be established.

Other cases where special factors have prevailed include *Smith* v *Inner London Education Authority* [1978] 1 All ER 411. Here the defendant was a public body and it was held that in such cases the interests of the general public must be considered. In libel cases where the defendant intends to plead justification, an interim injunction is unlikely to be granted on *American Cyanamid* principles.

Trade disputes are dealt with by statute. The Trade Union and Labour Relations (Consolidation) Act 1992 provides that the defendant in an application for an interim injunction may prove a prima facie defence under the statute. In *NWL Ltd* v *Woods* [1979] 1 WLR 1294 Lord Diplock observed that *American Cyanamid* was not dealing with a case where the grant or refusal of the injunction would dispose of the action. He stated that in such a case the consideration of the balance of convenience should take into account the likelihood of success had the case gone to trial.

There are two areas in which there have been important developments in the field of interim injunctions. These are search orders and freezing injunctions, formerly known as *Anton Piller* and *Mareva* orders (named respectively after *Anton Piller KG* v *Manufacturing Processes Ltd* [1976] Ch 55 and *Mareva Compañía Naviera SA* v *International Bulkcarriers SA* [1975] 2 Lloyd's Rep 509).

Search orders have been described as being of a 'Draconian nature' permitting a claimant to enter the defendant's premises and inspect evidence which it is believed may be removed or destroyed. They are available without notice so that the defendant is not forewarned. Ormrod LJ laid down three conditions, the first of which was that the claimant must have an extremely strong prima facie case. This is an exception to the *American Cyanamid* principles. Search orders are mandatory in nature. The courts are less willing to grant a mandatory order without an indication of the strength of the claimant's case.

Freezing injunctions are available to prevent a defendant moving assets or otherwise disposing of them in order to make the pursuit of the main claim fruitless. The claimant must have a legal or equitable right to protect and have a good arguable case.

The jurisdiction to grant search orders and freezing injunctions is now contained in the Senior Courts Act 1981, s. 37.

Thus, there are various situations where the principles in *American Cyanamid* have been refined or distinguished to meet the particular case.

Question 4

(a) Amelia, a sculptress, agrees with Belinda to make a bust of Belinda, a world-renowned child actress, for £500. When the bust is completed, Cindy, a film buff and fan of Belinda, offers Amelia £1,000 for it. Amelia, who is in severe financial difficulties, accepts Cindy's offer.

Advise Belinda on the availability of any equitable remedies for breach of contract in these circumstances.

(b) Delia took a long lease of the top flat on the 14th floor of a tower block being built two years ago. The service contract requires Easimoney Ltd, the freeholder, to undertake external building repairs, to have the outside of the windows cleaned once a month, and to install a lift within a reasonable period of time.

A recent gale has dislodged some tiles from the roof, and rain now leaks into Delia's flat. Despite Delia's repeated requests, the roof has not been repaired. The windows are never cleaned and the lift has not been installed.

Advise Delia of any equitable remedies that might be available to her.

Commentary

This is a straightforward question requiring a knowledge of the rules relating to specific performance. It is a good illustration of the need to read the question. For example, the claimant in part **(a)** is a child. This is not simply to add local colour to the question but is designed to raise the issue of mutuality. If you miss this point, your marks go down.

The second part of the question requires you to know the application of specific performance to contracts requiring supervision and construction contracts. You have to know the case law. Of particular importance is the decision of the House of Lords in *Co-operative Insurance Society Ltd v Argyll Stores (Holdings) Ltd* **[1998] AC 1**. (See also P. Luxton [1998] Conv 396.) If you can answer the first part, but know nothing about the cases relevant to the second, then it is too risky to tackle this question. A superb answer to the first part but zero on the second will barely earn you a pass.

However, if you have specific performance at your fingertips, then this question is fairly uncomplicated if you pick up all the points.

Answer plan

(a) • Discretionary nature of remedy of specific performance
   • Contracts for personal property
   • Effect of hardship

- Equity will not act in vain
- Need for mutuality

(b) • Specific performance of landlord's covenants

- Problem where need for constant supervision and exceptions
- Case law examples including *Co-operative Insurance Society Ltd* v *Argyll Stores (Holdings) Ltd*
- Application to the specific covenants in Delia's lease

Suggested answer

(a) The equitable remedy of specific performance is discretionary. It will not be available where damages provide an adequate remedy, or where the claimant has acted in an inequitable manner. Neither will the court grant the remedy unless it can be enforced; equity will not act in vain. If it is unjust to the defendant to grant the remedy, it will not be awarded.

Normally, contracts for the transfer of personal property will not be specifically enforced. They can usually be compensated for adequately by an award of damages. However, if the item of property has some particular rarity, or beauty or uniqueness, such as King Canute's hunting horn (*Pusey* v *Pusey* (1684) 1 Vern 273), then specific performance may be granted.

There is statutory authority for the remedy contained in the **Sale of Goods Act 1979**, s. 52. This enables the court to grant specific performance of a contract to deliver specific or ascertained goods where it is just to do so.

The contract between Amelia and Belinda is for personal property, a bust of Belinda. In order for the remedy of specific performance to be granted there must be something unique about the property. In *Cohen* v *Roche* [1927] 1 KB 169, a contract for the sale of eight Hepplewhite chairs was not specifically enforceable. The chairs were not considered to be of any special value or interest. On the other hand, a contract for the sale of a ship was enforced in *Behnke* v *Bede Shipping Co. Ltd* [1927] 1 KB 649, where the ship was of 'peculiar and practically unique value to the plaintiff'.

The bust of Belinda is unique: there is only one in existence. It is a case which falls within the ancient jurisdiction of cases such as *Pusey* v *Pusey*, where the goods are distinguishable because of their rarity, rather than *Cohen* v *Roche*, where the goods, though rare and valuable, are still no more than ordinary commercial articles.

However, Amelia is in severe financial difficulties, and, for that reason, accepts the offer from Cindy. Since the remedy is discretionary, the court would consider whether it is equitable in the circumstances to grant Belinda specific performance of the contract against Amelia. Where a hardship would amount to an injustice (if Amelia could show that it would put her out of business) then the court may be reluctant to award specific performance of the contract (*Patel* v *Ali* [1984] Ch 283).

Neither will the court act in vain. An equitable remedy will be granted only if it can be complied with by the defendant. In *Jones* v *Lipman* [1962] 1 WLR 832 the defendant attempted to defeat a contract for the sale of land by transferring the land to a company he had set up for this express purpose. The court awarded specific performance because the company was a sham. Normally specific performance would not be granted against a defendant who no longer owned the property. If Amelia has already delivered the bust to Cindy, then Cindy will take free of Belinda's claim to specific performance, assuming Cindy is a bona fide purchaser without notice. In these circumstances, Belinda will have to rely on the remedy of damages for breach of contract.

For specific performance to be awarded, it must be available to either party. If there is a lack of mutuality, there is a discretion to refuse the remedy. In *Flight* v *Bolland* (1824) 4 Russ 298, a minor was refused specific performance as it would not have been available against him. There is judicial authority for the viewpoint that the time to determine mutuality is at the time of the trial, not the contract. In *Clayton* v *Ashdown* (1714) 2 Eq Ab 516, it was held that where a minor attained majority at the time of the trial the remedy would be available. This principle was confirmed by the Court of Appeal in *Price* v *Strange* [1978] Ch 337.

There are, therefore, various grounds on which the court may refuse to exercise its discretion to award specific performance in favour of Belinda.

(b) Delia is seeking specific performance of her landlord's covenants. The general principle is that the court will not grant specific performance of a contract where constant supervision would be required: 'Specific performance is inapplicable where the continued supervision of the court is necessary in order to ensure the fulfilment of the contract' (Dixon J, *J. C. Williamson Ltd* v *Lukey and Mulholland* (1931) 45 CLR 282, at pp. 297–8). Equity will not act in vain and the court is unable constantly to supervise the performance of a contract. In practice, this means that if the court might have to give 'an indefinite series of rulings in order to ensure the execution of the order', the court will not grant the remedy (*Co-operative Insurance Society Ltd* v *Argyll Stores (Holdings) Ltd* [1998] AC 1). It will not, therefore, enforce a contract where such supervision would be necessary.

There are, however, exceptions to this principle and the courts, in some of the modern cases, are more willing to grant specific performance even where there are potential problems relating to supervision.

The earlier case of *Ryan* v *Mutual Tontine Westminster Chambers Association* [1893] 1 Ch 116 shows the application of the general principle. The lessor of a flat covenanted to appoint a caretaker who would be in constant attendance and would undertake cleaning and general portering duties. A caretaker was appointed but he was frequently absent. The Court of Appeal refused to grant specific performance as it would be unable to supervise the performance of the covenant. It awarded damages instead.

However, in *Posner* v *Scott-Lewis* [1987] Ch 25, specific performance of a similar covenant to employ a resident porter was awarded. The court held that if the obligation was sufficiently defined and the degree of supervision was not unacceptable, then, if the plaintiff would suffer greater hardship, the equitable remedy would be awarded.

Similarly, if the order can be defined with precision, so that the defendant knows exactly what is to be done, then the court will be more likely to grant the discretionary remedy (*Morris* v *Redland Bricks Ltd* [1970] AC 652, at p. 666, per Lord Upjohn).

The strength of the claimant's case is also a relevant factor given the equitable nature of the remedy (see Spry, *Equitable Remedies*, 8th edn, Thomson Reuters, 2009).

In *Co-operative Insurance Society Ltd* v *Argyll Stores (Holdings) Ltd* [1998] AC 1, a case concerning the enforcement of a covenant in a commercial tenant's lease to continue running the business, Lord Hoffmann distinguished between orders which require a defendant to carry on an activity and orders which require him to achieve a result. In the former case, which might involve an order to carry on running a business over an extended period of time, the possibility of repeated applications for rulings on compliance with the order may arise. Whereas in the latter case, where a result is to be achieved, however complicated, the court may simply look at the finished result and rule on whether compliance has been effected. So cases such as *Wolverhampton Corp.* v *Emmons* [1901] 1 KB 515, concerning a building contract, and *Jeune* v *Queens Cross Properties Ltd* [1974] Ch 97, concerning repairing covenants, are exceptions to the general principle because they involve the achievement of a result—a building, or specific repair.

The terms in Delia's lease are threefold. The first is to install a lift. In *Wolverhampton Corp.* v *Emmons* [1901] 1 KB 515, the Court of Appeal established three requirements: the building work must be clearly defined; damages would be an inadequate remedy; and the defendant has possession of the land. It would seem that these requirements are satisfied. The building work is clearly defined except that the time limit is vague. However, the court is unlikely to be unwilling to specify what would constitute a reasonable time. Since the work would have to be undertaken on part of the block of flats which is in the landlord's possession, it would be impossible for Delia to carry out the work herself. Damages would, therefore, be an inadequate remedy.

This exception was extended to landlords' covenants to repair in *Jeune* v *Queens Cross Properties Ltd* [1974] Ch 97. The **Landlord and Tenant Act 1985, s. 17**, now provides that specific performance of a landlord's repairing covenant may be granted. This overrides any equitable principles restricting the remedy. Delia would therefore be able to seek specific performance of the covenant to repair in respect of the damage to the roof caused by the gale.

The covenant to have the windows cleaned highlights the problem of supervision. Clearly, such a contractual obligation is ongoing and would require constant superintendence. However, applying *Posner* v *Scott-Lewis*, the work is clearly defined. If an order is issued requiring the landlord to appoint a firm of window cleaners to carry out the work, then the supervision required is no more than the appointment of the porter in *Posner* v *Scott-Lewis*. This falls into the category defined by Lord Hoffmann in the *Co-operative Insurance Society* case, as the achievement of a result. Damages might be an adequate remedy in that they would enable Delia to employ a window cleaner herself. However, to employ a window cleaner to clean the exterior of the windows on the 14th floor is not practicable and the court would no doubt take the view that it would cause greater hardship to Delia than to the landlord. Therefore, Delia has a reasonable prospect of success in enforcing this covenant.

Further reading

Luxton, P. [1998] Conv 396.

Dockray and Laddie (1990) 106 LQR 601.

Gray, C., 'Interlocutory injunctions since *Cyanamid*' [1981] CLJ 307.

16

Pick 'n' mix questions

Introduction

Your examination paper may contain one question which mixes a number of different topics. This may be upsetting at first sight. You may have carefully revised several topics which are covered in the question only to discover that it includes one topic which you thought safe to leave out. Assuming that each section in the question bears equal marks (and that is a reasonable assumption unless there is any contrary indication) then it is probably unsafe to tackle it in these circumstances. Most (if not all) questions in the paper will be discrete and you will find the question on charities or administration of trusts or whatever your favourite topic may be, without any difficulty. Once you have identified it then you are away.

However, the possibility of a mixed topic question is another reason why you should read the questions carefully before starting to write. A question might include two sections on charities, then a section on a private purpose trust with a question mark over its validity, and a concluding section on a gift to an unincorporated association. One question spotted in a university exam paper contained four problems: a secret trust; certainty of objects; certainty of intention; and wound up with the doctrine of election—not a pretty sight. If you glance at the question, think 'charities', and plough into it, only to discover 20 valuable minutes later that you have to deal with a subject about which you know nothing, you have wasted a great deal of effort and lost, probably, a class or worse.

Needless to say, if you know each of the topics then you do not have a problem. In fact, if your luck holds and you are thoroughly familiar with the case law for each point, this question may be a dream ticket.

Four questions have been selected to illustrate these points. Question 1 mixes charitable trusts, discretionary trusts and covenants to settle. Question 2 mixes constitution of trusts, *donationes mortis causa* and certainty of words and objects. Question 3 mixes the three certainties, secret trusts and trusts of imperfect obligation. Question 4 covers mutual wills and estoppel.

The main advice is: do not be taken by surprise by a pick 'n' mix question. Suspend disbelief: just because part (a) is on secret trusts does not mean the other sections must also be on the same theme. **Read the questions carefully**.

Question 1

Four years ago Alpha transferred £100,000 to Beta 'upon trust to provide, at his discretion, grants for law students in the United Kingdom, absolute preference to be given to my relatives'. One year ago, Alpha covenanted with Beta to transfer to Beta, upon the same trusts, any property he (Alpha) might subsequently acquire under the will of Gamma. One month later Gamma died, and in his will he bequeathed 10,000 shares in Delta Ltd to Alpha.

Alpha died last month, without having taken steps to transfer the shares in Delta Ltd to Beta. In his will Alpha gave all his property to his niece, Omega.

Discuss.

Commentary

The separate parts of the question are not intrinsically difficult, but the higher marks will be obtained by a student who can show how the different areas interact. Note that at the time of writing, the Charities Bill 2011 was still in the report stage. We have treated it in this question on the basis that it was successfully enacted in 2011, so all references are to the **Charities Act 2011**.

Answer plan

Entitlement to shares in Delta Ltd:

- Constitution of trust
- Breach of covenant to transfer and remedy of damages
- Rights of third parties
- Validity of trust for charitable purposes?
- Validity of trust as a private discretionary trust?

Suggested answer

It is first necessary to consider who is entitled to the shares in Delta Ltd. As sole beneficiary of Alpha's will, Omega is entitled to the shares if they formed part of his estate at his death. They will not comprise part of such estate if they are the subject-matter of a fully constituted charitable trust. Alpha, however, never transferred the legal title to the shares to the trustee, Beta, as he had covenanted to do. Furthermore, there is no evidence that he did everything necessary to be done by him in order to perfect the transfer in equity: see *Milroy v Lord* (1862) 4 De GF & J 264 and *Re Rose* [1952] Ch 499, CA. The trust therefore, remains incompletely constituted in respect of the shares. There is no evidence that valuable consideration has been supplied for the creation of the trust. As regards the shares, therefore, the trust is an incompletely constituted voluntary settlement. Equity will not compel Alpha's estate to transfer the shares to Beta, since equity will not assist a volunteer: *Re Plumptre* [1910] 1 Ch 609.

The decision in *Pennington* v *Waine* [2002] 1 WLR 2075, is unlikely to assist in this case. In *Pennington* v *Waine* a share transfer form had been executed but not delivered to the beneficiary. The beneficiary needed to hold shares in the company in order to be appointed as one of its directors, and, despite non-delivery of the share transfer form, he was still appointed. It was held that it was sufficient that the shares had been transferred by an instrument in writing in accordance with s. 1 (1) of the Stock Transfer Act 1963 and that it would be unconscionable for the transfer not to be effected.

The test of unconscionability is difficult to apply because of uncertainty—and that is a criticism of the decision. But it is arguable that *Pennington* v *Waine* is distinguishable from the current problem since no steps at all have been taken to transfer the shares and there appears to be no detrimental conduct undertaken on the basis of the promise which might render it unconscionable not to allow equity to assist the volunteer. In that case, the person entitled to the shares would be Omega.

Nevertheless, even though the shares are not themselves bound by the trust, it is still necessary to consider whether Beta can sue Alpha's estate for damages for breach of covenant. It has been argued that a covenantee of a voluntary covenant should be able to sue for damages for its breach and hold such damages in trust for the volunteers: see Elliott (1960) 76 LQR 100. The courts, nevertheless, are opposed to such a claim. In *Re Pryce* [1917] 1 Ch 234, the court would not direct the covenantees to sue, and in *Re Kay's Settlement* [1939] Ch 329 it positively directed them not to sue. There is no objection to such a claim if the covenantee is suing in respect of her own loss as beneficiary, as in *Cannon* v *Hartley* [1949] Ch 213; but this is not the situation in the problem. By contrast, in *Fletcher* v *Fletcher* (1844) 4 Hare 67, the court held that there was already a perfect trust of a chose in action: viz., the benefit of the covenant itself. This suggests that if Alpha intended the benefit of the covenant to comprise trust property, Beta will be obliged to sue Alpha's estate for damages for breach of covenant and to hold the substantial damages which he will recover upon the trusts declared. There is, however, no evidence that this was Alpha's intention.

An alternative explanation was proffered in *Re Cook's Settlement Trusts* [1965] Ch 902 by Buckley J. He considered that, whilst it might be possible to create a valid trust of the benefit of a covenant concerning property in existence and owned by the settlor at the date of the covenant, it is not possible to create a trust of the benefit of a covenant which relates to after-acquired property. If this view is followed, there can be no trust of the covenant in the problem.

Since the covenant was entered into only one year ago, it is enforceable by a third party whom the covenant purports to benefit, unless it appears that the parties intended otherwise (Contracts (Rights of Third Parties) Act 1999). If the specified purpose is charitable, this raises the question whether such a covenant is enforceable by the Attorney General. This seems unlikely, since he is not a person who is intended to benefit from the covenant. It also seems unlikely that the persons who might benefit under a charitable trust would have a personal right of action under the 1999 Act, since such persons do not have a beneficial interest under a charitable trust. The conclusion must be that the 1999 Act does not operate in relation to voluntary covenants to transfer property in favour of charity.

Even if a trust of a chose in action has been created, Beta will not hold it upon the trusts declared unless these are valid trusts. The Charities Act 2011, s. 3(1) lists 13 descriptions of purposes which will be charitable if they satisfy the 'public benefit' test which is set out in s. 4. The thirteenth category (para. (m)) includes all purposes previously recognised as charitable. It also preserves the ability of the courts to develop charity law by enabling new purposes to develop by analogy with, or within the spirit of, any of the purposes listed in paras (a) to (l). The limiting factor that the purpose be beneficial to the community is now apparently subsumed within the broader 'public benefit' test contained in s. 4. However, if a purpose has already been held to be for the public benefit then that requirement will already have been satisfied. New purposes under para. (m) will have to be shown to be for the public benefit.

Applying s. 3(1), clearly the primary purpose here (providing grants for law students in the United Kingdom) would be charitable under para. (b) of s. 3(1). It would also be charitable under para. (m) as education has always been a charitable purpose and was Lord Macnaghten's second category of charitable purposes in *Pemsel's Case* [1891] AC 531. Under the previous law, the requirement for public benefit excluded from charitable status a trust for a group of beneficiaries defined by a personal nexus (*Oppenheim* v *Tobacco Securities Trust* [1951] AC 297; *Re Compton* [1945] Ch 123), and this appears to be imported into the current law by s. 4 of the Charities Act 2011. Under the previous law, there was a qualification in that, provided that the primary class of beneficiaries was a sufficient section of the public, the courts allowed preferences for a class of beneficiaries which was not (*Re Koettgen* [1954] Ch 252 where a 75 per cent preference was allowed). *Re Koettgen* was much criticised (see *IRC* v *Educational Grants Association Ltd* [1967] Ch 993) and it remains to be seen whether the preference cases will survive the new public-benefit test. Although a preference of 75 per cent of the fund was accepted as a charity in *Re Koettgen*, a priority class on whom the whole of the fund can be spent is not: *Caffoor* v *ITC* [1961] AC 584. The words 'absolute preference' in the disposition may suggest a priority, in which case it will fail. The Attorney General's Reference to the Charity Tribunal on this issue was heard in November 2011, but an appeal is possible.

If it is not charitable, can the trust be valid as a private discretionary trust? It would probably satisfy the test for certainty of objects, since it would appear to be possible to say of any given person whether or not they are a law student in the United Kingdom: *McPhail* v *Doulton* [1971] AC 424, HL. It would probably also not fail for administrative unworkability, since the description of objects probably does form something like a class: *McPhail* v *Doulton*. Nevertheless, unless (which is unlikely) it can be construed as a trust for immediate distribution of capital, it would be void for perpetuity. Assuming this to be so, the benefit of any chose in action would be held by Beta on a resulting trust for the benefit of Alpha's estate. In practice, this means that the covenant is simply unenforceable.

If the purported trust is void, the money which Alpha transferred to Beta is also held on a resulting trust for Alpha's estate. Omega is therefore entitled to it.

Question 2

Discuss, with reference to decided cases, whether any of the following words create a valid trust. Indicate any problems which may have to be overcome before a trust can be imposed in these cases.

(a) Look, I am giving this cheque to our baby.

(b) The money in my deposit account is as much yours as mine.

(c) I hereby give to my executors and trustees £500,000 on trust to apply the said sum at their absolute discretion for the maintenance and support of red-haired women in London.

(d) It is my dying wish, Marjorie, that you should have my London flat. Here are the deeds and the keys, put them in your bag. My solicitor will sort out the details when I am dead.

Commentary

This question contains a mixed bag of problems relating to the constitution of a trust. It draws heavily on particular cases, which can make it very unattractive if you are not familiar with the exact case. In that sense, it is not a very sporting question. Many examiners try to avoid questions which rely on the student's knowledge of a particular case, preferring to test the understanding of general principles. However, if you are faced with a question of this type, and you know the relevant cases, then it can be a gift. Avoid the temptation of starting your answer with an immediate reference to the case. For example, do not start with: 'This is a *Jones Lock* problem . . .'. Instead, state the issue raised by the question, then the general rule with exceptions and then illustrate your answer with cases. Some questions of this sort can subtly vary the facts of the case. Watch out for those!

Answer plan

(a) • Necessity of intention to create trust

• Declaration of trust

• Imperfect gifts as evidence of intention to create a trust

(b) • Necessity of intention to create trust

   • Intention manifested by conduct

   • Intention manifested by words and conduct

(c) • Certainty of objects

   • Test for certainty in a discretionary trust

   • Problem of capriciousness

(d) • Deathbed gifts

   • Principle of *donatio mortis causa*

   • Whether land can be the subject of a deathbed gift

Suggested answer

(a) In order for a trust to be created there must be a clear manifestation of an intention to create a trust. Where the settlor makes a declaration of self as trustee, the trust is fully constituted. Where the settlor is to be one of co-trustees, the declaration constitutes the trust and it is not necessary for the property to be transferred into the names of all the trustees to give effect to it (*T. Choithram International SA* v *Pagarani* [2001] 1 WLR 1, PC).

The statement made implies a gift not a trust. The gift is imperfect since a cheque is merely an order to a banker; therefore, even if the cheque is handed to baby when the words are spoken, no property right is thereby transferred beyond the paper on which the cheque is written. In *Jones* v *Lock* (1865) LR 1 Ch App 25, an attempt was made to argue that, in effect, the donor had made a declaration that he was a trustee of the cheque for the beneficiary. It was held that a failed gift will not be construed in equity as evidence of an intention to declare a trust. Likewise, in *Pappadakis* v *Pappadakis* [2000] WTLR 719, it was held that an invalid assignment which did not identify the assignee who was to hold on trust could not operate as a declaration of trust.

Although there is present an intention to benefit the donee, there is no intention present to hold the property as trustee. This was confirmed in *Richards* v *Delbridge* (1874) LR 18 Eq 11, where words written on a lease which indicated an intention to give the lease to the grandson of the leaseholder were held ineffective at common law to effect the transfer. Since they were words indicating a gift, they were ineffective in equity to operate as a declaration of trust.

The gift will be perfected only when, and if, after presentation of the cheque, the funds are transferred to the credit of the payee's account.

(b) This statement again raises the issue of certainty of intention to create a trust. In this situation the holder of the deposit account has not made an attempt to transfer the account into joint names. It may be arguable, according to the circumstances of the case, that the account holder has manifested an intention to hold the account on trust by conduct. The words are not sufficient in themselves, but, coupled with the conduct of the parties, they may be. For example, in *Paul v Constance* [1977] 1 WLR 527, where money was put into an account in the sole name of Mr Constance, his assurances to Mrs Paul that the money in the account was owned jointly were held sufficient to indicate an intention by him to hold the account on trust for them jointly. In *Re Vandervell's Trusts (No. 2)* [1974] Ch 269, where money from a settlement was used to purchase shares in exercise of an option, it was held that the conduct of the trustees in using this money and paying dividends into the settlement constituted sufficient evidence of an intention to create a trust even though no specific words had been used. Compare *T. Choithram International SA v Pagarani* [2001] 1 WLR 1, where words which indicated an outright gift were construed in the context of the case as words of a gift to be held on the trusts of a settlement already constituted by the donor.

The decision in *Paul v Constance* was applied in *Rowe v Prance* [1999] 2 FLR 787, where a boat, which was held in the sole legal ownership of the defendant, was considered to be held on trust for the claimant and defendant in equal shares. The defendant had always referred to the boat as 'our boat' and had assured the claimant (his partner in an extra-marital affair) that her interest in the boat was her security.

There must, however, be a clear intention evinced, whether by words and/or conduct, to create a trust. In *Re B (Child: Property Transfer)* [1999] 2 FLR 418, where a house, further to a consent order, was transferred to the mother 'for the benefit of the child', no trust was created for the child. The relationship between mother and child had broken down.

Therefore, although it is difficult to state that the words are sufficient on their own to create a trust, coupled with other conduct there may be sufficient certainty of the requisite intention.

(c) In this gift there is a clear intention to create a trust. However, the issue is whether a gift to red-haired women in London is sufficiently certain to be carried out by the trustees. The trust appears to be discretionary. The test for certainty of objects in a discretionary trust was outlined in *McPhail v Doulton* [1971] AC 424, HL, where it was held that the test was the same as that established for powers in *Re Gulbenkian's Settlements* [1970] AC 508, HL. The test is, 'Can it be said with certainty that any given individual is or is not a member of the class?' The question is concerned with whether the concept is clear, rather than with any evidential difficulties. So, in *Re Baden's Deed Trusts (No. 2)* [1972] Ch 607, the question was whether the words 'relatives' and 'dependants' were conceptually certain.

The problem of definition arises, therefore, in respect of red-haired women. Can it be said whether any given person is or is not a member of the class? The problem is not, in this case, in proving evidentially whether a person is or is not within the class. Instead, the difficulty lies in defining the term 'red-haired'. Whereas all people may agree whether certain individuals are red haired, there may be some borderline cases where the trustees could not decide. The concept of what constitutes red hair may, therefore, be so unclear that it is impossible to carry out the trust.

Another problem might arise in relation to the width of the class. If a discretionary trust is so wide that it is administratively unworkable, this may invalidate it.

In *McPhail* v *Doulton*, Lord Wilberforce suggested that a discretionary trust for the residents of Greater London might be so wide that it was unworkable. This was followed in *R* v *District Auditor, ex parte West Yorkshire Metropolitan County Council* (1986) 26 RVR 24 (QBD), where a discretionary trust was purportedly created for the inhabitants of the county of West Yorkshire. The description of objects was considered to be so large that the trust was invalidated for administrative unworkability. This would be different if the gift was construed as a mere power (see *Re Manisty's Settlement* [1974] Ch 17).

The difficulties inherent in validating this gift to red-haired women indicate a capriciousness in the mind of the donor. While there is no general principle that a donor may not act capriciously (*Bird* v *Luckie* (1850) 8 Hare 301), where the gift involves the exercise by a trustee of a fiduciary obligation, the position is different. The difficulties, in the first instance, of defining red hair, and secondly, in the potential width of the class, indicate an element of caprice which may cause a court to invalidate a gift on that ground alone (see *Re Hay's Settlement Trusts* [1982] 1 WLR 202).

(d) It appears from the wording that this is a deathbed gift. In order to effect a transfer of land at common law there should be a deed (**Law of Property Act 1925, s. 52**). There would appear to be no deed transferring legal ownership in this case. Neither does there appear to be any consideration given. Marjorie is, therefore, a volunteer. The normal principle is that equity will not assist a volunteer in enforcing an imperfect gift.

However, there are some exceptions to this and one in particular, the principle of *donatio mortis causa*, may assist Marjorie. There are three conditions which must be satisfied before this exception will be allowed. The gift must be conditional on death, it must be made in contemplation of death and the donor must give the donee control over the gift (see *Cain* v *Moon* [1896] 2 QB 283).

Here, the question indicates that the gift is made in contemplation of death and it is not difficult to raise the presumption that it is, therefore, conditional on death (*Wilkes* v *Allington* [1931] 2 Ch 104). The donor states that the formalities will be dealt with after death. The subject-matter of the gift is land. Until recently, it was thought that it was not possible for land to be the subject of a *donatio mortis causa* (*Duffield* v *Elwes* (1827) 1 Bli (NS) 497). However, the Court of Appeal decision in *Sen* v *Headley* [1991] Ch 425 dispelled these doubts. In that case, someone who already had the keys of a house was given a bunch of keys including one to a steel box in the house containing the title deeds. It was held that the donor had parted with dominion over the house and the title deeds in circumstances otherwise satisfying the conditions for a *donatio mortis causa* and the gift was completed. It would, therefore, seem that as Marjorie has the keys, giving her physical control, and the deeds, this would be sufficient to give rise to the application of the rule that gifts made in contemplation of death are enforceable despite a lack of the appropriate formalities.

Question 3

Sam, who died recently, appointed Tick and Tack as the executors and trustees of his will and made the following dispositions:

(a) £50,000 to my sister Doris absolutely, feeling sure that she will give her son a reasonable amount.

(b) £30,000 to Tick and Tack for purposes of which I will inform them.

(c) My freehold property 'Dunroamin' to Tick and Tack upon trust to sell and to hold the net proceeds of sale for such worthy causes as they shall think fit.

Sam left his residuary realty to his son Percy and his residuary personalty to his daughter Mavis.

Advise Tick and Tack as to the validity of these dispositions, and as to who should benefit if any of them fail.

Commentary

This is a question which requires a fairly detailed knowledge of different parts of an equity and trusts syllabus. You may be lucky and find that you remember the relevant law and cases, but unless you feel fairly confident of doing well on two of the three parts, you might be wise to leave it alone. It is a question on which you might scrape a pass if you know some law, but would find it difficult to score well.

Hard-pressed examiners like to be able to see clearly which part of a question they are marking. It will help the examiner, therefore, if you number each part of your answer and leave a space between the different parts.

Answer plan

(a) • Precatory words and certainty of intention to create a trust
 • Certainty of subject-matter

(b) • Half-secret trust if sufficient element of obligation present
 • Problem regarding future communication
 • Problem regarding inconsistency on the face of the will

(c) • Trust of land under **TLATA 1996**
 • Power of sale under **s. 4(1)**
 • Invalid purpose trust as objects not charitable and infringes perpetuity rule

Conclusion

(a) • Goes beneficially to Doris if no certainty of intention; if certainty of intention still goes to Doris as uncertainty of subject-matter

(b) • Fails completely and results back to testator's estate for Mavis who is entitled to residuary personalty

(c) • Fails completely and results back to testator's estate for Percy who is entitled to residuary realty

Suggested answer

(a) It is unlikely that the words in the disposition to Doris are sufficiently obligatory to attach a trust to the property in the hands of Doris. Such words are precatory words and, since *Lambe v Eames* (1871) 6 Ch App 597 and the **Executors Act 1830**, the courts will not lean in favour of a trust: they simply construe the words in the context of the instrument to ascertain if a trust obligation is imposed. In *Mussoorie Bank v Raynor* (1882) 7 App Cas 321, the words 'feeling confident' were held to be precatory and failed to impose a trust, and the words 'feeling sure' used here would probably similarly fail. Doris would therefore take the gift beneficially.

Even if the words were sufficiently certain to impose a trust, a 'reasonable amount' would be too uncertain as regards subject-matter. Although the court held in *Re Golay's Will Trusts* [1965] 1 WLR 969, that a 'reasonable income' was capable of objective determination by reference to a person's lifestyle, a reasonable amount in this case would not seem to have any objective criteria by which it could be assessed, and it would therefore fail.

(b) This disposition could be an attempt to create a half-secret trust if it is found to have the necessary element of obligation. Although the words 'upon trust' are not used, it seems fairly clear from the face of the will that Tick and Tack are not intended to take the disposition beneficially.

In the case of a half-secret trust, the half-secret trustees must accept the trust before the execution of the will. This does not appear to have happened, as Sam refers to a future communication. Although communication of the identity of the beneficiary at any time before death would be sufficient for a fully secret trust, there are dicta in *Blackwell v Blackwell* [1929] AC 318, HL, and it was accepted in *Re Bateman's Will Trusts* [1970] 1 WLR 1463, that this must be before the execution of the will in the case of a half-secret trust. The reason given for this is that a communication after the will would allow the testator to change his mind and effectively make testamentary dispositions without complying with the **Wills Act 1837**. This is criticised as failing to take account of the fact that the secret trust arises from its acceptance by the trustees quite independently of the will.

Even if there has already been a communication of the purposes which Tick and Tack have accepted, it will still be invalid as there would then be an inconsistency on the face of the will, which is fatal to a half-secret trust: *Re Keen* [1937] Ch 236. The will clearly refers to a future communication and evidence of a prior communication would be inconsistent with it.

(c) This will impose a trust of land under the **TLATA 1996**. Even where the trust is expressed as a trust for sale, the power to postpone sale cannot be abrogated (s. 4(1)). It is a matter for Tick and Tack whether they decide to sell 'Dunroamin' or keep it for the beneficiary under the trust. There would appear to be a discretionary trust as regards the proceeds of sale, but the trust is a purpose trust. There are no objects of the trust who can, if necessary, enforce it against Tick and Tack. Moreover, a trust must be sufficiently certain for a court to enforce it if necessary and 'worthy causes' would be too vague. In *Re Atkinson's Will Trusts* [1978] 1 WLR 586, it was held that it would be impossible to confine worthy objects to charitable objects, so there is no possibility of this taking effect as a charitable trust. Although charitable trusts are purpose trusts, they are valid as they are enforceable by the Attorney General. A non-charitable purpose trust fails, however, for certainty of objects, and also if it infringes the rule against perpetual trusts. This trust will therefore fail.

The disposition in (a) will go to Doris beneficially if there is no certainty of intention to create a trust. If there is such certainty, but the purported trust in favour of Doris's son fails for uncertainty of subject-matter, Doris similarly takes the entire legacy beneficially as it is only the trust grafted onto it which fails (*Curtis v Rippon* (1820) 5 Madd 434). The dispositions in (b) and (c) fail completely, however, and will result back to the testator's residuary estate on failure.

The pecuniary legacy in (b) is personalty and will go as residuary personalty to Mavis. The doctrine of conversion, which applied to a trust for sale under the **Law of Property Act 1925**, was abolished by s. 3 of the **TLATA 1996**, and 'Dunroamin' would go to Percy, who is entitled to the residuary realty.

Question 4

Five years ago Olga, a spinster, married Clive, a widower with three children. They agreed to make wills in identical terms leaving their property to each other and then to Clive's two daughters, Amy and Bea. Wills in accordance with this agreement were executed by both of them shortly after they married. Clive had quarrelled with his son Nigel and did not want him to benefit from his estate.

About three years ago Clive became seriously and terminally ill. Amy was a nurse and Clive told her that if she would take unpaid leave to go and live with him to look after him, as Olga was not strong enough, he and Olga would ensure that his house 'Greensleeves' would be left to her. Amy took unpaid leave and nursed her father for nine months before he died. While living at the house, she paid for the modernisation of the kitchen and bathroom.

Some three months before he died Clive and Olga executed identical codicils to their wills, both signed on the same day, varying the ultimate disposition of 'Greensleeves' so that

Amy should receive it from the survivor of them and the remainder of their property should ultimately be divided between Amy and Bea.

After Clive died, Olga gave away considerable property which had belonged to Clive to charity. She also won £500,000 on the football pools. Nigel, who lived near to Olga, visited her regularly and did small jobs for her. Olga died recently and a will was found among her papers, dated a few days before she died, revoking all previous wills and testamentary dispositions and leaving all her property 'to my wonderful stepson Nigel'.

Advise Amy and Bea.

Commentary

This question raises some of the unresolved difficulties relating to mutual wills. You should be aware of these problems and also of the necessary requirements to establish mutual wills. Apart from this, however, the question is fairly straightforward.

The facts of the question disclose two possible causes of action available to one of the parties (Amy) whom you are asked to advise. If you come to the conclusion that Amy is likely to succeed on one ground, you should of course nevertheless go on to consider the other ground also. REAL cases are often pleaded in the alternative!

Answer plan

- The basis of mutual wills is a contract (*Olins v Walters*), the consideration for which is executory until the first person dies

- Is there sufficient evidence of such a contract (*Re Hagger*)?

- If disposing of land, does the contract have to comply with the **Law of Property (Miscellaneous Provisions) Act 1989, s. 2**? Even if it does not, it may be enforceable under a constructive trust (*Yaxley v Gotts*)

- Does a constructive trust arising from mutual wills attach only to the property the survivor receives from the first to die, or to all the survivor's property? If so, to what extent can the survivor use the capital of such a trust?

- Clive's agreement with Amy, upon which Amy acts to her detriment, gives rise to an estoppel under which Amy might claim 'Greensleeves'

Suggested answer

The enforceability of mutual wills depends upon an agreement between the parties making them: *Olins v Walters*. The agreement is that they will both make wills in substantially the same form, leaving property in accordance with the agreement, and they agree not to revoke the wills. It will be an unenforceable agreement until such time as the first of the parties dies, as it will not be supported by consideration until then. However, when the first party dies, the consideration is the benefit which the survivor receives under their will, and the agreement then becomes binding on the conscience of the survivor, who has received a benefit.

It is often difficult to find sufficient evidence of the agreement to establish that the parties did intend to make mutual wills. The fact that the wills are identical is some evidence but is not in itself sufficient (*Re Oldham* [1925] Ch 75) as there should also be an agreement not to revoke the wills. In the case of *Re Goodchild* [1996] 1 WLR 694, the Court of Appeal held that identical wills made by a husband and wife on the same date were not mutually binding as the necessary contractual obligation not to revoke the wills was lacking. However, in *Re Cleaver* [1981] 1 WLR 939, where two sets of wills were made by a husband and wife in identical form and a further will by the surviving wife consistent with her second identical will, this was held to be sufficient evidence of an agreement. Further, in *Olins* v *Walters* [2009], where reference to an agreement to enter into mutual wills was made in a codicil, the Court of Appeal held that this was sufficient to establish clear and satisfactory evidence of a contract between the testators. The identical wills made here, together with identical codicils giving effect to identical changes, would probably be sufficient evidence to establish the necessary agreement as in *Re Cleaver*.

A further problem with regard to the disposition of 'Greensleeves' to Amy under mutual wills is whether any such agreement is caught by the **Law of Property (Miscellaneous Provisions) Act 1989, s. 2.** In *Healey* v *Brown* [2002] EWHC Ch 1405, the judge decided that it was, and as there was no contract in writing signed by both parties (as here), the agreement was void. He held, however, that the agreement for mutual wills was nevertheless enforceable as it was a contract for a constructive trust which arose under the wills, and so, like *Yaxley* v *Gotts* [2000] Ch 162, was exempted from the formality requirement of s. 2(1) by s. 2(7). Presumably the agreement as to the mutual wills disposing of 'Greensleeves' might similarly be enforceable as the wills would give rise to a constructive trust.

It is probable therefore that Amy and Bea will be able to challenge Olga's will leaving all her property to Nigel, and require her estate to be administered according to the terms of her will and codicil made shortly before Clive died. The decision in *Goodchild* suggests that even if there is no legally binding obligation not to revoke a will, the moral obligation ensuing on the death of the first testator to die binds that person's property in the hands of the second testator, who is therefore under an obligation to deal with it as agreed.

There are a number of vexed questions with regard to the property which is subject to any trust created by mutual wills and there do not seem to be any very satisfactory answers.

Does any trust arising attach only to the property which the survivor receives from the other party to the agreement, or does it attach to all the survivor's property on death? If the latter, then the £500,000 which Olga won on the football pools would also be subject to any trust arising. As the survivor entered into an agreement to leave all their own property to the same third party too, this would seem to be a tenable argument. In *Re Dale* [1994] Ch 31, it was held that the trust attached to all the property held by the survivor at the date of the survivor's death. In *Re Hagger* [1930] 2 Ch 190, also a first instance decision, it was considered that the trust should at least attach to all the property held by the survivor at the date of the first death. In *Re Green* [1951] Ch 148, it was held that the trust attached only to the property received under the will of the first party to die, but this intention was clear from the terms of the will.

Does the trust arising prevent the survivor from disposing of any property they receive under the will of the first to die? If so, it would effectively be only a life interest in that property which the survivor has. In the Australian case of *Birmingham* v *Renfrew* (1937) 57 CLR 666, Dixon J said that the survivor could enjoy the property as if an absolute owner, subject to restrictions on his rights of alienability, but that on his death this 'floating obligation' crystallised and attached to the property. If this is correct, presumably an action could have been brought during Olga's lifetime to prevent her from disposing of any very large sums of money. This point did not arise and was not considered in *Re Dale*.

Additionally, Amy may have grounds to claim the house under the equitable doctrine of estoppel. This could apply to the circumstances of the question in two ways. First, it could apply to make the oral agreement between Clive and Amy enforceable notwithstanding the absence of the requisite formality for a contract for the disposition of land. Secondly, Amy's acting to her detriment in reliance upon a promise made by her father could found a claim in proprietary estoppel.

An oral agreement for the disposition of land will be void as it does not comply with **s. 2** of the **Law of Property (Miscellaneous Provisions) Act 1989**, which requires any such agreement to be in writing and signed by both parties. Before 1989, such an agreement had to comply with the formality requirements of s. 40 of the **Law of Property Act 1925**, but equity would enforce a purely oral agreement if there was a sufficient act of part performance by the party seeking to enforce it, and in *Wakeham* v *Mackenzie* [1968] 1 WLR 1175 a housekeeper was able to enforce an oral agreement to leave the house to her in return for work she had done. Section 40 was repealed by the 1989 Act and the Law Commission envisaged that the equitable doctrine of part performance would be replaced by estoppel. In *Yaxley* v *Gotts* [2000] Ch 162, an oral agreement that a builder who converted a building into flats should have one of the flats in return for his work was held to be binding not only on the person with whom he agreed, but also on his son who knew of the agreement and adopted it. The Court of Appeal applied estoppel, although Robert Walker LJ felt that the situation could also give rise to the imposition of a constructive trust. The agreement between Amy and Clive, whereby she gave up work to go and look after him, might therefore be enforceable against Olga and her estate.

Amy has also acted to her detriment by spending money on the house in modernising the kitchen and the bathroom. The doctrine of estoppel is much wider in its scope than the doctrine of part performance and may be used to enforce a promise upon which the promisee has acted to their detriment.

The promisor is then estopped from going back on the promise and an equity attaches to the property to which it relates, not only in the hands of the promisor himself but also in the hands of a volunteer acquiring the property from him. Thus in *Inwards* v *Baker* [1965] 2 QB 29, CA, a son who was persuaded by his father to build a bungalow on a plot of land belonging to the father was able to remain there after the father died and the land passed to his mistress. In *Pascoe* v *Turner* [1979] 1 WLR 431, a man who told a cohabitee with whom he lived that his house and contents all belonged to her, and was aware that she was spending her frugal savings on repairing and redecorating the house after he had left, was estopped from denying this and was obliged to convey the fee simple in the property to her.

Moreover, estoppel is not restricted by the fundamental premise of testamentary freedom (*Gillett* v *Holt* [2000] 2 All ER 289). The acquiescence relied upon to found a claim of proprietary estoppel should relate to the property. Amy has acted to her detriment in modernising the property and, if this was in reliance upon her father's promise, this may well be sufficient. Both Olga and Nigel are volunteers, so that Amy's claim to the house, which is necessarily equitable and not registrable under the **Land Charges Act 1972** (per Denning LJ in *E. R. Ives Investment Ltd* v *High* [1967] 2 QB 379), might succeed on this ground also.

Index